Critical Conversations

D0878594

Critical Conversations

Michael Polanyi and Christian Theology

Edited by

MURRAY A. RAE

◆PICKWICK *Publications* · Eugene, Oregon

CRITICAL CONVERSATIONS
Michael Polanyi and Christian Theology

Copyright © 2012 Wipf and Stock Publishers. All rights reserved. Except for brief quotations in critical publications or reviews, no part of this book may be reproduced in any manner without prior written permission from the publisher. Write: Permissions, Wipf and Stock Publishers, 199 W. 8th Ave., Suite 3, Eugene, OR 97401.

Pickwick Publications
An Imprint of Wipf and Stock Publishers
199 W. 8th Ave., Suite 3
Eugene, OR 97401

www.wipfandstock.com

ISBN 13: 978-1-61097-727-2

Cataloguing-in-Publication data:

Critical conversations : Michael Polanyi and christian theology / edited by Murray A. Rae.

x + 190 p. ; 23 cm. Includes bibliographical references and index.

ISBN 13: 978-1-61097-727-2

1. Polanyi, Michael, 1891–1976. 2. Knowledge, Theory of. 3. Religion and science. 4. Science — Philosophy. 5. Personalism. I. Rae, Murray. II. Title.

B945 R34 2012

Manufactured in the U.S.A.

*Dedicated to the memory of
the Revd. David J. Kettle—
faithful servant of the gospel*

Contents

Contributors

RICHARD T. ALLEN is the Editor of *Appraisal,* a refereed Journal dedicated to the discussion of the work of Post-Critical Philosophy and Personalism. His publications include *Polanyi* (1991); *Transcendence and Immanence in the Thought of Michael Polanyi* (1992); *Beyond Liberalism: The Political Thought of F. A. Hayek and Michael Polanyi* (1988); and *The Necessity of God: Ontological Arguments Revisited* (2008).

TONY CLARK completed a PhD thesis on Michael Polanyi at the University of St. Andrews in 2005. He was Teaching Fellow in the Divinity School at St Andrews in 2006 and is now Associate Professor of Philosophy and Ethics at Friends University, Wichita, Kansas. His monograph, *Divine Revelation and Human Practice: Responsive and Imaginative Participation,* was published in 2008.

PETER FORSTER is the Anglican Bishop of Chester. He is President of Council and Pro-Chancellor of the University of Chester. He has an MA in Chemistry from Merton College, Oxford and a BD and PhD from Edinburgh University. From 1983–91 he was Senior Tutor at St John's College, Durham.

BRUCE HAMILL completed a PhD thesis on Ethics and Michael Polanyi at the University of Otago, New Zealand, and is currently a parish minister in the Presbyterian Church of Aotearoa, New Zealand.

LINCOLN HARVEY is Tutor in Theology at St. Mellitus College in London. He completed a PhD at King's College London in 2008 in which he engages with the work of Michael Polanyi to construct a theological account of growth in knowledge. His publications include *The Theology of Colin Gunton* (ed. 2010).

DAVID J. KETTLE, who died in March 2011, was an Anglican priest and Coordinator of The Gospel and Our Culture Network in Great Britain (www.gospel-culture.org.uk). Among his published materials are *Beyond Tragic Spirituality: Victimhood and Christian Hope* (2005), and *Western Culture in Gospel Context* (2011).

MURRAY A. RAE is Professor of Theology and Ethics at the University of Otago, New Zealand. His publications include *Kierkegaard's Vision of the Incarnation* (1997), *History and Hermeneutics* (2005), and *Kierkegaard and Theology* (2010).

ALAN J. TORRANCE is Professor of Systematic Theology at the University of St. Andrews, Scotland. His numerous publications include *Persons in Communion: An Essay on Trinitarian Description and Human Participation* (1996); and *The Doctrine of God and Theological Ethics* (ed. with Michael Banner, 2006).

PAUL WESTON is lecturer in mission studies and homiletics at Ridley Hall, Cambridge. He teaches in the Cambridge Theological Federation and is an affiliated lecturer in the Cambridge University Divinity Faculty. He is Chair of the Management Council of the "Gospel and Our Culture Network" in the UK. His PhD is on the writings of Lesslie Newbigin, and he has edited *Lesslie Newbigin: Missionary Theologian: A Reader* (2006).

Introduction

Murray A. Rae

The philosophical writings of Michael Polanyi are concerned in the main with the nature and scope of human knowing. However, there are many other questions that are related intrinsically to this theme, including, for instance, the nature of the universe itself and the nature of human being. And, as Polanyi readily acknowledges, the epistemological inquiry requires consideration of theological questions too. An epistemologist and philosopher of science willing to acknowledge the theological dimensions of his inquiry quickly caught the attention of theologians who read Polanyi's work from the 1950s onward. Theologians have been encouraged, particularly, to find a philosopher of science critical of the rationalistic and positivist convictions that have dominated Western philosophical and popular conceptions of how we may learn the truth but that are antithetical to theological inquiry. They have been eagerly receptive of Polanyi's insistence that we need to recover an appreciation of the personal coefficients of human knowing, included among which are faith and belief, and they have seen resonances with their own work in Polanyi's emphasis upon the importance of tradition and the necessity sometimes of conversion.

These themes are explored further in the present volume, but so too is Polanyi's social and political thought, his anthropology, his hermeneutics, and his conception of truth. Polanyi's thought and writing ranges widely both in explicit discussion and in implication. While the dimensions of Polanyi's own thought are considered carefully here, so too is his reception by other thinkers. Several of the essays set Polanyi alongside the work of other thinkers, particularly Karl Barth, Lesslie Newbigin, Hans-Georg Gadamer, and René Girard, and they discuss points of comparison and contrast between the respective figures. While all the essays are appreciative of Polanyi's contribution they do not shy away from critical analysis. Polanyi is a stimulating thinker whose work gives significant support and encouragement to theologians in the investigation of their own particular subject matter, but as some of the essays show, appreciation does not entail agreement with all that Polanyi said. Polanyi himself spoke of the "conviviality" of learned societies upon which the advance of any discipline depends. He has in mind here the importance of trust in the authority of others, the readiness to submit one's work to the scrutiny of others and the maintenance of practices of mutual correction and endorsement. To some extent, though qualified in important ways, conviviality operates on a macro scale too, that is, across whole cultures and even between them. The conviviality within particular disciplines and essential to their epistemic progress is equally important across disciplines in order to serve the maturation and flourishing of a culture as a whole. It is to that end that the theologians represented in this volume have been willing both to learn from Polanyi and to critique him.

The volume begins with three essays that consider especially Polanyi's epistemology and trace the fruitfulness of that epistemology for the subject matter of Christian theology. Tony Clark's essay gives an outline of that epistemology, explaining in particular the seminal notions of "personal" knowledge, tacit knowledge, and indwelling, and exploring the continuities between knowing as it occurs in scientific practice and religious knowing. He then explores the importance of authority and tradition in scientific practice and again makes comparison with religious knowing. A particular point of interest here is whether Polanyi's claim that the progress of science relies upon the participation of its practitioners in something like a community of faith implies a relativistic view of truth. Clark argues that it does not, but it does encourage a more humble conception of the knowing process than that bequeathed by Enlightenment rationalism, a conception that takes seriously the fallibility of the human intellect and the inescapable dependence of all rational intellects upon the authority and tradition of a community of inquiry. We are not, in the sphere of knowing, self-made men and women. Far from undermining our search for knowledge and truth, however, these communities of dependence and trust are precisely the basis upon which genuine knowledge can be found.

Richard Allen, in the second essay, surveys some of the same epistemological ground as does Clark but probes further into the ways in which Polanyi's thought may be assimilated but also adapted to the task of theological inquiry. Allen here extends a line of inquiry introduced in his earlier published work and defends the claim that Polanyi's own interpretations of Christianity "need to be radically adapted for they too readily assimilate Christianity into the framework used for created and finite reality and a merely secular conception of human life, from which Polanyi did not properly liberate himself." Showing how such adaptation may work out in practice Allen goes on to explore two central and related themes in theology, the unity and simplicity of God, and knowing as a specification of love. Allen first explores how the being of God cannot be conceived within an ontology of form and matter and traces the pitfalls that have ensued when philosophers and theologians have attempted to do so. The Christian confession that God is Love constitutes an alternative ontology in which the attributes of God are conceived, no longer as parts of a whole, but as expressions of God's unitary essence. The confession that human beings are made in God's image suggests that love is central to the constitution of human being too. Having secured this point, Allen proceeds to explore, with more explicit reference to Polanyi now, how knowing may be conceived as an expression of love. Allen finds support here also from Max Scheler who, following Goethe, contends that "one can know only what one loves." This ought also to be the Christian view Scheler contends, but too often Christianity has assimilated itself to the alternative view, expressed here by Leonardo da Vinci but having much more ancient roots, that "[e]very great love is the daughter of a great cognition." Neglect of the former, authentically Christian, insight has led to the fateful assertion of the primacy of reason rather than love with resultant distortions in anthropology and epistemology, to say nothing *yet* of ethics. Polanyi, Allen contends, helps in the recovery of the Christian insight and shows how it in fact operates in the "unlikely sphere" of natural science. Allen then turns in a final section to the ethical implications of the Christian insight. For if knowing is an expression of love then ignorance is the result of a lack of love, and error that of hatred. Allen's essay serves well in showing the wide-ranging implications of Polanyi's thought and of the stimulus it provides to explorations beyond those that Polanyi himself undertook.

In chapter 3 Lincoln Harvey explores the persistence of detached objectivism in contemporary accounts of science and exposes the pretension to divinity that such an epistemology entails. He goes on to explain that such pretension, as well as being simply deluded, has the tragic consequence of depersonalising us and thus of undermining our humanity. If the detached, objectivist, view of knowing is in these ways problematic, must we accept pessimistically the alternative of relativistic subjectivism and abandon thus our longing to know the truth? Here the post-critical realism of Michael Polanyi offers another and more satisfactory account of the knowing process that recognises both its inescapably personal character and the genuine access it may provide to the object of our enquiries. Polanyi does not abandon the notion of objective truth, but contends that our access to it is facilitated rather than hindered by our tacit allegiance to a whole range of beliefs, our indwelling of and formation by particular traditions of inquiry, and our trust in established sources of authority.

In a final section, Harvey sets Polanyi's personalist epistemology alongside a theological account of the knowing process. The knowledge the Son has of the Father through the Spirit, and the Father of the Son, is a knowledge of relational acquaintance. It is a function of the indwelling of the Father and Son in the life of the other and is mediated by the Spirit. This is true of the incarnate Son, moreover, thus giving a basis to affirm that true knowledge can be had within the fabric of the created order. "Our flesh," Harvey observes, "is conducive to our knowing through the Spirit more than that which is merely ourselves." The Polanyian themes of indwelling (derived, of course, from John's gospel), integration and personal participation are explored in the theological light provided by Jesus' knowing of the Father through the Spirit to yield an epistemology more concordant than that of Modernity with the realities of human being.

While concerned still with Polanyi's theory of knowledge, chapter four shifts the focus of attention to Polanyi's social and political thought. After surveying Polanyi's account of the emergence of totalitarian socialism, attributed by Polanyi to a dangerous blend of scientific scepticism and moral perfectionism, Alan Torrance goes on to explore Polanyi's efforts to establish a proper theoretical relation between knowledge and the ethical. To begin with, Polanyi challenges the Enlightenment belief in the absolute, intellectual self-determination of humanity. We are unable to "sit back and choose at [our] pleasure a new existence" and so, as Torrance explains, "no political theory can be imposed from scratch or *ab initio* by the detached, sceptical subject." We are deeply immersed in communities and traditions and are simply not at liberty to begin as if with a blank slate. Instead, Torrance continues, "All theories and all corrections emerge through the gradual pressure of circumstance on participants within the community and the heuristic adaptations that result from this." Paul Nagy thus reports, following Polanyi, that ". . . the modern quest for moral perfection which is to be achieved through a supreme and universally applicable moral principle has proved futile."

Distrusting totalising political or ethical theory, Polanyi turns instead to the practices of the scientific community for a model of the healthy society based on "mediated consensus." He claims to find here an analogue for the development of the virtuous society. Torrance explores this suggestion at some length, but concludes that the disanalogies between the scientific community and society at large are such that the former holds little promise as a model for resolution of the ethical and political problems facing modern society. There is more promise to be found, Torrance suggests, in the community gathered for worship. Such a community lives, not in service of some totalitarian ideal, but within the *koinonia* of the Son's communion with the Father. Torrance traces the political implications of such convenantal relationality and emphasises that the patterns of life that characterise this relationship cannot be imposed in totalitarian fashion, but are lived out in service to the community as a whole.

Chapter five is the first of four chapters that offer critical comparisons between Polanyi and other leading thinkers of the twentieth century. Peter Forster, first of all, traces the deep agreements between Polanyi and Karl Barth, although neither thinker shows any evidence of familiarity with the other's work. Particular points of similarity between the two thinkers are found, Forster argues, in their respective epistemologies and ontologies. He contends, further, that the clarifications offered by Polanyi in the areas of epistemology and ontology allow us to take Barth's theology a little further than he himself was able to do. A number of themes in Barth's theology are considered in order to demonstrate the extension and enrichment that engagement with Polanyi's work affords. Forster considers, in particular, Barth's epistemology and rejection of natural theology, his doctrine of Scripture, his theology of baptism and his anthropology.

A further exploration of the fruitfulness of engaging Polanyi in conversation with other thinkers is undertaken by David Kettle in chapter six. This time the conversation partner is Hans-Georg Gadamer who, in common with Polanyi, offers a telling critique of the Cartesian account of knowing, affirms the personal, communal and historical dimensions of understanding and the roles of tradition and authority in the knowing process, and pursues an account of understanding that is open to the transcendent. Despite these commonalities, however, Kettle argues that there are weaknesses in Gadamer's account that leave him vulnerable to the charge of subjectivity and relativism. Utilisation of certain Polanyian insights enables a strengthening of Gadamer's fruitful exploration of "horizons" and, in particular, affords both a more adequate means of distinguishing truth from error and a more satisfactory account of how we are prone to evade the truth. Informing Kettle's discussion are the ultimate horizons of understanding disclosed in the life, death and resurrection of Jesus. In the concluding section of the chapter Kettle gives explicit attention to the ways in which a theological account of how we may be drawn into a communion in truth enriches and develops the lines of inquiry opened up by Gadamer and Polanyi.

In chapter seven, attention turns again to anthropology and this time it is René Girard who is engaged in conversation with the work of Polanyi. Bruce Hamill here considers how the writings of Girard and Polanyi respectively might help us towards a more finely tuned articulation of the assumption and redemption of humanity in Jesus Christ. Polanyi's thought is treated first. While critical of him in some respects, Hamill is appreciative nevertheless of Polanyi's "transcendentally-oriented epistemology," his affirmation of an order and meaning in the world that is not of our own making, and his relational account of the knowing process. Hamill also detects in Polanyi something like an account of human sin, a recognition, at least, of the human propensity to evade the truth. According to Hamill, however, Polanyi's account of redemption is fundamentally Pelagian in character. Hamill therefore turns to Girard where he finds a more Augustinian approach to the problem of redemption.

Girard, of course, employs a quite different vocabulary than does Polanyi and is concerned fundamentally not with human knowing but with desire. In common with Polanyi's account of the knowing process, however, Girard considers the development of desire to be crucially dependent upon our social existence. Desire is, indeed, a mimetic activity. It is also ambiguous. Girard explains that our existence as social beings catches us up in the fallen structures of the world and becomes often enough a source of rivalry and violence. Only the new sociality established in communion with Christ, the crucified yet risen scapegoat, provides hope of redemption. "The community formed in conformity to this risen victim is precisely the new social order," Hamill writes, "and God's new creation by the Spirit."

In a final, substantial, section of his chapter Hamill returns to Polanyi's conception of the knowing process and, drawing upon insights from Girard, considers the extent to which the knowing process involves both a desire for the truth and an act of self-giving. Both aspects are functions of love. What is desired, furthermore, is something "to which the self is subordinated and in which the self participates freely." There are intimations here, Hamill suggests, of the redemption of the relational self and of the kingdom of God in which "we will know as we are known" in the loving attention of God.

Paul Weston contributes the final chapter of this volume in which he traces the influence of Michael Polanyi upon the work of Lesslie Newbigin, especially upon Newbigin's later missiology. That influence, Weston argues, is more pervasive than is often supposed. Newbigin's reference to Polanyi's work began early in Newbigin's writing career and remained important throughout. On reading Polanyi in the 1960's, Weston explains, Newbigin found strong support for his own efforts as a student thirty years earlier to develop an account of the personal nature of religious knowing. Newbigin was especially impressed by Polanyi's analysis of the emergence and demise of the Enlightenment project and considers that analysis to provide vital assistance in the task of proclaiming the gospel to the modern, Western, mind.

Weston proceeds to show how a number of Polanyian concepts are deployed in Newbigin's own writing to shed light on the nature of Christian discipleship and on the missionary task. Particularly fruitful are the notions of "tacit knowledge" and "indwelling," that are used by Newbigin to describe the relation of the disciple to the biblical story. The ecclesial community constituted by this indwelling of the biblical story becomes, furthermore, a hermeneutic of the gospel and witness to the world. "By indwelling the bible's story," Weston writes, "the Church meets the crisis of the hour by providing both the fiduciary starting point for cultural renewal, and by demonstrating within an alien culture what this epistemological renewal looks like in practice."

"Heuristic passion" and "universal intent" are two further Polanyian concepts developed by Newbigin in service of his concern with the gospel as "public truth." Developing these themes, Weston shows how Polanyi's "language and grammar were consistently conducive to [Newbigin's] own interests, and transferable to his own particular missiological concerns."

To the extent that Newbigin stands in the mainstream of the orthodox theological tradition and remains an important voice in contemporary missiology, his fruitful utilisation of Polanyi's work constitutes a strong recommendation for continuing theological engagement with the work of this seminal thinker. It is to that task that the essays of this volume are dedicated. It is not the purpose of this volume, however, to advocate for theology an uncritical adoption of Polanyi's thought. Its purpose is to show forth, rather, the continuing value for theology in engaging a thinker whose account of our human situation and epistemic capacity has given to contemporary Christian theology renewed confidence in articulating its own *distinctive* understanding of the God who, in making himself known, brings about our transformation and recovers our true humanity.

1

Knowledge in Science and Religion

A Polanyian Perspective

TONY CLARK

INTRODUCTION

WITHIN THE PARADIGMS OF thought bequeathed to us by the Enlightenment, it has been held that the ways in which scientists and religious people come to establish the knowledge that they claim must be clearly distinguished. The differentiation between the status of scientific and religious knowledge has become, indeed, one of the established dogmas of Western society. My intention, in this essay, is to consider some of the ways in which the thought of Michael Polanyi calls this view into question.

It will be helpful to note at the outset that Polanyi's agenda is not the defense of religious beliefs.[1] His concern is to establish an authentic philosophical description and justification of scientific work *as it is actually conducted.* This he sought to do in a context in which the positivism of the philosophy of science did more to conceal than illuminate scientific practice. It is out of *this* concern that Polanyi expresses his own distinctive—and in part unique—epistemological insights.

Paul Ignotus—a friend of Michael Polanyi's—said of him, "while others excelled in extolling science, he excelled in practising it."[2] Indeed,

---

1. While Polanyi does remark on religious and theological themes in some of his writings, these are not at the heart of his concern.

2. See Shils, *The Logic of Personal Knowledge,* 12.

for the first half of his working life Polanyi was a physical chemist, establishing an international reputation as a scientific researcher. It was only in his fifties that he turned his mind more fully to questions of economics, social science, and philosophy. Polanyi's philosophical thought was more than an explication of his scientific work, but his life and experience in science was the springboard, and remained an important source, for his philosophy.

It is with this in mind that we might read Polanyi's opening comments in the preface to *Personal Knowledge*, his *magnum opus* published in 1958: "This is primarily an enquiry into the nature and justification of scientific knowledge. But my reconsideration of scientific knowledge leads on to a wide range of questions outside science."[3]

Polanyi's philosophical work represents a new theory of knowledge. But it is a theory of knowledge that takes, for its point of departure, the *practice* of science. The significance of this will become apparent as some of the contours of Polanyi's thought emerge.

KNOWLEDGE: DETACHMENT OR COMMITMENT?

In making a comparison between scientific and religious knowledge one cannot avoid acknowledging the significance of the Enlightenment. This is not the place to offer an account of Enlightenment thought, but it is necessary to make some general observations in order to identify the kinds of conceptualization that Polanyi is challenging.

Scientific and religious thought may be distinguished in various ways. The distinction upon which I will focus concerns the *relationship* between the scientific and religious "knower" and the knowledge that is claimed.

It is generally thought that relationship between the scientist and scientific knowledge is typified by a high level of *detachment*. The personal beliefs of the scientist play no part—or at least *ought* to play no part—in scientific method and inquiry. In contrast, religious knowledge is typified by a high level of *commitment*: the personal beliefs of religious people are regarded as intrinsic to the methods of religious inquiry.

In science, fact is established through empirical observation and strictly logical inductive or deductive reasoning. As such the *personal* motivations, interests, and beliefs of the scientist are held to occupy no le-

3. Polanyi, *Personal Knowledge*.

gitimate place in scientific inquiry. Indeed, the exclusion of such personal factors provides an important plank for its claims to "objectivity." It is precisely *because* of the impersonal nature of scientific method that its results may be held with a high degree of certainty. In sharp distinction, religious knowledge is regarded as, *de facto*, a matter of personal beliefs. What is faith if it is not a personal commitment? As such, religious knowledge is "personal," and the very personal nature of religious knowledge undermines any claim to "objectivity." To talk of "belief" and "faith" is to imply personal commitment and, therefore, some degree of "subjectivity."[4]

In the philosophy of the Enlightenment the distinction between scientific and religious—or theological—knowledge is that (in very general terms) the former is impersonal and objective, while the latter is personal and subjective. One of the consequences of seeing things in this way is that the former is regarded as "universal" in a way in which the latter cannot be. Polanyi notes in an essay of 1947, "People who believe in science do not usually regard this as a personal act of faith. They consider themselves as submitting to evidence that by its nature compels their assent and which has the power to compel a measure of assent from any rational human being."[5] But Polanyi challenges this distinction. The form of his challenge will occupy the greater part of the remainder of the essay.

POLANYI'S EPISTEMOLOGY: A COUNTERPROPOSAL

a) Challenging the Concept of Impersonal Objectivity

Recalling that Polanyi's primary concern is the nature and justification of scientific knowledge, I will now consider how he confronted the idea of science that I have just outlined. Polanyi sets the scene early in *Personal Knowledge*:

> [T]he prevailing conception of science, based on the disjunction of subjectivity and objectivity, seeks—and must seek at all costs—to eliminate from science . . . passionate, personal, human appraisals of theories, or at least to minimize their function to that of a negligible by-play. For modern man has set up as the ideal of knowledge the conception of natural science as a set of statements

---

4. The terms "objectivity" and "subjectivity" are problematic. Polanyi goes a long way in showing why this is so and goes a long way towards resolving the difficulties associated with such terminology.

5. Polanyi, "Science, Observation and Belief," 10.

which is "objective" in the sense that its substance is entirely determined by observations, even while its presentation may be shaped
by conventions.[6]

But Polanyi argues that such "personal" aspects are *intrinsic* to scientific work, and believes that the claim that scientific work is detached and
impersonal is mistaken.

In what ways is scientific work *personal*? In the first instance the
scientist must decide what to do. What avenues are to be pursued, and in
what ways? If the scientist is to have any hope of success, it is necessary to
identify a "good problem." Having identified such a problem, the scientist
must postulate a hypothesis as a means to solving it. A hypothesis is a
kind of informed "guess" that the scientist makes. The scientist is not a
disinterested "fact-gatherer," but one who anticipates as yet hidden realities. Of course, the scientist may be wrong, and a line of inquiry may "go
cold." But it is such intuitions, or guesses—cast in the form of hypotheses—that direct the scientist's work and suggest the kinds of experiments
and observations that are likely to uncover what is at present concealed.
Science, *per se*, can determine neither what must be investigated, nor the
way in which to proceed. This is the personal judgment of the scientist.
Polanyi writes, "[T]he act of knowing includes an appraisal; and this personal co-efficient, which shapes all factual knowledge, bridges in doing so
the disjunction between subjectivity and objectivity."[7]

The disjunction between the objective and the subjective, central to
the objectivist outlook that has permeated Western culture in so many
ways, is—according to Polanyi—untrue to the way in which science does
and *must* proceed. Scientists must, in an imaginative and disciplined way,
decide how they will employ their various skills in tackling a problem that
is deemed (according to a personal evaluation) to be worthy of attention.
Which facts are going to be regarded as significant? What sort of experiments will be undertaken? Before observation and data-collection begin,
the significance of the *personal* aspect of the process is already apparent.

The factors that determine the procedure will be many: the interests of the scientific community (influenced by inherited traditions and
currents of contemporary concern) will inevitably have a bearing on the
matter, as will a particular scientist's interests, experience, aspirations and

6. Polanyi, *Personal Knowledge*, 15f.

7. Ibid., 17.

capabilities. But this process cannot be purely "objective"—if by that we mean: "no personal involvement." Conceiving a problem and determining how to approach it is necessarily *personal* in that it draws upon the skills and imagination of the scientist.

Another factor that undermines the supposed impersonal and "objective" conception of science may be located in the potential for experimental and observational error. How can scientists be sure that observations that they make are correct? Observational mistakes can be made, and experimental equipment can malfunction. Such errors may impede the scientist's progress either by masking the truth of a correct hypothesis or by supplying support for an erroneous one. A scientist must evaluate the quality and reliability of experimental-observational work undertaken. Again, this task is not an impersonal one that can be resolved by following explicit, "objective" criteria. It is an evaluative task that necessarily draws upon a plethora of scientific skills, and an informed intuition. Such a task is both personal and substantially unspecifiable.

b) The Tacit Dimension

In the section above I have shown something of how scientific work, far from being impersonal, draws in a profound way upon the insights and imagination of the scientist. There may be certain routine elements of scientific work in which what Polanyi calls the "personal co-efficient" is less pronounced,[8] but in the work of scientific discovery these personal elements are very much to the fore, as are the particular personal qualities of individual practitioners.

I have already hinted at the significance of the community—the "interests of the scientific community," "inherited traditions" and "currents of contemporary concerns." Polanyi recognizes that the scientist does not work as an isolated individual but as part of a community. In Polanyi's thought this emerges as a central epistemological concern, as we shall see. In order to appreciate fully this point it is necessary to introduce a unique aspect of Polanyi's epistemology—his theory of tacit knowledge.

At the heart of Polanyi's theory of tacit knowledge is the postulation that "we know more than we can tell."[9] This, according to Polanyi, is basic to the way in which we come to know things. It is certainly true of scien-

---

8. One might think, for example, of some routine mathematical calculations.

9. See Polanyi, *The Tacit Dimension*, 4.

tific inquiry, but its operation can be identified in just about any sphere of human knowing. A survey of this crucial element of Polanyi's thought will reveal more of the significance of the scientist's personal participation in the many and diverse aspects of scientific practice.

The key to Polanyi's theory of tacit knowledge is to be found in the distinction that he makes between two types of knowledge and the dynamic relationship that exists between them. Polanyi calls them "the two terms of tacit knowing." We rely on our knowledge of the first term in order to attend to the second. While the second term is explicit, the first term is not: although we "know" the first term (we only know the second term by way of it) it is knowledge that can be articulated only in part. Our knowledge of the first term transcends our ability to express it: it is tacit. Polanyi writes: "The new theory of knowledge recognizes that our *explicit knowledge of a thing invariably relies on our tacit awareness of some other things*."[10]

Polanyi's meaning will be clarified by an example: the recognition of a facial expression.[11] The particular features of a face—the many physical phenomena manifested in it—comprise the first term of tacit knowledge and it is in our reliance upon these clues that we are able to establish the second term: the mood of the face indicated by them. As this example shows, the function of the two terms is clearly distinguishable. Polanyi writes: "[I]n an act of tacit knowing we *attend from* something for attending *to* something else."[12]

In Polanyi's terminology the first term of tacit knowledge is "subsidiary," while the second term is the "focal."[13] It is the first term, the subsidiary, of which we have knowledge we may not be able to tell. Thus, in terms of the example, we have knowledge of the features of the face (the features that indicate an identifiable mood), but it is unlikely that we will be able to describe those features, except in the most general terms. It is important to emphasize that this does not represent a failing; it merely demonstrates the significance of the tacit in our epistemic processes. It *does* imply that there is a shortfall of *explicit* knowledge, vis-à-vis the

10. Polanyi, "Science and Religion," 5. Emphasis Polanyi.

11. This goes, too, for recognising a person.

12. Polanyi, *The Tacit Dimension*, 10. Emphasis Polanyi.

13. He also adopts the parallel terms "proximal" and "distal," respectively.

knowledge that we claim to have, and this is precisely Polanyi's reason for claiming that "we know more than we can tell."

The tacit process by which we integrate subsidiary clues into focal knowledge is not infallible. Expanding on the example, there may be certain circumstances in which I might mistake a grimace for a smile. Any ensuing social interaction between myself and the bearer of that particular facial expression may be adversely effected by such a mistake. The person may shout at me, angrily, "You may think that it's funny, but I don't!" This may alert me to my error. However, despite the possibility of such mistakes, I retain the belief that my social interaction with others is enhanced by attempting to interpret, or "read," the facial expressions of others. Just because I am occasionally mistaken does not invalidate my belief that my interpretation of facial expressions yields knowledge.

In this example the features of the face are known subsidiarily. But this does not mean that all the features of the face are necessarily beyond the reach of our focal knowledge. For example, I might stare intently at a particular minute feature of a face and gain focal knowledge of it. But in doing this I will cease to be aware—or will be only hazily aware—of the nature of the facial expression to which the detail observed makes some contribution. By becoming focally aware of the particular feature, that feature is no longer functioning as a clue to the expression of the face, and my awareness of the expression of the face is obfuscated. At any one time the focal and subsidiary forms of knowledge are, *functionally*, mutually exclusive.

c) Indwelling: Subsidiary Knowledge as Skilful Performance

We attend *from* our subsidiary knowledge in order to attend *to* a focus. This is what Polanyi refers to as the "from-to" function of tacit knowing. This "from-to" relationship also operates in the use of tools, probes, machines, and the like. It will be useful to introduce another example in order to draw out some other features of tacit knowledge: consider driving a car.

In order to drive a car it is necessary to master a number of skills. One might think, for example, of the gear change and clutch use, "balancing the engine," the operation of the accelerator, steering, braking, recognition of road signs, and so on. When one is learning to drive it is easy to be overwhelmed by the many tasks that must be performed. The new driver is confronted with the task of having to do several things at once. One may have a profound sense of achievement at putting the car into first gear, balancing the engine and accelerating away smoothly—perhaps for the first time—only to find that one is heading directly for a lamppost! The problem is, of course, that it is difficult to focus on several things all at once. And, in Polanyi's terminology, that is precisely what the *new* driver is doing: giving *focal* attention to the various operations that are necessary in order to drive the car. So why is the intense difficulty felt by the learner not the continuing experience of the experienced driver (after all, the experienced driver must continue to perform all the same actions)? The answer is that experienced driver no longer *focuses* on the operations. When one has learned to drive the operations that are the focal concern of the learner driver are no longer thought about *explicitly*: they are rendered part of the driver's subsidiary knowledge. The experienced driver does not need to look down to locate the position of the brake pedal because she "just knows" where it is and how much pressure must be applied to it in any given situation. The driver knows this even though she would be hard pressed to articulate such knowledge with any precision. She knows more than she can tell.

The learner driver is *learning*. Driving a car is a skill and it is fair to say (in a rough and ready way) that one has "learned" to drive when one no longer needs to focus on what might be called the "basic driving operations" and can concentrate instead upon the road ahead and the task of moving safely and efficiently from one place to another. We might say that the driver who has achieved this has "assimilated" or "interiorized" the necessary skills. Polanyi calls this "indwelt" knowledge. The difference between the learner and the experienced driver is that the former must focus on the basic operations of driving the car, while the latter "indwells" those operations as learned skills. Here the "from-to" structure of tacit knowing is again evident. One attends *from* indwelt knowledge—tacit skills—*to* a particular task. When we have such knowledge we cause it to function, according to Polanyi, as an extension of our own bodies.

Polanyi makes the observation that our body is the "ultimate instrument" by which we attain our practical and intellectual knowledge, and comments: "Our own body is the only thing in the world which we normally never experience as an object, but experience always in terms of the world to which we are attending from our body. It is by making this intelligent use of our body that we feel it to be our body, and not a thing outside."[14]

In the skilful use of tools, probes, machines, and the like, we come to indwell these things and, in doing so, they function—as it were—as an extension of our bodies. And so the car, that for the learner driver is a strange, awkward piece of complex machinery, is, for the experienced driver, an extension of her own body through which she is able, in some degree, to express herself.[15]

d) Indwelling: Thought and Theory

I have offered two examples that illustrate the function of the tacit dimension in visual perception and in the skilful use of tools and equipment. I now want to say something about the function of the tacit in respect of theoretical knowledge. This is an interesting case, since theoretical knowledge is generally thought to be, by its nature, explicit. Is this an example in which the tacit does not operate?

Polanyi is certainly not opposed to the theoretical formulations of knowledge. After all, the first part of his working life was spent developing such formulations. However, for Polanyi it is vital to distinguish between scientific theory and scientific knowledge. He believes that it is a profound mistake simply to equate the two. In an almost confessional statement, Polanyi makes the following comments about the theoretical formulations ("logical rules") of science:

> The discoveries of science have been achieved by the passionately sustained efforts of succeeding generations of great men and women who overwhelmed the whole of modern humanity by the power of their convictions. Thus has our scientific outlook been moulded, of which these logical rules give a highly attenuated summary. If we ask why we accept the summary, the answer lies in the body of knowledge of which they are the summary. We must reply by recalling the way each of us has come to accept that knowledge and the reasons for which we continue to do so. Science will appear then as a vast system of beliefs, deeply rooted

14. Ibid., 16.

15. Oddly, the learner driver may be in a better position to *articulate* the operations of driving than the experienced driver as a result of having to think about those operations in explicit terms. Nevertheless, it is the experienced driver who *knows* how to drive. The *knowledge* here is substantially tacit. It is wrong to assume that, because knowledge is articulate, it is *necessarily* at a "higher level"!

in our history and cultivated today by a specially organized part of our society. We shall see that science is not established by the acceptance of a formula, but is part of our mental life, shared out for cultivation among many thousands of specialized scientists throughout the world, and shared receptively, at second-hand, by many millions. And we shall realize that any sincere account of the reasons for which we too share in this mental life must necessarily be given as part of this life.[16]

For Polanyi, the theoretical formulation of science is an "attenuated summary" of a form of life nurtured and developed within the scientific community. It is this "vast system of beliefs" (and accompanying skills) into which the scientist is apprenticed and within which, after a diverse and lengthy training, the scientist is able to participate. While the explicit formulations of science have their part to play—and an important part at that—they ought not to be mistaken for a deep participation within the scientific community, with all the beliefs, skills (theoretical, practical, and social) that are implied in it.

New discoveries and advancements in science come out of such a rich indwelling. By way of an historical example, one might think of Isaac Newton's dramatic discoveries that he made from his own rich and imaginative indwelling of the heliocentric view of the universe. It was through his indwelling of *this* view of the universe, among other things, that Newton was able to discover the laws of gravitation. In making his discovery, he was not looking *at* the Copernican view but looking *with* his own sophisticated development of it. Had he indwelt a Ptolemaic view he would not have made his discovery, because what he was able to uncover was not implied in a geocentric view of the universe.

In view of these examples it becomes clear that the knowledge that we indwell—that we cannot fully articulate—provides the basis for all that we *can* articulate. Polanyi writes: "To apply a theory for understanding nature is to interiorize it. We attend *from* the theory *to* things interpreted in its light."[17]

16. Polanyi, *Personal Knowledge*, 171.
17. Polanyi, "Science and Religion," 8. Emphasis Polanyi.

e) The Ubiquity of Tacit Integrations

As I have noted, Polanyi's work is, primarily, an inquiry into the nature and justification of science. But he is aware that what he says of scientific knowledge has implications for other spheres of knowledge. Towards the end of his life Polanyi turned his thoughts to a more explicit treatment of some such matters. Evidence of Polanyi's background in science is never far from view in his writings but in his last book, *Meaning*[18]—that he co-authored with Harry Prosch—his engagement with the implications of his theory of knowledge for subjects outside science is more sustained. In it, Polanyi explores an extension of his theory of tacit knowledge in specific areas, including metaphor, art, myth, and religion.

In this book, Polanyi demonstrates the ubiquity of the processes by which subsidiary clues are integrated into focal knowledge. In his later writings, Polanyi's favored phrase for describing the tacit assimilation of a subsidiary into a focus is "tacit integration."[19] This broader application of his understanding of the process of integration is one of the major themes of his last published book. The point that emerges from this work is that there is a much greater degree of continuity in the ways of knowing, across a variety of disciplines, than has generally been recognized.

In *Meaning*, Polanyi argues against the rigid distinctions that, it is often supposed, separate the arts and the sciences, and science and religion. He insists that, even in the empirical aspects of science, the imagination of the "artist" is at work: "We may conclude quite generally that no science can predict observed facts except by relying with confidence upon an art: the art of establishing by the trained delicacy of eye, ear, and touch a correspondence between explicit predictions of science and the actual experience of our senses to which these predictions shall apply."[20] Polanyi points out that even Kant was prepared to give a nod in this direction:

> [E]ven a writer like Kant, so powerfully bent on strictly determining the rules of pure reason, occasionally admitted that into all acts of judgment there enters, and must enter, a personal decision that cannot be accounted for by any rules. Kant says that no system of rules can prescribe the procedure by which the rules themselves

18. Michael Polanyi and Harry Prosch, *Meaning*.

19. This was not a phrase that Polanyi adopted in *Personal Knowledge* and other earlier writings, although the central function of tacit integration *was* present if articulated somewhat differently.

20. Polanyi and Prosch, *Meaning*, 31.

are to be applied. There is an ultimate agency that, unfettered by any explicit rules, decides on the subsumption of a particular instance under any general rule or a general concept. And of this agency Kant says only that "it is what constitutes our so-called mother wit" (*Critique of Pure Reason*, A.133). Indeed, at another point he declares that this faculty, indispensable to the exercise of any judgment, is quite inscrutable. He says that the way our intelligence forms and applies the schema of a class to particulars "is a skill so deeply hidden in the human soul that we shall hardly guess the secret trick that Nature here employs." (*Critique of Pure Reason*, A.141)[21]

Polanyi was puzzled that a critique of pure reason could admit such a powerful agency without subjecting it to more rigorous analysis. His conclusion was that, "both Kant and his successors instinctively preferred to let such sleeping monsters lie, for fear that, once awakened, they might destroy their fundamental conception of knowledge. For, once you face up to the ubiquitous controlling position of unformalisable mental skills, you meet difficulties for the justification of knowledge that cannot be disposed of within the framework of rationalism."[22]

The "sleeping monster" that Kant and his successors left undisturbed is roused in Polanyi's theory of tacit knowledge, and in it the rationalistic framework is, indeed, undone. Polanyi is not rejecting rational thought, but he is claiming that the pursuit of fully formalized knowledge is mistaken because it is logically unobtainable. Additionally, the Cartesianism of Enlightenment philosophy, in which the rational thought of the isolated thinker—devoid of the influences of tradition and authority—is undermined in the recognition that rational processes are facilitated by participation (and substantially tacit participation) in communities of practice. Here a very different picture of how knowledge is established emerges, both in science and in other spheres of life.

One profound implication of this is, in Polanyi's words, "a far-reaching relaxation of the tension between science and the nonscientific concerns of man."[23] If we see all knowledge in terms of such dynamic structures, we cannot uphold the rigid distinctions that have been drawn between science and the humanities and, not least, science and religion.

21. Polanyi, "The Unaccountable Element in Science," 1.
22. Ibid., 2.
23. Polanyi and Prosch, *Meaning*, 33.

This is the conclusion we must reach, according to Polanyi, once we have "recognized personal participation as the *universal* principle of knowing."[24]

For Polanyi all knowing is personal—a participation through indwelling. Once this is grasped one of the gaps supposed to exist between the natural sciences and the humanities (and science and religion) is bridged.

COMMUNITIES OF PRACTICE:
AN ALTERNATIVE EPISTEMOLOGICAL PARADIGM

Polanyi's theory of tacit knowledge fundamentally undermines a conception of science as a discipline of detached "objectivity" in which the personality of those engaged in it can be safely and appropriately regarded as an inconsequential epiphenomenon. It is also clear that science cannot be fully represented in explicit formulations. But further, and significantly, science cannot be understood individualistically because it is a communal activity. It has its own traditions, conventions, and authorities. I want to consider this point in a little more depth now as it provides another important way for understanding continuities between religious and scientific knowledge.

The significance of community, authority, and tradition has gone largely unacknowledged in the philosophy of science. Although such things are intrinsic to scientific life, philosophical reflection upon science has generally disregarded them. Enlightenment thinkers were united in the belief that the employment of reason and critical thought was a prerequisite for the pursuit of truth and the establishment of greater human freedom and dignity. The concomitant negative belief was that uncritical submission to authority in general, and to the dogmatic and authoritarian beliefs of the church in particular, was to be rejected. As such *criticism* and *autonomy* were two of the most significant principles of thought for the eighteenth century and the two centuries that followed. Although science did not, and could not, operate according to such principles alone, it clearly was possible to ignore the importance of community, authority, and tradition in science or, alternatively, to dismiss them as elements of an inconsequential by-play. Science had, in any case, shaken itself free of the shackles of church authority and tradition that were the principal focus of concern.

24. Ibid., 44.

How did this happen? How could scientists fail to see the inadequacies of a philosophy of science in which the scientist and the scientific community have no substantive role to play? Polanyi writes, "The decisive reason why such obviously inadequate formulations of the principles of science were accepted by men of great intellectual distinction lies in a desperate craving to represent scientific knowledge as impersonal."[25] It was felt, as I have noted already, that by establishing science as an enterprise of impersonal detachment, the high claims of scientific "objectivity" could be justified. In sum, science was misrepresented because the philosophers of science were so gripped by a philosophical agenda that it was difficult, if not impossible, for them to see the truth.

Polanyi was convinced that once this distorting, prescriptive thinking of the philosophy of science yielded to a more reflective, *a posteriori* approach the *actual* practice of science would be apparent. Polanyi felt that, in an important way, his book, *Personal Knowledge*, was little more than a call to a "common-sense" point of view. He writes:

> [My] aim is to re-equip men with the faculties which centuries of critical thought have taught them to distrust. The reader has been invited to use these faculties and contemplate thus a picture of things restored to their fairly obvious nature. This is all the book was meant to do. For once men have been made to realize the crippling mutilations imposed by an objectivist framework—once the veil of ambiguities covering up these mutilations has been definitively dissolved—many fresh minds will turn to the task of reinterpreting the world as it is, and as it then once more will be seen to be.[26]

I will now offer some comments on Polanyi's understanding of the importance of authority and tradition in communities of practice both in their capacities to transcend themselves and to nurture new practitioners. Once again, the principal focus will be upon the scientific community but the significance of what is said for other communities of practice will be readily discernible.

25. Polanyi, *Personal Knowledge*, 168f.
26. Ibid., 381.

a) Self-Transcending Tradition

The breadth and complexity of the body of scientific knowledge is such that no one scientist can understand any more than a small fraction of the totality in any depth. Each member of the scientific community is competent to judge the work of colleagues working in the same or closely related fields and in this way, Polanyi believes, the self-regulating structure of the scientific community is established and maintained. Hence, there is a consensus across the scientific disciplines, and within the confines of this consensus it is possible to say whether a new contribution is "scientific" or not. In this way, the more radical scientific debates are cast in the form of a conflict between established authority and a challenger to that authority; and the one challenging may not be credited with the status of scientist—at least with regard to the issue in dispute.

It is important to realize that challengers do not attack the authority of scientific opinion in general but only in respect of a particular detail. Paradoxically, "[E]very thoughtful submission to authority is qualified by some, however slight, opposition to it."[27] Hence the advancement of the body of scientific knowledge is dependent upon challenges being made to it, while its stability is dependent upon recognition, on the part of scientists and—to some degree—of society as a whole, of the authority of the scientific tradition. Anyone who rejects the authority of the tradition *in a general way* would find no basis on which to resolve their disagreement with those who accept it.

In this description of science it is clear enough that scientists are not autonomous but, in a significant way, are beholden to their colleagues within the scientific community. Factors such as the publishing policies of academic journals and the research policies of scientific departments— established by eminent and respected practitioners in any given field— guide and direct the work of the scientific community. Commenting on the practice of scientists to ignore evidence incompatible with current scientific theory, Polanyi says: "The wise neglect of such evidence prevents scientific laboratories from being plunged for ever into a turmoil of incoherent and futile efforts to verify false allegations. But there is, unfortunately, no rule by which to avoid the risk of occasionally disregarding thereby true evidence which conflicts (or seems to conflict) with the current teachings of science."[28]

27. Ibid., 164.
28. Ibid., 138.

As such the scientific community is one in which tradition and authority have an essential role to play. This is not to deny a degree of autonomy to the practitioners, nor is it to deny the critical aspect of their work (if these elements were absent there would be little progress in science); it is, rather, to suggest, that scientific autonomy and scientific criticism function within a broad framework of tradition and authority, *and must do so*, if science is to avoid degenerating into chaos.

b) Nurturing Tradition

A further implication of Polanyi's insights concerns the nurture, or apprenticeship, of scientists. If a person wishes to work within science—in whatever specialized field—they must submit themselves to the training, authority, and the traditions of the scientific community.

The precise nature of the apprenticeship will, of course, depend upon the field of specialization. But any aspiring scientist must acquire the necessary skills. This will certainly entail "book-work"—learning the theory of the discipline and the mathematical apparatus required to express it. But the process of assimilating such explicit, articulate, knowledge will occur *alongside* the development of practical skills. The student may have to learn to use an array of experimental equipment; this will be achieved less through the reading of books and more through observing the practice of those already skilled in the use of such equipment. These essential formal elements of scientific training must be supplemented by submitting to the practices and mores of a particular scientific department or research institute, and coming to an understanding of how to work within it.

This rough sketch demonstrates how such an apprenticeship is a nurturing within a tradition. It may also be apparent that, for the greater part, a scientist's knowledge of these things will be substantially tacit. Like the car driver, the competent scientist (having completed his apprenticeship) may know how to proceed, but will not be able to articulate fully this knowledge.

Polanyi makes the significant point that the life of the scientific community has grown and developed over many years in the pursuit of scientific truth. This is achieved through a commitment to such truth. And, of course, the scientific community is one of many communities whose life has grown up in the service of truth. The judiciary, the various humanities, the arts, religious communities, and others are similarly committed, if in other spheres of life. Polanyi writes: "Our adherence to the truth can be seen to imply our adherence to a society which respects the truth, and which we trust to respect it. Love of truth and of intellectual values in general will now reappear as the love of the kind of society which fosters these values, and submission to intellectual standards will be seen to imply participation in a society which accepts the cultural obligation to serve these standards."[29] The significance of such commitments becomes painfully clear when they break down: think, for example, of the state of a country when its judicial system has become riddled with bribery and corruption.

Because participation in such communities is substantially tacit, it is not possible to offer a full and explicit explanation of them. Nor is it possible to offer a fully articulate defense or justification of them. Polanyi's theory of tacit knowledge demonstrates that the standard of a fully articulate defense is *logically* impossible. It is not a lack of rigor: there is *necessarily* an unaccountable element because of the tacit component of our participation in such communities. Polanyi writes:

> Take two scientists discussing a problem of science on an equal footing. Each will rely on standards that he believes to be obligatory both for himself and for the other. Every time either of them makes an assertion as to what is true and valuable in science, he relies blindly on a whole system of collateral facts and values accepted by science. And he relies also on the fact that his partner relies on the same system. Indeed, the bond of mutual trust thus formed between the two is but one link in the vast network of confidence between thousands of scientists of different specialities, through which—and through which alone—a consensus of science is established which may be said to accept certain facts and values as scientifically valid.[30]

The purpose of an apprenticeship in science is to attain the knowledge required to participate in the scientific community. In order to gain such knowledge one must *submit* to the tradition and *trust* that, in the personal transformation that results from such nurture, one is significantly equipped with know-how that will facilitate scientific inquiry.

29. Ibid., 203.
30. Ibid., 375.

To offer a "rough and ready" parallel, look at the way a child learns to speak within a family. The child must perceive that the noises that it hears when its parents speak are somehow meaningful. On this basis, the child seeks to mimic words and phrases and, in time, perceive how they function in the context of the life of that family. Like learning to play a game, the child "picks up" the idea of how to use language by seeing how it is done. The child will learn the "rules" of how to speak without any explicit knowledge of the rules of grammar. They may even be learned from parents who also lack such knowledge. Nevertheless, there *are* rules and they must be adhered to if language is to function effectively. The parents know these rules, even if they cannot explain them, and these are the rules that the child must learn if it is to speak. As the parents function as the authority in the child's acquisition of speech, and the "tradition" of speech is mediated through them, so the teachers represent the authority for the student. The student may often not understand why the teacher does things in particular ways, but she must, nevertheless, trust that the teacher's actions are purposeful and meaningful. The student must strain to understand "why"—even when there is no explicit explanation—and gain insight into why the teacher proceeds in a particular way. The student must learn to "play the game."

However innovative one's playing of a game may be (whether the use of language for speech, the deployment of scientific "know-how," or any number of other skills), learning to "play the game" must be a submission to authority and the imitation of an inherited tradition.

Thus science is conceived as, and funded by, a commitment to a vast body of beliefs and practices. Such a commitment implies a very substantial degree of trust. It must be acknowledged that such trust might conceivably be mistaken. This possibility cannot be circumvented, as it is intrinsic to tacit knowing.

POLANYI AND RELATIVISM

Polanyi leads us to think of science as something like a "community of faith." It is plain to see that as a community of faith, the modern Western scientific tradition has no significant rivals. While there are, of course, many internal conflicts within science, it experiences no significant challenges from "competing" or "alternative" scientific communities. This situation may be contrasted with many other spheres of human engagement where there *are* "competing" or "alternative" communities. This is obviously the case with religious communities. Although one religious tradition may predominate in particular geographical regions, no religious faith community dominates globally in a way that parallels the dominance of modern western science.

Modern Western science represents an extraordinary community that has transformed much of the way in which we see the world. It has established itself over a period of three hundred years, across cultures and continents. From the perspective of the twenty-first century, the credentials and stability of modern Western science may appear unassailable, but this appearance may be deceptive.[31] Science grows within a society of practitioners whose skills are predominantly unspecifiable. Because of the unspecifiability of the body of scientific knowledge, the safe passage of the tradition from one generation to the next is by no means assured. Science is not a body of explicit knowledge: the knowledge of its practitioners is predominantly tacit and, as such, cannot be abstracted from the life of the scientific community and the beliefs that sustain it. Furthermore, science, as a "community of faith," can make no *absolute* claims about its own veracity. It is, in Polanyi's terminology, an "indwelling" through which its practitioners engage with reality. It is, for all its longevity and its stunning achievements, a community whose beliefs and commitments can never be fully and finally validated according to any explicit criteria.

This being the case, two important questions arise: firstly, is it conceivable that another body of science could develop—rooted in a distinct community and tradition—that, in time, might challenge the dominance of modern Western science? Secondly, is Polanyi's philosophy inherently relativistic? To the first question, it is clear that Polanyi wishes to give an affirmative answer, although, in the absence of any *actual* challenge, it is difficult to say more. To the second question, a more nuanced response is required.

Polanyi is aware of a problem implicit in his theory. If the pursuit of truth is facilitated by the indwelling of a tradition, what justification can be offered for indwelling any *particular* tradition? In the case of science, at least, one might proffer the defense that it is the only one available. But the dilemma remains: if I hold convictions on the basis of a received authority they do not appear to be *my* convictions. On the other hand, if I

31. See Ibid., 181ff.

actively affirm them, it appears that my affirmation is arbitrary: why *these* convictions rather than others? Further, as Polanyi notes, "The exercise of authority will tend to appear as bigoted or as hypocritical, if it asserts as universal what is only parochial."[32]

Does this imply that every affirmation is made in bad faith? It will do so only if it is made on the basis of an ill-founded received authority, or if, as the objectivist has done, we propose a standard of impersonal knowledge. Polanyi, by illuminating the fiduciary and tacit elements of knowing, has shown that a standard of impersonal knowledge is illusory. Consequently, he accepts that knowledge established through participation in any particular community of practice—whether the scientific community or another—is necessarily fallible, but he does not conclude that such knowledge is, thereby, rendered invalid or relative. He writes, "I accept these accidents of personal existence as the concrete opportunities for exercising our personal responsibilities. *This acceptance is the sense of my calling.*"[33]

Polanyi's position is not relativistic but it does acknowledge the particularity of a person's "calling," whether that calling is the culture in which one has been nurtured, or, in addition, one's participation in a particular community of practice within the wider community—scientific, religious, or some other. It is from within such callings that a person must bear their responsibility in the search for truth.[34] Polanyi illustrates this point by reference to the role of the judge in the law courts:

> By seeking the right decision the judge must *find* the law, supposed to be existing—though as yet unknown. This is why eventually his decision becomes binding as law. The judge's discretion is thus narrowed down to zero by the stranglehold of his universal intent—by the power of his responsibility over himself. This is his independence. It consists in keeping himself wholly responsible to the interests of justice, excluding any subjectivity, whether of fear or favour. Judicial independence has been secured, where it exists, by centuries of passionate resistance to intimidation and corruption; for justice is an intellectual passion seeking satisfaction of itself, by inspiring and ruling men's lives.[35]

32. Ibid., 204.

33. Ibid., 322. Emphasis Polanyi.

34. This is the responsibility of which objectivism sought to relieve us, in its claims to impersonal objective knowledge.

35. Polanyi, *Personal Knowledge*, 308f. Emphasis Polanyi.

The judge indwells the legal system that he administers. This is the judge's "calling." There can be no final and incontrovertible justification of this system. Indeed, there are many distinct legal systems across the world, and all of them are necessarily open to revision in that they must be responsive and adaptive in the face of new cases. However, out of the possibilities that are open to him from within the system that he indwells, the judge seeks to establish new law. It is by this process that the incremental growth of the law is facilitated. Polanyi suggests that there are parallels between the work of the judge in making a decision and the course of scientific discovery:

> In both cases the innovator has a wide decision of choice, because he has no fixed rules to rely on, and the range of his discretion determines the measure of his personal responsibility. In both cases a passionate search for a solution that is regarded as potentially preexisting, narrows down discretion to zero and issues at the same time an innovation claiming universal acceptance. In both cases the original mind takes a decision on grounds that are insufficient to minds lacking similar powers of creative judgment. The active scientific investigator stakes bit by bit his whole professional life on a series of such decisions and this day-to-day gamble represents his most responsible activity. The same is true of the judge, with the difference, of course, that the risk is borne here mainly by the parties to the case and by the society which has entrusted itself to the interpretation of its laws by the courts.[36]

The scientist, engaged in the pursuit of a discovery, gropes towards that which is hidden but that he believes *may* be accessible. The choices made in this process are the scientist's own but the scientist is constrained by many things—not least the "shape" of the problem by which she is confronted.

Insofar as they are acting responsibly, their personal participation in drawing their own conclusions is completely compensated for by the fact that they are submitting to the universal status of the hidden reality that they are trying to approach. Accidents may sometimes bring about—or prevent—discovery, but research does not rely on accident: the continuously renewed risks of failure normally incurred at every heuristic

36. Ibid., 309f.

step are taken without ever acting at random. Responsible action excludes randomness, even as it suppresses egocentric arbitrariness.[37]

Scientists and judges are not free to do as they wish; they act as they must, as the reality that confronts them constrains the ways in which they deploy their skills, knowledge, and imagination. This is a strictly disciplined work. It is a personal action that draws from a deep participation within a community of practice, whether scientific or legal.

Polanyi's philosophy is not relativistic but it does acknowledge that every form of knowing is funded by tacit knowledge that is established through some form of communal participation. There is no "view from nowhere," to borrow Thomas Nagel's phrase. The "God's-eye view" is not one that is available to us. Humans know as humans are: intelligent, but fallible, communal creatures.

CONCLUSION

The title of this essay indicates that its purpose is to deal with the question of knowledge in science and religion from a Polanyian perspective. The greater part of it has been concerned with scientific knowledge as it is established within the scientific community. I make no apology for the one-sidedness of this approach, but in concluding I will re-emphasize some of my reasons for tackling the issue in this way.

As I have been attempting to offer a "Polanyian" perspective on this theme I have, largely, followed Polanyi's own trajectory of thought. He is not primarily concerned to develop a "general epistemology," but to articulate how knowledge emerges and is established within science. He adopts a strongly *a posteriori* approach and was able to do this with considerable proficiency because of his own extensive experience within the scientific community.

The epistemology that Polanyi establishes calls for a significant remapping of epistemological categories. It challenges many epistemological assumptions; in particular, the disjunction between subjective and objective, and the standard of explicit justification. He achieves this primarily through the development of his theory of tacit knowledge, in which he expounds the "from-to" nature of knowing, and the central importance of indwelling—participation within communities of practice— as the means by which tacit knowledge is established.

37. Ibid., 310.

The kind of epistemology that emerges from his reflections upon science bears a much greater resemblance to the ways in which it has been *generally* accepted that knowledge is established in the humanities and religion. Polanyi shows that knowing in science, as well as humanities and religion, is facilitated by participation in what might be called "faith communities." The beliefs and commitments that sustain such communities can neither be fully justified nor exhaustively articulated.

Of particular interest is Polanyi's description of scientific discovery as the outcome of a highly disciplined—but, also, highly imaginative—engagement, or participation, within such a community. Discovery is the successful integration of clues hitherto unseen or unnoticed, opening up new possibilities and extending a paradigm of thought. All of this is deeply personal—the outcome of profound commitments that *could* be mistaken. Polanyi writes:

> The understanding of science we have achieved . . . enables us to see that the study of man in humanistic terms is not unscientific, since *all* meaningful integrations (including those achieved in science) exhibit a triadic structure consisting of the subsidiary, the focal, and the person, and all are thus inescapably *personal*. This observation . . . can be understood to constitute the first step in bridging the gulf that supposedly separates scientific from humanistic knowledge, attitudes, and methods. In view of what we have now seen . . . we can surely bridge this gulf completely. We now see that not only do the scientific and humanistic both involve personal participation; we see that both also involve an active use of the imagination. That the various humanities are heavily entangled with the imagination has always been very clear to almost everyone; but that imagination has an essential role to play in science as well has rarely even been glimpsed.[38]

Thus, in radical discontinuity with an Enlightenment view, Polanyi shows that the kinds of knowledge that are established in science stand in substantial continuity with the kinds of knowledge established in religion. At least, there is no differentiation to be made on the basis of the supposed presence or absence of personal participation or imagination.

Polanyi *does* acknowledge *certain* distinctions between the ways of knowing established in science and elsewhere. In *Personal Knowledge*, he suggests that it may be appropriate to speak of *verification* of science by experience, while speaking of the knowledge gained elsewhere (his

38. Polanyi and Prosch, *Meaning*, 63f. Emphasis original.

examples are mathematics, religion, and "various arts"[39]) as the outcome of "a process of *validation*."[40] This suggestion is made on the basis that the bearing of science on facts of experience is more specific than in other spheres. He also acknowledges that the level of personal participation is generally greater in validation than verification. He writes, "The emotional coefficient of assertion is intensified as we pass from the sciences to neighbouring domains of thought."[41] But this is as much as he will concede, and he affirms, "both *verification* and *validation* are everywhere an acknowledgement of a commitment: they claim the presence of something real and external to the speaker."[42]

This is the way in which Polanyi sees *particular* commitments and "indwelling" facilitating a genuine "knowledge-forming" engagement with what is external to the mind of the knower. Polanyi's critically realistic epistemology does acknowledge a differentiation between the ways of knowing in science and elsewhere—including religion—but it is clear that it will in no way admit the radical disjuncture established in the forms of Enlightenment thought that remain influential in the present day.

The reader will be aware that I have referred to science and "religion." This is only satisfactory up to a point because "religion" is a generic term that applies to a variety of religions. But, of course, there is no "religion in general," only particular religious or faith communities.

It is necessary to stress that religious knowledge is established, primarily, through participation in a particular religious community. Even in religions where the expressions of explicit belief (cast in the form of doctrines, dogma, theologies, "spiritualities," and the like) are highly developed, they represent, to recall Polanyi's phrase, an "attenuated summary" of what is known through participation within the life of commitments and indwelling—participation within a community.

I am aware that this essay leaves open vast and pressing questions about the truth claims of different religious communities. The present essay is clearly not the context in which such issues can be taken up. The task of this essay has been limited to looking at the radical continuities that exist between scientific and religious ways of knowing; continuities that, for too long, have gone substantially unrecognized.

39. See Polanyi, *Personal Knowledge*, 202.

40. Ibid. Emphasis Polanyi.

41. Ibid.

42. Ibid. Emphasis Polanyi.

2

The Dialectic of Assimilation and Adaptation Revisited

R. T. ALLEN

INTRODUCTION

IN A NEAT TWIST of Hegel's dialectic, those who would sever theology from philosophy and, specifically, deplore the use of Greek philosophy in patristic times, are likely to find themselves committing what they would abjure. For, thinking that they are free of philosophy in general and of Greek philosophy in particular, they are bound, without realizing that they are doing so, to use the terminology and thought-forms of ancient philosophy—"substance," "essence," "form," "idea," "matter," "being," "existence," "science," "concept," "quality," etc.—that have deposited themselves into "ordinary" language, and thus to employ them wholly uncritically.

The lesson to be learned from this is that Christian thinkers should neither pretend that they can dispense with philosophy nor uncritically adopt any one philosophy. Rather, they should be ready to take up, and adapt as necessary, anything that they find compatible with their profession and useful for their work (indeed, to deride human reasoning as irredeemably corrupt is equivalent to Gnosticism). The philosophy of Michael Polanyi, because it is a thorough-going personalist philosophy, is one that especially commends itself to Christian thinkers, who, as always, should be prepared to adapt it.

Back in 1992, I published a revised version of my PhD thesis, in which I sought to do what seemed to me not to have been done thitherto: to apply Polanyi's philosophy directly to some themes of Christian doctrine rather than only to retrace his own steps in removing Objectivist obstacles to Christian faith, thus "clearing a path to the porch" but not himself going inside the church.[1] Re-reading it recently, I saw that this theme of assimilation and adaptation runs through it. Explicitly discussed on pp. 19, 29, and 49–50, yet omitted by me from the Index of the book, the theme reappears with almost every topic treated, as the particular aspects of Polanyi's philosophy are shown to need some adaptation in order to be able to accommodate Christian doctrines, or, from the reverse direction, for Christian theology to be able to assimilate and employ them. The invitation to contribute to this collection now gives me an opportunity to revisit, partly to correct and then to elaborate, what I have already written about Polanyi on the dialectic of assimilation and adaptation, and then to apply it further to a specific topic within the Christian doctrine of God and consequently to one within Christian epistemology.

POLANYI ON ASSIMILATION AND ADAPTATION

I shall now briefly summarize, and add to, what I have already written about assimilation and adaptation in Polanyi's work.

a) Because his overall aim in *Personal Knowledge*, the central text for our theme, is to confute Objectivism and to show that the knower necessarily plays a part in his knowing, Polanyi decisively rejects any account of the mind as a passive *tabula rasa*. For example, though he draws much from Gestalt theory, he rejects the account of some Gestaltists that recognition and construction of Gestalts are accomplished by some automatic and impersonal process within us.[2]

---

1. King's College, London, 1982. Published as Allen, *Transcendence and Immanence*. Breaking out of frameworks is a very important theme even though "breaking out" itself appears only twice in Polanyi's *Personal Knowledge*, 6.13. I also welcome this opportunity to say more about it, for the neglect of which my friend, Endre Nagy, has chided expositors of Polanyi—myself among them—in Nagy, "The Hungarian Background to Michael Polanyi's Thought." This neglect was evident in my short book *Polanyi* that, because of size, was necessarily selective. I have said something about the topic, however, in my *Transcendence and Immanence*.

2. Polanyi, *Personal Knowledge*, 98.

b) Our activity in knowing is shown by our (tacit) construction of what he calls "interpretative frameworks" or "conceptual frameworks," and what others have called "absolute presuppositions," "categories," "categorial frameworks," "schemata," etc. With these we apprehend, comprehend, and act within the world around us, as is shown by Piaget's studies of child development[3] and Ames' and others' experiments with persons placed in abnormal situations.[4] We cannot simply open our eyes and see, or our ears and hear, as Empiricists and Positivists have assumed, but we have to learn to apprehend the world and to discover order and meaning in our experience of it. Summing up the personal efforts and judgments that we made as infants (e.g., as to whether a rattle in the fist either grew larger or smaller or retained its size as we moved it towards and away from us), and the preferences we employed (e.g., for distinct shapes), he writes: "[w]e eventually constructed a universal interpretative framework that assumes the ubiquitous existence of objects, retaining their sizes and shapes when seen at different distances and from different angles, and their color and brightness when seen under varying illuminations."[5]

c) Polanyi uses "indwelling" to refer to our relation to our frameworks. We use them, but they are more than *tools*. For a tool is an external object that is temporally incorporated into the body when it is used, and thus when our attention is redirected, not focally *to* it, but subsidiarily *from* it and focally *to* what we are doing with it, just as we primarily attend *from* our bodies and *to* the world and our actions in it.[6] In using it, we indwell a tool and then cease to do so when we stop using it. But our relation to

---

3. I particularly recommend Piaget, *The Child's Conception of the World*, that empirically demolishes the dogmas of Empiricism and much other philosophy, (for example, that children start off by perceiving a merely physical world and then learn, by analogy with themselves, that some things in it are animate and of them some are personal). In fact, as Piaget demonstrates, they start by interpreting everything as personal and then learn to depersonalise some things. See also what Piaget calls the child's "realism," that is the child's original lack of distinction between the real and the unreal, a distinction that has to be learned and applied, and that, in history, is shown to be applied in different ways. (Piaget was very aware that he and his assistants were studying the modern European child.) We are all, and necessarily so, tacit metaphysicians and epistemologists, forming, employing and adapting tacit ontologies, cosmologies and standards for knowing.

4. Cited in Polanyi, *Personal Knowledge*, 96.

5. Ibid., 97.

6. Ibid., 59.

our bodies is permanent and more intimate. Likewise our relation to our interpretative frameworks. Moreover, our frameworks can determinate what sorts of person we are, and to change them may require, or result in, a radical change of oneself. Hence to change them, "breaking out," can involve a radical change of personality, as becomes clear in the political examples that Polanyi mentions.[7]

d) Polanyi also uses Piaget's terminology: we now *assimilate* our experience with perceptual, and other, interpretative frameworks, and simultaneously we *adapt* those frameworks to cope with new experiences or to clarify confusions.[8] The former is a routine and relatively impersonal operation, but the latter is an heuristic act that requires personal judgment and decision "to modify the premises of our judgment, and thus to modify our intellectual existence."[9] Such modification of a framework cannot be conducted wholly from within it; it is a matter of "breaking out" from the framework, or significant parts of it, and not of its continued application.

e) Here Polanyi significantly departs from what seems to be the fixity of Kant's categories as the necessary and sufficient conditions for any experience whatsoever (curiously and more explicitly asserted also by those Relativists and Post-Modernists who state that we are entrapped within our own categories and so cannot comprehend any others).[10] Apart from

7. See his articles "Beyond Nihilism" and "The Message of the Hungarian Revolution" in *Knowing and Being*.

8. Polanyi, *Personal Knowledge*, 105: Polanyi substitutes "adaptation" for Piaget's "accommodation."

9. Ibid., 106. See also 267: commenting on St Augustine's use of *nisi credideritis, non intelligitis*, Polanyi writes: "It says, as I understand it, that the process of examining any topic is both an exploration of the topic, and an exegesis of our fundamental beliefs in the light of which we approach it; a dialectical combination of exploration and exegesis". That is equivalent to a dialectical combination of assimilation of the topic into our existing framework and of adaptation of that framework to the topic.

10. Compare the Wittgenstein of the *Tractatus*: "*The limits of my language* mean the limits of my world" (Wittgenstein, *Tractatus Logico-Philosophicus*, Proposition 5.6 [emphasis Wittgenstein]), which would be true if all knowledge were explicit. For then we would have no tacit awareness of anything for which we did not already have the words, and so our current vocabulary would be fixed and unchangeable: "Whereof one cannot speak, thereof one must be silent" (ibid., Proposition 7). Compare also Winch, *The Idea of a Social Science*, based on the declaration of the later Wittgenstein that "this language game is played;" from which it is inferred that no "language game"—and with it, its

other obvious errors, such assertions contradict the very historicity that they invoke. For as infants we had continuously to create and adapt our frameworks, and hence retain the power to do so today.

f) This tacit power to create, modify, and abandon intellectual and conceptual frameworks, etc., is in turn possible only because it enables us to sense aspects of reality that do not fit what we already focally (and perhaps explicitly) know. The from-to structure of knowing (*A* attends from *B* to *C*) makes it possible for us to bring into focus hidden realities suggested by that which we already know, and thus to strain to attend *from* the latter and *to* the former and thus to bring them into focus. This is Polanyi's answer to the problem of the *Meno* (that learning is either redundant because we know already what we are looking for, or impossible because we do not know what we are looking for and so cannot recognize it when we come across it).[11] Reality does not consist of a collection of logical atoms, each enclosed within itself, but of overlapping networks in which each node is a clue to others.

g) Consequently, although Polanyi does not himself make this wholly explicit, we all share at least one framework or absolute presupposition at the highest level: that there is a real world to which we need to attune ourselves and make our beliefs adequate.[12] We change both lower and higher level beliefs because of growing dissatisfaction with them, and that means their *adequacy to reality*. As Polanyi shows,[13] it is necessary, in natural sci-

---

constitutive framework or set of presuppositions—can be criticized from outside it. A theological invocation of the later Wittgenstein can be found in Phillips, *The Concept of Prayer*. It did not occur to the author that the same principle also legitimizes witchcraft, "magic," and astrology. Atheism and secularism would not have worried Prof. Phillips, for his account of religion and prayer is itself wholly secular and hence *not* the "language game" that is being played.

11. Polanyi, *The Tacit Dimension*, 21–24.

12. Those who still ask, "Was Polanyi a realist?," or even answer, "No," either have failed to read him (see "reality" in the Index to Polanyi, *Personal Knowledge*, e.g., note 13 below; and likewise see the "pseudo-substitutions" for "truth," such as "regulative principles," "simplicity," "economy," and "fruitfulness"; and his explicit article "Science and Reality"), or are still stuck in the Objectivist framework in which any involvement of the knower in his or her knowledge renders that knowledge hopelessly "subjective," in which case they have never read the findings of the empirical psychology of perception and child development.

13. Polanyi, *Personal Knowledge*, 284–94; cf. 106: "To learn a language or to modify its meaning is a tacit, irreversible, heuristic feat; it is a transformation of our intellectual

ence as elsewhere, to maintain the stability of our beliefs—up to a point. For this there are several devices, with legitimate and illegitimate uses. Nevertheless, difficulties and contrary evidence can accumulate to such an amount that, if we are honest with ourselves, we do need to modify our current frameworks, perhaps radically, so as to adapt them to what so far we have implicitly or explicitly denied, such as the movement of the earth around the sun, action at distance or quantum leaps.

h) To return to (d): Between one framework and a modification of it or the adoption of another one, there is a logical gap that cannot be crossed by use of the premises and evidence of the old. Hence for the pioneer to cross it in the first place, he needs "heuristic passion" and then "persuasive passion" to convince others that they should follow him, and this leads to controversy, in science as elsewhere, in which these passions often get out of hand.[14] The pioneer has to try to win sympathy for his discovery or innovation although, in the nature of the case, he cannot explain it in terms of existing conceptions and frameworks. On the hand, he must teach others a new language, yet, on the other, they may be unwilling to acquire it if they are not convinced that it will mean something. And so, "demonstration must be supplemented . . . by forms of persuasion which can induce a conversion."[15] And even an appeal to "the facts" may not suffice, for the facts can appear very differently when viewed from within the old and new frameworks, and in the one may not be accredited as facts at all.[16]

i) But, perhaps because Polanyi is discussing the crossing of these logical gaps in the context of "intellectual passions" (the title of chapter 6 in his *Personal Knowledge*), Polanyi does not deal with possible attempts by the pioneer to try to adapt his language so as to make his discovery or innovation a little more intelligible within the existing framework of his audience, and thus to narrow somewhat the logical and linguistic gap. For this one can try analogously to extend existing terms, or metaphorically to apply them, so that some meaning (albeit probably with existing

life, originating in our own desire for greater clarity and coherence, and yet sustained by the hope of coming by it into closer touch with reality."

14. Ibid., 142–45 and 150–60.

15. Ibid., 151. On similar innovations and controversies in art, see 201–2; and note 7 above for conversions in politics.

16. Ibid., 167.

but now misleading associations and implications) is conveyed to one's audience, or to employ models and visual analogies, such as the planetary model of the atom and the double-helix for DNA. Such adaptation of the new, so that it may in part be assimilated by those still holding to the old and thus induce them to begin to adapt their beliefs and frameworks to it, is probably needed in the first place by the pioneer himself so that he can more clearly understand what he has discovered. This secondary use of "adaptation" applies to the language (and models) used rather than to the framework itself, and to the one who has already crossed the gap.

j) Polanyi himself uses "breaking out," not so much for abandoning one framework for another, but for what he thinks is an abandonment of frameworks altogether in favor of "vision" or "contemplation."[17] Scientific discovery, resulting in the formation of a new framework to replace the old, bursts the bounds of disciplined thought in an intense if transient moment of heuristic vision. And while it is thus breaking out, the mind is for the moment directly experiencing its content rather than controlling it by the use of any pre-established modes of interpretation: it is overwhelmed by its own passionate activity.[18]

> That is, the new aspect of reality, to which the scientist now attends, is grasped directly—though almost certainly confusedly—until he has formed new categories, schema, conceptions, etc., appropriate to it or has radically modified existing ones. Such direct vision is sought most radically in the desire to break through "all fixed conceptual frameworks" in "the act of ecstatic vision," as when an astronomer, forgetting his astronomy by which he would see the stars merely as instances of types and of astronomical laws, simply looks *at* them in the night sky. Vision, or contemplation, dispenses with the "screen" that the conceptual framework—used for observation and manipulation—interposes between ourselves and the sensuous properties of things: "we cease to handle things and become immersed in them." Then we achieve an "impersonality," equal but opposed to that of complete detachment.[19] Yet it seems to me that this is true only of specific frameworks, such as those of practical life, in which things are viewed in relation to our desires and intentions, or of specialised intellectual disciplines. Perhaps here even the framework of aiming at truth and reality is

17. Ibid., 6.13.

18. Ibid., 196.

19. Ibid., 196–97.

abandoned (or "bracketed" as Husserl would say), but not in "the transient moment of heuristic vision" wherein our tacit power to attend from what we already know brings into view something real (or taken to be real) for which we have yet no adequate framework or conceptions. And even in aesthetic vision when we simply contemplate what we already know, our visual, auditory and tactile frameworks—by which we distinguish and recognise shapes, colours, sounds, and textures—are being used to the full and are not being set aside. So also, other frameworks are retained by which we recognise what is presented or represented. Without frameworks of some sort, we would end up in that pure consciousness of non-dualist mysticism in the Indian tradition, which, not being a consciousness of anything, is no consciousness at all.[20]

THEOLOGICAL APPLICATIONS

The further questions and theological implications flowing from this aspect of Polanyi's thought are many and various. Some of them I have already treated in my *Transcendence and Immanence*:

a. whether or not different frameworks (e.g., religion in general and Christianity in particular) can be, at least partly, understood and legitimately criticized from the outside;

b. theology as the axiomatization of Christian belief and practice, the articulation of its conceptual framework or absolute presuppositions;

c. the possibility of a "presuppositional" and "dialectical" natural theology, that would argue from acceptance of specific frameworks (of modern science, ethics, play, the upbringing of children) to the existence of God as in turn presupposed by them;

d. the theological extension of "ordinary" language to bridge the ontological gulf between created realities and God, and to adapt, in the secondary sense noted in paragraph (i) in the previous section, the language of theism and Christianity, or the existing language and conceptions of those outside the faith, in order to narrow the gap of understanding between them and the faith.

20. See the text and the comment in the *Chandogya Upanishad*, xi: "When a man is sound asleep, integrated within himself and quite serene, when not conscious of dreaming—this is the Self, the immortal, the free from fear: this is Brahman . . . Such a man it seems to me, has no present knowledge of himself so that he could say, 'This I am' . . . Surely he might as well be a man annihilated. I see nothing enjoyable in this."

In addition, I argued that some central aspects of Polanyi's philosophy, especially the structure of tacit integration in knowing, speaking, and being, can be suitably adapted to enable us the better to comprehend the ways in which we can know God, how he is related to the world, and the relations among the three divine persons.

I also argued that some of Polanyi's own interpretations of Christianity, such as his assimilation of it to a visionary experience without any ontological import (as in paragraph (j) above) and as a desire never to be satisfied,[21] need to be radically adapted, for they, too, readily assimilate Christianity into the framework used for created and finite reality and a merely secular conception of human life, from which Polanyi did not properly liberate himself.

I do not intend to repeat anything that I have said about such matters. Yet there are two connected topics that I would like to develop here: the unity and "simplicity" of God, and knowing as a specification of love, for both of which Polanyi's philosophy offers some assistance, plus two further topics that I shall now simply mention.

One extension of the question raised in paragraph (d) above is a deeper and fully personalist understanding of the evangelist's task, and, indeed, of God's self-revelation to humankind. The language of the Christian message has to be adapted to its audience (but without compromising the content). Here Christianity has had a great advantage over its one missionary rival, Islam. For its central texts—the Gospels—already contain translations from the Aramaic words of the Master into koiné Greek. Therefore it does not have a "sacred" language, whereas the Koran's own statements of its verbal inspiration to Mohammed have rightly entailed that the very words are sacred and thus untranslatable. And so Muslims have had to submit themselves to the learning, often in parrot-fashion, of the original Arabic text, accompanied, if possible, by some explanation in the vernacular. Only competition from the Bible in the local vernaculars has brought about the translation of the Koran. But Islam, as "submission" and with a Code of very specific injunctions and prohibitions, remains mostly the adaptation of the believer to the message of the Prophet with but little adaptation of that message to the believer. Consequently, it is generally a much less *personal* religion than Christianity.

21. Polanyi, *Personal Knowledge,* 198–99; and the whole treatment of these themes in Polanyi's writings.

Furthermore, the same applies to our understanding of God's relation to humanity. Just as the human evangelist, truly to convert the unbeliever, must appeal to his conscience and reason so that he can lay hold of the gospel and make it is own, so too God does not displace the human person but condescends and adapts himself to our level and speaks, indirectly or directly, in language and terms that we can at least partially understand. The Incarnate Word spoke in everyday Aramaic (and perhaps even in Greek) and used homely and familiar analogies, and thus could be understood by all who had ears to hear. Moral appeal and honest persuasion, not sheer psychological power and "possession," were his means. Yet there is always the danger of a lapse into theological Objectivism, in which the believer is supposed to contribute nothing to his or her faith (since that would be human presumption) and to be instead a passive receptacle for, and conduit of, a message that is all God's doing.

There, again, the church has the advantage. For the prophets of the Old Testament, the authors of the New, and Christian theologians, teachers, and missionaries today, remain finite persons who themselves have personally to appropriate what they are called to pass on. Hence it can be freely admitted that at times the Word of God has been mixed with and expressed through—as it has to be—the fallible and inadequate words of human beings, and has even been distorted by them.[22]

THE DIVINE UNITY AND SIMPLICITY

In *Transcendence* I began my treatment of this theme by suggesting that God, not having a collection of attributes, is not a person with powers, nor without powers, nor powers without a person, but "a super-integration of person and powers, that unity which becomes distinct and liable to division in finite beings."[23] That is, I was suggesting that the from-to structure of mental powers and levels of being in us (each higher level determining the boundary conditions of the next lower one and not being determined

---

22. I find it objectionable that, in some churches, the lessons are closed with the simple and unqualified statement, "This is the word of God." Biblical "fundamentalism" and literalism have no place at all in Christianity. One thing wrong in the *Book of Common Prayer* is the recitation of the full text of Exodus 19:4, the Second Commandment, despite the clear recognition of individual responsibility in Ezekiel 19. The latter, and not "visiting the iniquity of the fathers upon the children," is a word of God undistorted by the words of men in which it is expressed.

23. Allen, *Transcendence and Immanence*, 136 and 149.

by it[24]) has, as it were, God at the top of a scale of increasing integration of the levels. This, I now see, was a failure properly to break out of the framework of finite being. For it still implied that, in some way at least, God is a whole of parts, whereas what is required is a conception of unity that is not "partitive" at all.

This is an old problem in theology. In European history it goes back to Plotinus, and in India to earlier still, where it is the question of whether Brahman has "ragas" ("determinations") or not. In Greek thought, the forms are principles of finitude that make determinate, and hence real, an otherwise formless "matter," the *apeiron*, that we may call the "lower infinity." Plotinus, fully realizing that the forms are finite and finitizing, confined them to his Second Hypostasis, *Nous*, that both looks to The One and contemplates the forms. Yet The One, being above forms, is simultaneously the "higher infinity" and yet formless and therefore nothing. But that Plotinus rightly could not allow, for he knew that The One is "He" rather than "It," and is more than just good but is Goodness. But he found no solution. This problem has been with us ever since. It has been given canonical formulation in Cusanus' dictum: *omnis determinatio est negatio*—to be is to be *something*, some *one type* of thing, and therefore *not* something else. His proposed solution, that God is the coincidence of opposites, is sheer nonsense. Contrary "determinations"—and all "determinations" are held to have others incompatible with them—cannot be combined. Therefore either God is finite, being *this* but *not that*, or nothing at all: the third way, of being everything is, *ex hypothesi*, impossible. The way of negation, again found in Europe and earlier in India ("*neti, neti*"), makes sense only as we have a tacit idea of what God positively is, a positive idea that we should at least try to articulate in terms appropriate to it.[25] I then went a little way beyond finite categories altogether by challenging, in effect but not in name, the Cusanian thesis.[26] And now I shall expand a little upon that.

It is precisely personal attributes that are not exclusive and so not inherently finite. That is, they have no contraries and exclude only their absence or distortions: knowledge, for example, excludes only ignorance

24. See Polanyi, *The Tacit Dimension*, 35ff, and many of Polanyi's later longer essays, as reprinted in the later parts of Grene, *Knowing and Being*, and Allen, *Science, Economics and Philosophy*.

25. Allen, *Transcendence and Immanence*, 82.

26. Ibid., 149–50.

and error, whereas physical attributes, such as color and shape, necessarily exclude others in the same range (if red, then not green in the same place; if square, then not rhomboid or circular). Again, personal unity is not a unity of parts but of expression of one and the same intention or character that necessarily takes different forms in different circumstances precisely in order to stay the same and be *one* continuing intention or character. A commander's aim is victory, and so now he attacks and then he retreats; now harbors his reserves and then commits them. To perform the same "material" act in different circumstances is necessarily really to do different things. Likewise the Socratic-Platonic doctrine of the unity of virtue shows that all the supposedly distinct virtues are expressions of the one virtue, not so much of "wisdom" (still too much intellectualism) but of whole-hearted devotion to what is right and good, in different contexts: as justice with regard to rights, as generosity to those in need, as courage and fortitude in face of danger and suffering. It is not the case, as might be easily assumed, that they *limit* each other, but that they maintain the integrity of each other, or, rather, the one virtue expresses itself appropriately on all occasions *in an through them.* Thus justice does not *prevent* us from being generous with others' money, for that is a specious generosity (as of politicians who congratulate themselves upon giving away the tax-payers' money and never give their own), but ensures that generosity is genuine, or, rather, the one virtue expresses itself in *genuine* generosity and so does not commit injustice.[27] Only as expressions of the one virtue can the seemingly distinct virtues be what they are. This, then, is the "non-partitive" idea of unity, of a *self* and its *self-expression,* appropriate to persons, who are *defective* when their unity is one of "parts," as in the compartmentalization of life, and, at the extreme, in schizophrenia and "multiple personalities."

27. The heroic virtues of courage, fortitude, determination, etc., do have a genuine independence and can be shown in the service of evil causes; that is their tragedy. They are like the "natural virtues" that constitute the carefulness required for success in any course of action, whether it be good or evil: had the members of the SS, the KGB and their like been lazy, careless and slapdash, and not disciplined, committed and efficient, the twentieth century would have been spared its worst nightmares. All virtues can be displayed in some contexts but not in others: on the occasion of the parable of the Good Samaritan, what the lawyer (typically!) really wanted to know was who was *not* his neighbor, whom, therefore, he had no need to love as he loved himself. To the extent that we compartmentalize our lives and behave properly in some and not in all, we are therefore not truly good in any.

None of the above owes anything directly to Polanyi, but his personalism in general, and his dialectic of assimilation and adaptation in particular, should warn us against assimilating higher levels of being to lower ones and instead should encourage us to adapt, or break out of, our frameworks and find new categories and concepts appropriate to them. Metaphysics has been far too much meta-*physics* and dominated by the ontology of things: substance and quality, cause and effect. Even then, it has not been appropriate to processes and their phases, still less to personal being. Even Plotinus, of whom it has been said that his metaphysics was a metapsychology, remained too much within the ontology of form and matter, appropriate to the products of craft.[28]

So then, what is God? Being, He Who Is—yes, indeed. But that still leaves his being blank and empty. Christianity gives us the final answer: God is Love (1 John 4:8). God's attributes are not parts of a whole, but expressions of his unitary essence of love. His mercy, justice, wrath towards sin, and forgiveness are all ways in which he, as love, diversely expresses himself towards different actions on the part of human beings. It follows also that, not only these moral attributes, but all others as well, are specifications or expressions of love. How can this be? Since humanity is made in the image of God, and God is love, it follows that humanity too is love,[29] and so a deeper knowledge of ourselves should tell us something about him who made us. Here we must beware of the rationalism that is the *déformation professionelle* of philosophers, and thus of theologians who too quickly assimilate their theology to the concepts and categories of a

---

28. See Collingwood, *The Principles of Art*, chapter 2. Plotinus' problem was experienced earlier in the Advaita (non-dualist) conception of Brahman, that nevertheless was held to be *sat chit ananda* (being, consciousness, bliss). Francis Bradley's Absolute, beyond (i.e., *less than*) personality, God, and all attributes whatsoever (that are finite and hence not reality), is all the same affirmed as being Experience and Spirit. Hegel's solution, followed but modified by Hartshorne with his "di-polar" conception of God, was to conceive the infinite as including the finite, but that is simply to finitize God or *Geist* and not to break out of the Cusanian framework altogether.

29. This was worked out by Max Scheler, in his philosophical prime, from his *Ressentiment in the Construction of Ethics* (1912), through *Formalism in Ethics and the Non-Formal Ethics of Value* (1913, 1916) and *The Nature of Sympathy* (1913, 2nd ed. 1923), to *On the Eternal in Man* (1921, 2nd ed. 1923). This is the period of his second marriage and between his two divorces, when he was reconciled to the Roman Church and drew much of his inspiration from St Augustine and Pascal. After that he lapsed into an immanentist and emergent conception of God and a more naturalist and wholly secular conception of humanity.

philosopher and philosophy affected by that error. It has often resulted in reason being taken as the distinctive nature of humanity and God, and hence, for example, the vision of God has sometimes been too closely interpreted in terms of Aristotle's purely intellectual contemplation. Such a presupposition in the study of humanity and God, is one that we shall need to overcome. Obviously I cannot tackle the whole theme here and now, but I can say something, with Polanyi's aid, about one topic—knowing as an expression of love—that will also help to liberate us from the narrow frameworks of rationalism and intellectualism.

KNOWING AS AN EXPRESSION OF LOVE

While, as in the rest of philosophy, Christian epistemology will properly coincide with or adopt (and adapt) conceptions and principles from other philosophies, it should have its own distinctive features. One of these should be a thorough-going personalism, and that should include an emphasis on the whole person: we should expect human beings to manifest, in a finite form, something of the unity of God. Consequently, Christian epistemology should not confine itself to finding a place for faith alongside reason, as if there could be an autonomous reason without faith. For one thing, that would concede too much to secularists who take human beings to be capable of self-sufficiency. On the contrary, a properly Christian epistemology would look for and articulate what is really there: the necessary role of faith in all human reasoning.[30] So, too, it should go

---

30. For Polanyi's fiduciary philosophy, see Polanyi, *Personal Knowledge*, chapters 8–10 (especially 8.12, "The Fiduciary Programme," with its references to St. Augustine, and 10.1, "Fundamental Beliefs"), and his later essays such as "Faith and Reason," (reprinted as "The Scientific Revolution" in Allen, *Science, Economics and Philosophy*, 329–43), and "Science and Religion," 4–14. The great merit of Polanyi is that, unlike many others (including such personalist philosophers as Scheler and John Macmurray, who tended to regard natural science as a merely intellectual or technical mastery of nature and not as a penetrating understanding of it; those Idealists of the nineteenth century who sought to safeguard the mental, moral and spiritual spheres by arguing that the natural world is only a mental creation; and Dilthey and his school, who separated the human from the natural sciences; and who all thereby conceded the whole sphere of natural science and its prestige to materialists and reductionists), he overcame this dichotomy by showing that in natural science itself faith plays a central and necessary role (along with all our other personal activities of judgment, valuing, feeling, imagination, insight, etc.), an aspect of his work that others have already treated in depth. See also the Augustinian and Anselmian approach of Collingwood, "Reason is Faith Cultivating Itself" and his "Faith and Reason" both in *Faith and Reason*.

even further, and with Polanyi and others discern the equally necessary role of a range of constructive emotions in all our knowing.[31] Following on from the previous topics of the unity of God, and of love as his essence, I shall now seek to show, with Polanyi's aid, that human knowing is itself an expression of love and thus is a clue for understanding the unity of God's nature.

At first sight, it seems nonsensical to state that knowing is a function or expression of love, for, apart from conventional beliefs that love is blind or distorts our knowing, surely one must know something or someone first before one can love it or him. Yet among Max Scheler's most important works is a paper, "Liebe und Erkenntnis"[32] in which he reverses these assumptions. Scheler begins with a quotation from Goethe: "One can get to know only that which one loves and the deeper and fuller the knowledge is to become, the stronger, more forceful and livelier must the love, indeed the passion be." Scheler then contrasts this with a claim from Leonardo da Vinci: "Every great love is the daughter of a great cognition." (Both, again, are contrasted with the common opinion that love is blind.) Scheler's main argument is that the former represents the Christian relationship and the latter the Greek (and to some extent the Indian), but that, except for Augustine and some later followers such as Malebranche and Pascal, Christian thinking has submerged what should be its great insight and has assimilated itself too much to the Greek view, in which love is a desire and striving for something yet to be attained—from the lower to the higher, from "not being" to "being," from man to God (and hence Socrates' "love of wisdom" instead of "[possession of] wisdom," that must disappear once its object, e.g., knowledge, is attained). This is opposed to the Christian view that love is a movement downwards from God to man, who first loved us. Scheler criticizes Aquinas for maintaining the Greek views that love of an object presupposes knowledge of it, that values are only functions of being ("every being is good insofar as it is"), that love is not a fundamental act of the person but only a special activity of striv-

---

31. I have summarized some of this, and combined the contributions of Polanyi, Macmurray, *Reason and Emotion*, Scheler, and Stephan Strasser, *The Phenomenology of Feeling*, who draws upon Aquinas and phenomenology, in Allen, "Passivity and the rationality of emotion;" Allen, "Governance by Emotion;" Allen, "The cognitive functions of emotion;" and Allen, "Polanyi and the rehabilitation of emotion."

32. In Scheler, *Gesammelte Werke* Bd.6, 77–98. The original was written in 1915. English translation in Max Scheler, *On Feeling, Knowing and Valuing*. I am using a private translation.

ing and willing, that the primary forces of the self are the *vis appetitiva* and the *vis intellectiva*, and that every act of striving must be preceded by one of the intellect.[33] Scheler also criticizes Aquinas for saying that God created the world for his own glorification and not out of love, to which the striving of his creatures is a response. Accordingly, God's revelation in Christ is no longer the result of his redemptive act of love and grace, but only the central theme of the wholly intellectually conceived "revelation" itself, i.e., not the *act* of God but only the *message about* that act. He also states that the dispute—between Thomists, on the one side, and Franciscans, Scotists, and Occam, on the other—about the primacy of reason or will in God is a side issue. For Augustine, it is *love*, and not will, that is primary. It is from love that all other activities follow—judgment, perception, the development of ideas, memory, etc.; and so love is the essence of God. Scheler also credits Augustine with holding that things only come to their full being and value when they reveal themselves to, and thus become known, by us, a "natural revelation" that, as it were, redeems them from their self-enclosedness.

Whether or not we go as far as that last point, Scheler, if he is correct, has indicated that Christian philosophy and theology has too often assimilated itself to, instead of adapting, an inadequate philosophy. He has also made the case for a revival of this Johannine and Augustinian centrality of love as the nature of God and thus of man, and for the need to carry it through in detail in philosophy, psychology and other disciplines. Scheler's own essay is itself a manifesto and, though he wrote studies of the functions of rue and remorse, shame, and sympathy, and of other functions of love, a study of love's own cognitive functions has yet to be done.

It is at this point that we can turn to Polanyi (*Personal Knowledge*, 8.2), who, in effect, has carried it through in a sphere that some would see as the most unlikely, namely, natural science. We have already glanced at the heuristic and persuasive functions of intellectual passions, and

---

33. Cf. Franz Brentano, who revived the Scholastics' doctrine that all mental acts, including desires and emotions, have objects (what he, but not they, called "intentionality"), and thus relaunched the proper philosophy of mind and prepared the way for phenomenology, yet who still declared that all other mental acts must be preceded by acts of presentation. Brentano, *Psychology from an Empirical Standpoint*, 8. I shall not comment upon Scheler's historical accuracy, save to say that he probably did not do justice to Plato, for there is evidence to show that Plato was at least on the brink of acknowledging outgoing love on the part of God: see Rist, *Eros and Psyche*.

elsewhere[34] I have formalized Polanyi's scheme of the three functions—selective, heuristic, and persuasive—along with what is, in effect, the fourth, viz. satisfaction. These more or less coincide with those of the roles of emotion in all our activity, as set out by Strasser, himself adapting and extending a simpler scheme of Aquinas, and I have brought them all together in what, I hope, is a yet more comprehensive scheme. What concerns us now is Polanyi's selective function plus a prior valuing of science itself.[35]

Science, claims Polanyi, is like the other systematic endeavors of humanity in claiming that certain emotions are right and in trying to impose and evoke them. They are the valuing of science itself and of its own standards and specific forms of value. Science needs to be valued, not only by its own practitioners, but by the general public: it "can no longer hope to survive on an island of positive facts, around which the rest of man's intellectual heritage sinks to the status of subjective emotionalism."[36] What this means is that the love of both the natural world, and of the endeavor to understand it, is the fundamental prerequisite of scientific research. Without this prior love and without taking an interest in the world and the understanding of it, no intellectual discipline can get under way or be sustained. When people are not interested in the world, or some aspect of it, and in the attempt to know it, then natural science and other sciences either do not arise or else eventually decay.

Secondly, Polanyi argues that within science there is the need to select, out of the manifold facts, those that are of scientific value and those which are not. Without such a prior selection, scientists would dissipate their energies in the pursuit of trivialities and dead-ends, as can be seen in the earlier history of scientific investigation. Yet, equally, important lines of investigation may be closed off for the same reason that they do not fit into the prevailing framework. No rule, or set of rules, can decide such matters, but only the individual and collective personal judgments of practicing scientists. (Again, science requires the dialectic of assimilation by, and adaptation of, interpretative frameworks.)

34. Allen, "Governance by Emotion".

35. In my scheme in ibid., these are replaced by Primary Experience of Desire (that should be "of Valuing"), Motivating Emotion towards or away from the object, and Deciding Emotion to act or abstain.

36. Polanyi, *Personal Knowledge*, 134.

Polanyi distinguishes three specific values within science: certainty or accuracy, systematic relevance or profundity, and intrinsic interest. The first two are integral to natural science, and the third is extra-scientific. A deficiency in one can be outweighed by the other two. As usual Polanyi gives examples of these. One is the exact measurement of atomic weights that gained a Nobel prize in 1914, but then came to be seen as having little significance because atomic weights arise from the accidental proportions of the constituent isotopes, and not from anything truly profound and with systematic relevance. As for intrinsic interest, that increases as investigation moves from the inanimate matter of physics, through the living entities of biology, to ourselves in history and human sciences. And, as it increases, so the other two values, of accuracy and systematic relevance, decrease. Any scientistic preference for the latter pair over the former consequently results in the trivialization and distortion of the studies of life and man, of which Polanyi gave many examples in his subsequent publications. The paradigm of that mistaken preference is Laplace's formulation according to which a complete knowledge of the locations and velocities of all the atoms constituting the universe would yield a complete knowledge of everything that exists and will happen. Its error is that "it substitutes for the subjects in which we are interested a set of data which tell us nothing that we want to know."[37] It would give us only strings of co-ordinates $(p(1) \ldots p(n))$ and velocities $(q(1) \ldots q(n))$ at time t, and from them only other such strings could be computed. It would not even tell us of what element the atom at any given location was an instance, nor anything of its chemical properties, let alone what physical object a group of adjacent atoms composed, such as a pebble, bacterium, plant, animal, or person. "Yet behind these specific values, and especially the first and second, lies the intellectual beauty of a scientific theory as a token or manifestation of its truth, its contact with reality, a beauty akin to and often embodying that of mathematics."[38] This raises the question of whether this intellectual beauty is merely the elegance, simplicity, and economy of a formal system, and thus that, as proclaimed by Ernst Mach, scientific theories are neither true nor false but only simpler, more economical, and more fruitful ways of summarizing and dealing with observed facts. Such was Osiander's interpretation of Copernicus,

37. Ibid., 140.

38. See the many references in the Index of ibid. What immediately follows is taken from ibid., 8.4, "Elegance and Beauty," 145–50. On the intellectual beauty of mathematics, and the need for love of that beauty, see ibid., 192–93.

one vigorously rejected by Bruno, Galileo, and Kepler. But all these alternatives are "pseudo-substitutions" for truth, and tacitly trade upon being understood in terms of what they are supposed to replace: "fruitful" is tacitly taken to mean "fruitful of *true* (and not *false*) results." And, moreover, that fruitfulness arises, not by accident and in despite of the theory's errors, but because the theory is itself *true*. Furthermore, it is truth, not fruitfulness, that is the more concrete; for, before the theory or discovery can be used and thus bear any fruit, scientists have to decide if it is *true*, thus to be adopted and applied. This, we may add, is an example of the standard Utilitarian fallacy—that we shall meet again in a moment—of identifying consequences with motives or intentions.

So, then, what does animate scientific investigation? Routine science, like any other routine activity, can be conducted in a more or less mechanical and sub-personal manner. But the establishment of a routine cannot be itself simply a matter of routine, for it requires the doing of something new and hence the exercise of personal powers—imagination, judgment, decision—to a greater degree. As for whole domains of human culture, such as natural and human sciences, they can be developed in the first place, and maintained in the second, only by deep personal engagement and commitment on the part of pioneers and then by influential and inspiring successors: routine will discover nothing really new, only more of the same. Therefore an interest in scientific investigation is required. But what sort of interest? This is where we encounter the Utilitarian reduction of all values to utility, all motives and intentions to ulterior ones, and all actions and means to something else. This, of course, sets up an infinite and meaningless progress of means to means to means . . . To stop it, the Utilitarian has to invoke a value that is not utility, and an intention to do something for its own sake. The usual candidates are pleasure or general welfare. And so science becomes regarded as technology, or valuable only as it results in better technology. Polanyi encountered this in the 1930s on his visits to the USSR, and realized that freedom in general, and thus the freedom of science, was itself valued in Utilitarian terms. Hence his confrontation of Marxist and other calls for the planning of science to promote technological progress and thereby welfare.[39] I shall not repeat his detailed arguments here, save to say that he showed that natu-

39. See especially ibid., 6.8; Polanyi, "Rights and Duties in Science" in Allen, *Science, Economics and Philosophy*; Polanyi, "Science and Welfare" and Polanyi, "Planned Science" in Michael Polanyi, *The Logic of Liberty*.

ral science and technology have different aims; that technology employs conceptions, such as "efficiency," of which physics and chemistry are ignorant; that until the middle of the nineteenth century, natural science had contributed almost nothing to technology; that it could not have foreseen the uses to which, often much later, it would be put; that technological applications are primarily the by-products of fundamental research—as into the structure of DNA—carried out without reference to them. To value science for, and to confine it to technology, would inevitably be to stunt it and would thus be counter-productive. Moreover, it is a universal law of personal life, as expressed in the old paradox of happiness, that to attain one thing, insofar as anything can be attained amid the sundry and manifold changes of this life, we have to aim at something higher: "Seek ye first the kingdom of God, *and then* all these things will be added unto you."[40] The Utilitarian concedes the main point: that natural science will be cultivated only in so far as its practitioners, and the wider public, take an interest in it, but errs in taking that interest to be in its technological utility. So, too, in their own ways do those who take scientific research to be animated by ulterior motives such as personal prestige, power, or class ideology. But abuses are parasitic upon uses, and ulterior motives upon genuine ones, without which science, and every other practice, would not exist in the first place. Only genuine interest in the subject-matter itself, love of the natural world, can get scientific research under way, keep it on its proper path, and counteract anything that would deflect or distort it.

As we have seen, Polanyi takes intrinsic interest in the subject-matter to be extra-scientific. In some ways this is correct. For an interest in the natural world need not take a scientific form but could remain satisfied with looking at it, and with capturing and expressing moments of contemplation in works of art. As regards what is inanimate, there is little interest to be taken in any example rather than another. It is precisely because their structures are uniform and their interrelations can be stated in laws, and those laws in equations, that any given sample of inanimate objects is viewed just as a specimen of its type and any event as an instance of the law and a result of the relevant equations. Hence natural science can create an edifice of systematic, wide-ranging and precisely expressed theories about the structure and laws of the natural world. It is this, the achieved scientific vision of the natural world and the intellectual

40. Matt 6:33.

beauty of that vision, that is the object of the scientist's interest, rather than nature as directly perceived. In contrast, in the historical sciences, it is the subject-matter itself—the persons, their actions, and their productions—that interests the investigator and is the prime object of his or her knowledge.

Our conclusion, with Scheler and Polanyi, is that knowing is a function or expression of love. Without a prior interest in what we perceive, we would remain with the fragmentary and ephemeral colors, noises, and bodily sensations of our earliest days. Yet again, the reductionist conceptions of human inquirers distort this interest as one in "survival." But the infant knows nothing of "survival," only present pains and pleasures, and one of the latter is making sense of his experiences. That such an interest has "survival value" is obvious, but that is a by-product. Indeed, at birth we are manifestly unfitted to survive, having only the two "instincts" (pre-formed habits) of grasping whatever touches the palm of the hand and sucking whatever touches the lips, and needing constant care and attention by adults over a long period. It is because of these biological deficiencies that we are open to the world and are not closed within the ambit of purely physical needs. We have already broken out, millennia ago, of the framework of the merely biological.

The thesis that knowing is an expression of love has the corollary that, *ceteris paribus*, ignorance is the result of lack of love and error that of hatred. This requires a detailed study that would go well beyond anything that Polanyi wrote, but I shall offer a few brief comments and examples following on from passages in his writings that do bear on this corollary.

If we, individually or jointly, can know but do not know something, it is, in the end, because, as in the old musical hall routine, we "do not wish to know that." Either we have no interest, or other interests get in the way or take up our time. In chapter 6 of *Personal Knowledge*, Polanyi cites examples of when this has happened in natural science and mathematics and of how it could happen again. A non-scientific example is that of the Enlightenment's attitude towards the "Dark Ages"—the Enlightenment was the one period to name itself. These ages were "dark," not because they could not be known, but because the Enlightenment held them not to be worth knowing, being the interval of savagery and superstition between that first flickering of enlightenment in Greece with its afterglow in Rome, and its rekindling in the Renaissance. Today, the "dark ages" have been illuminated by archaeology, and so only a brief period—that of the early Anglo-Saxon settlement in respect of British history—remains comparatively dim. If we really want to know, we shall, and sooner rather than later in these days, find ways to do so.

As for systematic error and distortions of knowledge, we can cite again the manifold reductionisms that we have already mentioned and against which Polanyi constantly argued. They amount to, I would suggest, an inverted Gnosticism. Whereas the Gnostics of old sought escape from this world, that was regarded as evil because physical, and sought such escape by way of knowledge of how we came to be here and of how to retrace our way back to the Light, contemporary reductionists hate some or all aspects of man's spiritual nature and so seek to deny them or interpret them as the epiphenomena of his sub-spiritual levels of existence. Why do they indulge in this self-hatred? I would suggest that it follows from the fundamental error of the Enlightenment (taking that term to include its predecessors in the sixteenth and seventeenth centuries). In Kant's words, "Enlightenment is human being's emergence from his self-incurred minority. Minority is conceived here as the inability to make use of one's own understanding without direction from another."[41] It is this assertion of human autonomy in a radical sense, one that acknowledges nothing (a) superior to man collectively, to human reason and human will, out of the form of which any human duty is to be spun, nor (b) anyone superior to the individual, such as tradition—what Edmund Burke called "the capital and bank of men and ages." Human beings are to achieve their own felicity for and by themselves and thence in this life on earth. This pride turns to hatred when frustrated, as must inevitably happen. It is also reinforced by, and reinforces, the surge in the feeling of power, first intellectual and then physical, that the new, mathematical, science of nature gave. Power over nature soon turned into power over humanity. For how could the immanentized *eschaton* be realized except by power to reconstruct human nature to fit the Utopia now to be achieved? Hence human beings are simultaneously the unconditioned conditioners (of others) and are themselves wholly conditioned by natural laws, "man a machine,"

---

41. Immanuel Kant, "What is Enlightenment?" 11. Of course, Kant is systematically ambiguous about human self-sufficiency. But note that in his *Religion within the Limits of Reason Alone*, the whole content of Christianity and any theism is steadily whittled away: to be of moral worth, a man's action must be wholly his own (40); and God's grace cannot be admitted except as a man earns it (40, 107, and 159); and then can help him only over the "last lap" (47); so that it is given only when it is superfluous.

in the title of de La Mettrie's book.[42] And the saving knowledge of modern Gnosticism is the knowledge of how the human machine works, individually and socially, and thus of how it can be changed. The spiritual and free nature of human beings must necessarily hinder the achievement of secular salvation, and hence must be simultaneously denied and hated.

Let us note one further example of the dialectic of assimilation and adaptation raised by this mention of hatred: the rationalization of evil. For hatred is an underived phenomenon. It may seem to presuppose a good against threats to which it responds, but that is not so. Hatred, in contrast to indignation, abhorrence, and revulsion, is active and aggressive—it seeks to destroy not to redeem; and it hates simply in order to hate. Scholastic philosophy remains too close to Greek rationalism in its formula that all things are sought and willed *sub specie boni*. That, once more, subsumes sin under error, a mistake in thinking, a confusing of false goods with real goods. It has no place for genuine evil, the gratuitous willing of harm and destruction in hatred, malice, and envy. Shakespeare had a better grasp of the facts of human life, as he showed in the characters of Richard III, Iago and Edmund. Evil is ultimately unmotivated and irrational, and cannot be explained, only explained away. But we know it in our hearts and understand it from the inside: "I do not do the good I want, but the evil that I do not want is what I do."[43] The facts of life do turn out to be Christian and our moral and other frameworks need to be adapted to them.

Note that these reflections do not entail a "debunking" of others' assertions by discrediting their motives instead of refuting the assertions themselves, as is practiced by some forms of reductionism. On the contrary, we begin by noticing a sustained ignorance or distortion of some aspect of reality, and then conclude that, *ceteribus paribus*, it issues from a desire not to know it or from hatred of it. It would take much longer to show that all other personal activities are expressions, specifications, or functions of love, but Scheler has indicated how in general it can be done with respect to knowing, and Polanyi has shown that it is the case with our scientific knowledge of the natural world, a very significant first step on the road.

42. A contemporary version is Skinner, *Beyond Freedom and Dignity*, in which the technological ambition of psychology is paramount and explicit. In Kant, the division runs within each person: as "phenomenal" each of us is subject to natural laws and so can be studied by a Newtonian psychology, but as "noumenal" we are not known not to be free.

43. Rom 7:19.

3

The Theological Promise
of Michael Polanyi's Project

An Examination within the Contemporary Context of
Atheism and the Constructivist Critique of the Natural
Sciences[1]

LINCOLN HARVEY

THE DANGER OF PLAYING GOD
WHEN YOU DON'T KNOW WHAT HE IS LIKE

IN A RECENT BRITISH television program, James Dewey Watson—the American biologist who, together with Francis Crick, proposed the double helix structure of the DNA molecule—addressed a small crowd informally over drinks. Their subject matter was genetic engineering and Watson was ridiculing those who argue that man must not play God by interfering with genetic codes. Watson's counter-argument was short and succinct. He asked simply, "if we do not play God then who do we think will?"[2]

---

1. This paper was presented at the day conference *Christian Theology and Michael Polanyi*, hosted by the Department of Theology and Religious Studies, King's College, London, in association with The Gospel and Our Culture Network, Friday, May 2, 2003. It was my honour to share the platform that day with my doctoral research supervisor Professor Colin Gunton, four days prior to his sudden death. My indebtedness to his theological thinking will be clear throughout.

2. "DNA: The Story of Life," Channel 4, March 8, 2003.

56

Watson's response is honest. If you believe that man inhabits a fluke, meaningless universe and that, as individuals, we are no more than chance by-products of a distant explosion, little more than sacks of water and chemicals fizzing around for three-score years and ten, then what possible wrong can there be in us playing God? Watson thinks there can be none. Yet what is really interesting about Watson's response is the rhetorical character of the question. His audience had to remain silent. The possibility that one of the crowd might suggest that God himself play the role of God seemed well beyond Watson's belief. As a result, Watson provides a clear example of the atheistic character of modern Western society.

The entrenched nature of contemporary atheism can be further illustrated. The well-known Cartesian notion of the evil demon—the metaphysical trickster whose possibility drives our doubt to its radical totality[3]—has been updated. Doubt is no longer fed by the speculation of a deceiving demon but is instead driven by the possibility that the thinking subject is a brain in a vat—that is, a brain in a vat that receives various electrical and chemical stimuli to make it think that it is actually a person with a body living in a world. This means that philosophers no longer postulate the spiritual demon in service of a sceptical agenda but imagine instead the possibility of a "super-scientist."[4] This modern translation of Descartes' thought-game reveals both the ease with which the contemporary mind conceives reality as subject to human control, and its simultaneous difficulty in imagining a malignant spiritual being. What is of note, however, is that, in a similar way to our previous example, the modern scientist displaces the creator of the world.[5]

Within the skeptical thought experiment, however, a clearly determined function exists for the "super-scientist." The "super-scientist" has to create an imaginary world in order to trick the brain-in-a-vat. But is

---

3. Descartes, *Meditations on First Philosophy*, 17–24.

4. The actual term "super-scientist" is lifted from Larry Lauden's imaginary conversation between a positivist, realist, pragmatist and relativist in the philosophy of science. See Lauden, *Science and Relativism*. Dennett in *Consciousness Explained*, 3, confesses that the tale of the brain-in-a-vat is "a modern day version of Descartes' evil demon"; Nicholas Jardine opts for the more technical-sounding term, "the malevolent neurophysiologist." See Jardine, *The Fortunes of Inquiry*, 10. For other contemporary uses, see Williamson, *Knowledge and its Limits*, and Devitt, *Realism and Truth*.

5. For an account of modern society in which the displacement of God is central, see Gunton, *The One, The Three and the Many*.

the function of the scientist clearly determined in our initial example? To a certain extent, this must be the case. Watson is not thinking of the scientist and then using his knowledge of a scientist to define God. Instead he is operating within some pre-existing framework that the modern scientist must fill. God is displaced and the scientist steps in, yet God is not redefined in the process. I want to suggest that this is problematic, not only because the God and Father of our Lord Jesus Christ actually exists, but also because the pre-existing definition of God places an unbearable burden upon the scientists' shoulders. Not only does the pre-existing definition carry an obvious connotation of creating (that is perhaps Watson's intended reference with regard to genetic engineering) but it also brings with it a problematic conception of knowledge—a god's-eye view-from-nowhere.

I want to suggest that the pre-existing definition of divine omniscience tends to depict a god's-eye view-from-nowhere.[6] This view-from-nowhere will then be translated into a desire for impersonal objectivity, that through the process of displacement becomes the throne upon which the scientists must sit to fulfill their God-like role. My argument is simple: this is not only an offence to the God who exists but is also, because of its loaded definition, fundamentally anti-human.[7]

A THEOLOGICAL CONSIDERATION
OF THE SCIENTISTS WHO PLAY GOD

Leaving to one side the problematic attribute of inhuman objectivity entailed by Watson's assertion of divinity, I will apply to Watson's "theology" the established theological principle of reading from the economic to the immanent being of God. I shall thus seek to discover, by examination of

6. For example: Boethius' classical definition of omniscience: "[T]he state of God is ever that of an eternal presence, His knowledge, too, transcends all temporal change and abides in the immediacy of his presence. It embraces all the infinite recesses of past and future and views them in the immediacy of its knowing as though they are happening in the present . . . [I]t is better called providence or 'looking forth' than prevision or 'seeing beforehand.' *For it is far removed from matters below and looks forth at all things as though from a lofty peak above them.*" Boethius, *Consolations of Philosophy*, V.6, cited in Helm, *Eternal God: A Study of God Without Time*, 96. Emphasis added.

7. The creative and epistemic connotations of the displacement of God could well merge together in the anti-realist thrust of the more extreme post-modern narratives within the philosophy of science, where we encounter a strange epistemic creation *ex nihilo*. For a good example of this, see Woolgar, *Science: The Very Idea*.

scientific practice, the nature of the divine being allegedly at work in the scientist who plays God. By this means, I hope to highlight the fundamental discrepancy between the reality of the scientist and the procrustean framework of god-likeness that Watson thrusts upon him.

Such a method is sympathetic to the course of action constructivist sociologists and certain philosophers of science have recently undertaken.[8] On the whole, their work is a reaction against what may be termed the "tabloid" view of science. This tabloid view should remain in our minds throughout this paper because it constitutes the caricature of the scientist that Michael Polanyi attacked. The tabloid view of science finds its roots deep in the modern mindset. The Enlightenment schools of rationalism and empiricism sought to justify scientific knowledge through the secure foundation of incorrigible mental or sense data; data that was strictly impersonal, stripped of prejudice, and unauthorized by tradition. More recently, the tabloid view has traded on Karl Popper's attempt to demarcate science from the pseudo-sciences. The genesis of Popper's work lay amidst what he termed the "explanatory power" of the Marxist and Freudian systems that set out to explain *everything* in their own terms.[9] This meant that no risky predictions were ventured because *any* event provided evidence for the truth of the interpretative system.[10] In contrast, Popper argued that the dynamic of conjecture and refutation lies at the heart of true science. In other words, true science is marked out from pseudo-science because its predictions are open to falsification rather than finding verification in everything that is seen. A true scientist predicts through a theory and tests it through experimental observation. The hypothesis remains if it passes the test and falls by the way if it fails.

This model of hypothesis, risky prediction, and possible refutation soon became the dominant model of science. But the trouble—especially in Michael Polanyi's eyes—was that a false picture of the scientist was smuggled into the mix: a view of the impassionate white-coated lab-

8. See for instance Collins and Pinch, *The Golem*; Latour and Woolgar, *Laboratory Life: The Construction of Scientific Facts*; Feyerabend, *Against Method: Outline of an Anarchistic Theory of Knowledge*; and Knorr-Cetina, *The Manufacture of Knowledge*.

9. Popper, *Conjectures and Refutations*.

10. For example, a Marxist can explain a *rise* in wages in terms of the capitalist's strategy to appease the workers, whilst a *fall* can be explained as an exploitation of the workers. Either way the interpretative system can adapt (ibid.). See also the discussion of Freudian and Stalinist interpretative flexibility in Polanyi, *Personal Knowledge*, 7.15 and 9.8.

dweller, coldly and rationally submitting random theories to the harsh judgment of empirical testing, with experimental observation overriding any particular favorites, and prejudice being defeated in the cold light of day. In effect, scientific knowledge had become a knowledge that was purged of the personal through its strict methodology. The human element was cut out of the picture.

In critical response to this ideal, some philosophers and sociologists have re-examined the actual practice of modern science. To understand their method, we should bring to mind a picture of a travelling ethnologist and a newly discovered tribe.[11] The ethnologist lives alongside the tribe and observes at close hand its life and times, attempting to record what is seen without importing any prejudice. Constructivist sociologists do this with the modern tribe of scientists. They try to see the work of scientists as if for the *first time*.[12] Some of their number take on mundane jobs in a lab so that the practice of science can be observed at close hand.[13] More often, however, the method involves a re-examination of key historical events. Old controversies are unearthed, evidence sifted and sorted, diaries and letters scanned and searched in an attempt to enter the mind-set of the protagonists and thereby access the reality of the event.

Limitation of space prevents me from looking at any particular cases in this paper; however, extensive examples are available within Polanyi's writing, as well as those offered by numerous social scientists and philosophers of science.[14] Such case studies show quite clearly that the tabloid ideal is wrong. Science is much messier than is usually imagined. Experiments are often ambiguous and frequently depend on the skill and resources of the practitioner. Experimental repetition is not straightforward and the resultant inconsistencies allow refuting evidence to be dismissed as "bad practice" by one side while counting as proof of false conjecture for the other. Such ambiguities mean that both individual

11. For anthropological method, see Evans-Pritchard, *Social Anthropology: Past and Present,* 82, and the discussion in Feyerabend, *Against Method,* 250.

12. Richard Jennings calls this "the stranger perspective." Jennings, review of "Leviathan and the Air-Pump: Hobbes, Boyle, and the Experimental Life."

13. See for instance the celebrated case of Bruno Latour in the first chapter of Latour and Woolgar, *Laboratory Life,* and Knorr-Cetina, *The Manufacture of Knowledge.*

14. For an excellent range of examples, presented in a style and language that is easily accessible for the non-specialist, see Collins and Pinch, *The Golem.* See also the novel by William Boyd, *Brazzaville Beach* in which the subjective influences at the frontline of research are revealed.

and institutional reputations are at stake, and the defense of one's reputation becomes a decisive factor in the resolution of scientific controversy. "Settlement" of such controversies can depend heavily on pride, egos, career moves, peer pressure, and the competition for available funding. In consequence, issues are seldom settled decisively: hypotheses are rarely proved definitively, and, instead, a socially constructed winner emerges from the mess, and finds its way into the textbooks, finally being read as some cut-and-dried fact and shoring up the mythical edifice of clinically-observed objective induction.[15]

Such complications at the frontiers of science are illustrated by the interdependent relationship between theory and measurement. In practice the dominant theory in the mind of the experimenter marks out the boundaries defining error within the experiments. That is, the theory defines which data is dismissed as bad practice and that is accepted as evidence. Consequently, as science progresses and groundbreaking theories turn into facts, the "correct" experimental result automatically supports the theory that led to its interpretation as "correct" in the first place.[16] But that is not all. The actual practice of experimental science is complicated further by the age-old problem that Plato raised in the *Meno*: how are we to search for the unknown?[17] If we know what we are looking for then we have not got a problem, but if we do not know what we are looking for, how on earth can we expect to find it?

Michael Polanyi, through his theory of personal knowledge and the tacit integration of indwelt subsidiary clues into a meaningful whole, offered an alternative solution to Plato's doctrine of reminiscence. We shall come to Polanyi shortly. But the numerous case studies made by Collins and Pinch highlight the practical relevance of this problem in modern science. They call it the "experimenter's regress."[18] If a theory suggests, for instance, that such things as gravity waves exist, then the scientist must search for them as evidential proof of the theory. The trouble is that despite not knowing whether gravity waves exist, some equipment must be built

---

15. As Paul Feyerabend has argued, the skills of propaganda carry more weight in arbitration than any fairy-tale conception of pure facts. See Feyerabend, *Against Method*, and also the discussion of the persuasive function of the passions and the role of propaganda in conversions to a new world-view in Polanyi, *Personal Knowledge*, 150ff.

16. For a clear example of this, see Collins and Pinch, *The Golem*, especially chapter 2.

17. Plato, "Meno," 80d.

18. Collins and Pinch, *The Golem*, chapter 5.

that will identify them. But how can we know whether the equipment is correctly identifying the conjectured reality? If gravity waves exist, then the equipment that demonstrates their existence is good equipment. On the other hand, if gravity waves do not exist then the equipment that does not identify them is better. As Collins and Pinch have argued, this means that defining what counts as a good gravity wave detector and establishing whether gravity waves actually exist are essentially the same process. The one cannot simply determine the other; in some real way they are mutually dependent.[19]

Constructivists argue that such a regress is only ended when an authoritative individual or institution makes an underdetermined judgment that effectively crystallizes majority opinion and allows the community to say which reading is in fact the fact. But such social determination, and the theory laden-ness of all scientific observation, opens the door to the extreme relativism and anti-realist ontology that we encounter in some constructivist circles today.[20] However, here is not the place to air such radical arguments. Of interest instead is that these recent case studies unveil that which is normally kept hidden by the tabloid view. That is, the open-ended underdetermined struggle for acceptance in scientific controversies brings into clear focus the role of the protagonists. Controversy in science reveals the presence of the *human*—personally involved— scientist at every level and at every stage of the scientific process.

This situation has many implications. One is fairly obvious: if demarcation on the grounds of impersonal method is impossible then science ends up looking like any other human enterprise. Therefore, the question our imported theological method must ask of James Dewey Watson and his like, is whether they are prepared to accept that their God looks as messy, un-clinical and un-objective as empirical research suggests, or whether instead they are prepared to let go of the god-like self-image and embrace the limited human being, warts and all? Whichever way they go, it would appear that they need a new theory of knowledge.

---

19. Ibid., 101.

20. For a good example of such ontological conclusions in the sociology of science, see Woolgar, *Science: The Very Idea*.

FINDING THE HUMAN HOME BETWEEN A ROCK AND A HARD PLACE: THE VALUE OF THE EPISTEMOLOGICAL PROJECT OF MICHAEL POLANYI

Let me briefly rehearse the argument thus far. Some humans think they have discovered that God is dead. Humans decide to step into the vacant space. Such a space has a particular shape. Conformity to this shape requires that humans be purged of their human characteristics if they are to assume the role. Central to this remolding is the modern epistemological project and its desire for impersonal objectivity and certainty. Science is then heralded as the embodiment of this paradigm. Science alone can attain the god-like view-from-nowhere.

However, trouble arises because, as we have seen, even a brief study of the practice of science reveals that the discipline falls well short of the ideal. The god-like view-from-nowhere is debunked and we must recognize instead that it is always a human *person* who sees, and seeing (for us human beings) is always undertaken from a particular time and place, is loaded with choices, and is motivated by a set of background beliefs. Such, it is now commonly maintained, also holds for the rationalist's notion of pure mental data; that is, rationality has likewise been localized. The combined result, therefore, is that we are confronted by the parochial *humanness* of all our epistemic projects. The days of the naïve universal are over.[21]

Given such a situation, it would seem best for Watson and his like to re-embrace our humanness. Denial can only be destructive. The illusion that we are Atlas can only ever crush us. That, in a nutshell, is the argument so far. But a further question must be asked given such a contemporary climate. Put simply, it is this: does the rehabilitation of the personal coefficient in our epistemic projects mean that we must relinquish any claim to objectivity? That is, if our foundation is but the sand of the personal, can we ever hope to rise above the subjective, to claim any objective voice?

The acceptance—indeed celebration—of both objectivity and the subjective human being are central to the work of Michael Polanyi. On one hand, knowing is a subjective event. Knowledge is always *our* knowl-

---

21. For an old and succinct summary of the lack of necessity in inferential logic, see Carroll, "What the Tortoise said to Achilles," 278–80. For a good discussion of these issues, see Barnes and Bloor, "Relativism, Rationalism and the Sociology of Knowledge."

edge. That is, no knowledge is without the personal coefficient. Utterly objective knowledge, void of a personal aspect, is an illusion. In other words, knowledge is always constituted in part by the tacit commitment of the knower.[22] Not even the act of perception is void of such passionate commitment. We see things as we see them because we tacitly indwell presuppositions that are outside our focus. Numerous experiments scattered throughout Polanyi's work will convince us of that.[23] Yet the reality of knowing—as a personal event even at this most simple level—means that it is something that we do, an activity, a craft, a skilful performance achieved through time that can be done well or performed badly. This is important for us to note. Knowing is a diachronic activity, and reason a skilful performance, the maxims of which are socially determined, passed on and learnt as we are apprenticed in a community.

This dynamic combination of the personal and the active is at the heart of the structure of personal knowledge. The notion of commitment within Polanyi's doctrine of indwelling is the key to understanding it.[24] Knowing is not a passive event (in the way that the subjectivity of pain is); instead it is a passionate move, a commitment driven by the emotional love of truth.[25] This passionate commitment is the distinction of the personal; it is neither subjective nor objective but transcends the two.[26] The person is a passionate knower who pours herself out, commits herself, and indwells subsidiary clues before drawing them together into a meaningful whole through an act of integration. The logical structure of such personal knowing is very important. It is best illustrated by the example of the blind person using a stick.[27] The stick becomes an extension of the person, a subsidiary clue tacitly indwelt in order to focus on the meaning beyond. In concrete terms the vibrations of the stick are not felt on the palm of the hand but instead are translated into the meaning of the environment at the end of the stick.[28] The blind person exteriorizes herself,

22. Polanyi, The Tacit Dimension.

23. Polanyi, Personal Knowledge, 5.2.

24. Ibid., 4.8.

25. Ibid., chapter 6.

26. Ibid., 300.

27. Ibid., 62.

28. "The rower pulling on an oar feels the resistance of the water; when using a paper-knife we feel the blade cutting the pages. The actual impact of the tool on our palm and fingers is unspecifiable in the same sense in which the muscular acts composing a skilful

indwelling the tool and shifting her focus outwards, seeing *through* the stick to the world beyond: this is how she knows. Our language, concepts, and theories, the activities of art, craft, science, and religious ritual are likewise to be understood as tools for knowing the world, and all depend on this dynamic structure.[29] In every case we give ourselves in trust to the tradition of a community; we tacitly indwell its practices and norms, its language and theories, and then, through these indwelt tools, we attend to the focal meaning beyond. In effect these indwelt clues become the spectacles we see through. We pour ourselves into them, and by an act of integration we gain sight of the world that is real.

However, this choice of spectacles and their use is not purely subjective. Polanyi argues that the event of knowing rises above the subjective parochialism suggested by our occupation of a particular community—our "calling" as Polanyi terms it [30]—because our enquiry is always guided by beauty (an aesthetic ideal), that amounts to faith in the inherent rationality of the world. It is, therefore, this intimation of the world's knowability that shapes our epistemic activity into *responsible decisions* made with *universal intent* as we integrate clues into a meaningful whole.[31] In other words, we hold our own beliefs to be true and, in so doing, we hold all people accountable in terms of them. Underlying Polanyi's conception of calling and universal intent is the reality of an *objective truth*. This is a realist epistemology; that which we seek to know stands independent of our knowing it.

In contrast, relativism equates the ubiquity of the subject—the self-accredited passions and drives of our commitment—with an unavoidable *pollution* of our motives (the Christian doctrine of the Fall, we may

---

performance are unspecifiable; we are aware of them in terms of the tool's action on its object, that is, in the comprehensive entity into which we integrate them." Polanyi, "Knowing and Being," 127.

29. Polanyi does argue that some knowledge is *outside* this framework, notably in the moment of breaking out in discovery when a form of immediacy is experienced. Polanyi likens this immediacy to the apophatic mystical contemplation of God in worship claimed by some. Polanyi, *Personal Knowledge*, 6.13.

30. Ibid., 10.10.

31. "Intellectual commitment is a responsible decision, in submission to the compelling claims of what in good conscience I conceive to be true. It is an act of hope, striving to fulfil an obligation within a personal situation for which I am not responsible and that therefore determines my calling. This hope and this obligation are expressed in the universal intent of personal knowledge." Ibid., 65.

note, may make us sympathetic to this view); but the problem, as Michael Devitt has argued, is that such polluted motives compromise the purity of the outcome.[32] That is, radical relativists argue that because the motive is impure, objective truth cannot result; ontology is collapsed into the subjective ideal and the end is confused with the means. However, Polanyi's discussion about the personal coefficient is always situated within a realist ontology, that is not itself confused with subjective questions of access to it. Polanyi will not allow imperfect motives uncovered by empirical research to collapse reality into the subjectivity of anti-realism. Truth, for Polanyi, is always part of something bigger than the person. Ontology is always prior and distinct from any question of semantics and epistemology.

In order for us to understand the objective pole of this knowing event and our attraction to it, we will be served best by a brief excursus. Karl Popper has argued that two key doctrines operate throughout the history of Western philosophy.[33] These two key doctrines transcend traditional divisions. That is, they are found in both classical and modern thought, in both rationalism and empiricism. The first doctrine is characterized by its broadly optimistic character. It amounts to the notion that we know truth when we see it. Whether it is the immediacy of the eternal vision of the Platonic Forms, the Cartesian clear and distinct ideas or the sense data of the empiricist, the underlying belief is that truth as truth is *manifest*. The second ubiquitous doctrine is, in contrast, pessimistic. This doctrine asserts that something stops us seeing this manifest truth. Again we may cite as example here the Platonic notion of imperfect matter that keeps us chained up in the cave, or more recent Enlightenment dogmas of the evil of tradition and hegemonic authority. Whatever the particular evil, the narrative is structurally the same: the truth is obvious when we get there but we must overcome the impeding obstacle.

The combined result of these two dogmas can be disastrous. If this messy material world cannot provide the certainty of manifest truth, then the latter practice of overcoming obstacles becomes an otherworldly flight. Dualism is the by-product. Human beings are divorced from their rightful place in the world and seek the alternative realms of either the Platonic Forms or the modern inner mind. Even the empiricist, after Hume, ends up by being separated from the thing-in-itself, being trapped

32. Devitt, *Realism and Truth,* 159.

33. Popper, "On the Sources of Knowledge and Ignorance," in Popper, *Conjectures and Refutations,* 3–39.

in some cognitive immediacy, an unbridgeable distance from that which is beyond. Whichever way we go, we soon become disembodied and dehumanized.

But Michael Polanyi's theory of knowledge is radically embodied *and* this-worldly. In achieving this, the two doctrines are refuted. First, with regard to pessimism (i.e., the belief that something prevents us from grasping the truth), Polanyi argues that the reality of personal knowledge, and its tacit rooting in un-formalized belief, is possible because we trust in the inherent rationality of the universe. All our acts of knowing, of discovery, of understanding meaningful wholes in the light of fragmented clues are made possible by an *a priori* belief that order exists. In effect, we trust that the world is structured so that it can be known. It is this faith that fuels the process of commitment and indwelling. And here the optimism in Polanyi's project is most apparent because this is not a blind faith. Instead, Polanyi paints a picture within which the objective universe calls us, enticing and encouraging us to find the meaningful patterns and order inherent within the kaleidoscope of experience. That is, reality is the sort of place where knowing is possible. This world, in effect, wants to be known and is structured to meet our enquiry, is geared up to facilitate our probing and exploring, and in some real way facilitates our cognitive integration. It is in light of this objective element that one recent commentator calls Polanyi's project "resonance realism."[34] This phrase attempts to do justice to the importance of the aesthetic ideal of inherent harmony. This harmony is that to which we become attuned. We do not create it, or impose it, as Kant would have us believe; neither are we able completely to formalize it in some abstraction from it. Instead we know it in continuity with it, through a process of echoing and tuning, a process we realize in the tacit act of indwelling, and in the intellectual satisfaction our best theories provide. This is what Polanyi means by passions. They guide us; the beauty of truth attracts us. In effect, Polanyi argues that certain of our emotions are, in themselves, simply *right*.[35] Thus the twin doctrines of indwelling and integration are broadly optimistic.

But now I must return to the second epistemological doctrine: the doctrine of optimism (i.e. we know the truth when we see it). We must tread with more caution here because Polanyi does accept a version of

34. Puddefoot, "Resonance Realism."

35. For a clear statement of the correctness of an emotion, see Polanyi, *Personal Knowledge*, 134.

this doctrine. What is known as "the Eureka moment"—the moment of illumination when troubling clues fall into place and we know we've got it—does feature in Polanyi's account. What must be noted, however, is that this conception of illumination is not collapsed into a static vision of truth, a truth known once and for all, manifest, grasped, complete—certain, if you like. Instead, truth is much more supple and elusive; it lies both behind and before us, and is always much more than we can tell.

To understand this we must remember Polanyi's definition of the real. It is this conception that qualifies Polanyi's optimism. For Polanyi, that which is real will always manifest itself in yet more surprising ways.[36] Our theories are only ever attuned to *an aspect* of reality, while reality as a whole continues to open itself up and unveil areas previously hidden. Reality as such is never wholly evident at any moment of discovery. We never see the totality in the moment. Instead the truth is known only *through* time and not by its immediate clarity. Consequently, we cling to beliefs we now hold to be true, ever aware that they may conceivably be false, ever aware that they are but partial and never complete. This is not the straightforward optimism of manifest certainty. It is the alternative humility of fallible exploration.[37]

THE THEOLOGICAL PROMISE OF MICHAEL POLANYI

A short paper such as this can never be exhaustive, yet the foregoing discussion does allow me to highlight certain key points. First, Polanyi's description of the event of personal knowledge happens within a realist universe. There *is* something out there—a truth, a rationale—to which we move in discovery. It is true that our movement towards objective reality is fuelled by the subjective, driven by our passions and our parochial calling, but this can never amount to more than a semantic relativism (across both space and history); it is never ontological. As mentioned earlier, imperfect motives need not rule out the *telos* of our activity. Instead

36. "[R]eality is something that attracts our attention by clues that harass and beguile our minds into getting ever closer to it, and that, since it owes this attractive power to its independent existence, can always manifest itself in still unexpected ways." Polanyi, "The Unaccountable Element in Science," in Grene, *Knowing and Being*, 119–20. See also his essay "Knowing and Being" in the same collection, 123–37.

37. For Polanyi this is the principal purpose of his work: "[T]o achieve a frame of mind in which I may hold firmly to what I believe to be true, even though I know that it might conceivably be false." Polanyi, *Personal Knowledge*, 214.

we must hold that our words and theories *do* engage with objective reality. Relativism is thereby qualified. Reality itself does not change along with our theories. The distinction between rival theories instead becomes one of better or worse fit. That is, reality is only ever *more* or *less* known. Realism thus recognizes a constant in our epistemic endeavors. One result of this is that commensurability between theories is made possible. It is possible because—leaving to one side any questions about the new heaven and the new earth—God created one world, one world within which the communities of history all live.

We have to admit that an understanding of difference and continuity, of better-or-worse fit, does allow talk of progress—itself very unfashionable in this day and age. But, we may note, though the goal of our enquiry is fixed and real, and progress into it is real and possible, this progress is not inevitable. Polanyi's conception of the character of human progress into knowledge, into a better fit with the world, will be better understood through the employment of a metaphor, that of a craftsman. A sculptor provides the best example for sculptors have often spoken of a finished work emerging from the stone rather than being imposed upon it. In her work the sculptor imagines the figure of the statue somehow already inside the rock she faces. She conceives it as there before her, and she approaches the stone in order to uncover it—the "already-figure" somehow shaping her work, as her work in turn shapes the rock in which it lies. At each stage, at each blow, the sculptor gets nearer and nearer, deeper and deeper, more precise and more exact, not thereby making the earlier blows wrong, but instead driving forward the continuous event of discovery. Each movement of the sculptor's chisel is dependent on the earlier work that the current moment inherits and achieves an end less exact than the work that is still to come. This progress, as we mentioned above, does not proceed according to some Hegelian necessity. This is no unstoppable march through history.[38] Instead, as part of an artistic process, the practitioner can use what is received with more or less *skill*. Mistakes can be made, progress may be held up and the work may be abandoned or even futilely smashed.

The craft-based metaphor of fragile progress towards an objective entity with which the work is—in some way—continuous illustrates well

38. Other forms of necessary locomotion are Marxist dialectical materialism, Darwinian survival of the fittest and Adam Smith's concept of the invisible hand at work in the free market place.

Polanyi's account of epistemic progress. Polanyi describes each generation, each individual, receiving from the past an ongoing project and working responsibly with it, refining and improving it, and trying to approach the truth, ever responsible also to a future that depends on this work. This is a picture of continuity; yet it is also a picture that allows for change. Change does not come about through the violent revolutions of Thomas Kuhn's all-or-nothing incommensurable paradigm shifts, however.[39] Instead, Polanyi offers a theory of knowledge built on the transcendent reality revealing itself more and more across time and space. One result is that earlier theories—such as geocentric cosmologies and the like—can be said to have had an element of contact with reality. Truth and error are not all-or-nothing categories. For instance, older cosmologies did talk of the earth, moon, sun, and stars whatever the problems now associated with the order or system within which they were discussed. The point is, instead, that contact with reality can increase or decrease over time through the continued refinement, adaptation, and change of our cognitive tools and our skill in using them. Further, such a model of continuity and change allows us to posit *hypothetical* percentages to clarify the conceptual scheme, as Michael Devitt has done.[40] To paraphrase the work of Devitt, we can say that science in 1705 had 10 percent fit, 1805—20 percent, 1905—30 percent, 2005—who knows? The percentages are arbitrary; the point instead is that the famous meta-induction of Hilary Putnam is not necessary.[41] Putnam argues that because entities posited in the past do not exist, it must follow that the entities we posit now will be shown in due time not to exist either. But this is not so. Just because some entities of former times are held not to exist we do not have to say that all entities posited yesterday and today do not exist. As Devitt argues, *most* objects of common sense—such as the sun, moon, and the stars—have been held to exist throughout history. If that is so, then the question of the relativity of truth claims is best addressed through Polanyi's notion of keying into a fixed structure via the skilful use and adaptation of cognitive

---

39. Kuhn, *The Structure of Scientific Revolutions*. I am not denying paradigm change. Instead I am questioning the *suddenness* and *totality* of such shifts. I agree with Lakatos' analysis. He argues that a new worldview needs a "breathing space" in which auxiliary disciplines can develop to support the new theory whilst it is still in its counter-inductive form. Imre Lakatos, "History of Science and its Rational Reconstructions," *Boston Studies for the Philosophy of Science*, VIII: 113. Cited in Feyerabend, *Against Method*, 183.

40. Devitt, *Realism and Truth*, 147.

41. Ibid.

tools, rather than sidestepped by collapsing ontology into epistemology via the cry of incommensurability and the impossibility of translation.

Let us consider now this picture of historical convergence on a structural rationale from a theological perspective. It will be helpful here to draw upon the famous trinitarian model of Irenaeus, that of the Son and the Spirit as the two "hands" of God mediating his will to and in creation.[42] This model relies upon a distinction of the persons of the Trinity that is based on their activity in the economy. That is, the distinction between the Son and the Spirit is known through their different actions within the one divine work: it is the Son who becomes human, with all things being made through him, holding together in him, and being shaped towards him, but, as Basil has argued, it is the Spirit who is the perfecting cause, who brings creation to its fullness, who enables it to be itself and who brings the divine work to its completion.[43] This is the eschatological work of the Spirit: the work of resurrection, of scriptural inspiration, of shaping the church, distributing gifts and drawing the dispersed people of God together. With this image in mind (of the two hands of God, creating and perfecting) let us recall the earlier metaphor of the sculptor and now imagine the two hands of the sculptor in light of the divine economy. Or better still for our purpose, let us re-imagine the metaphor in terms of the work of a potter. One hand is dropped into the clay, the clay clinging to it, yet somehow wanting to fall and slip away, as the other hand shapes the clay, molding it around the first hand, fixing it upon that which it hangs, on that which it depends, on that which its shape is based.

By using this metaphor I offer a necessary corrective to James Dewey Watson's atheistic assertion with which I began this paper. That is to say, a trinitarian doctrine of creation—along Irenaean lines—allows us to stand at ease within our limits, no longer suffering under the illusion of being either creators, on the one hand, or meaningless chance by-products, on the other, but existing instead under the reality of God's creative and formative action. Such a theological conception of our reality encourages creaturely humility; it reminds us that we are not God, that we ourselves—and our *knowledge*—are but a part of the divine act of creation. This is to recognize that the reconciliation of God and humanity in

42. Irenaeus, *Against the Heresies*, cited in Colin E. Gunton, *Father, Son and Holy Spirit*, 77.

43. Basil of Caesarea, *On the Holy Spirit*, XV.36 and 38, cited in Gunton, *Father, Son and Holy Spirit*, 81.

Jesus Christ does have epistemological impact. In the divine economy, the Father knows the Son and the Son knows the Father *through* the Spirit. Knowledge, in this model, is a relational acquaintance that is mediated by the person of the Spirit. This knowing as acquaintance through the Spirit is also an event that happens in the *flesh*. It is Jesus who knows the Father through the Spirit. This knowing happens in this world, in this humanity, in this matter, in this flesh. That being so, the creation must be the sort of place within which such an epistemic event *can* happen. That is, the fabric of the created order is one in which a person, through the Spirit, *can* be in a relational acquaintance with an other (i.e., our flesh is conducive to our knowing through the Spirit more than that which is merely ourselves). Therefore, this incarnated trinitarian model can be used the same way as Colin Gunton, drawing on Coleridge, uses the Trinity as the Idea of ideas.[44] That is, the christological trinitarian model can provide resources that allow us to re-imagine the relation between the subject and the object, between the enquirer and reality, and thereby open up new ways of imagining the event along lines of acquaintance—an acquaintance that is achieved through time, by an act of indwelling and mediated by the Spirit.

Once again here, we find promise in the work of Michael Polanyi. First we have the resource of his notion of indwelling and the person's continuity with the other. Attention has already been paid to this above. Second, and of more interest to us here, we have his somewhat mysterious auxiliary doctrine of integration, that I introduced earlier, whereby indwelt clues are brought together into a meaningful whole. Such integration is a ubiquitous element in knowing. Like justice for Plato in the *Republic*, it is best seen in the large—in, for example, the paradigm leap across logical gaps into the unknown that is achieved by men and women of genius: a Copernicus, an Einstein. The crossing of a logical gap is involved, however, in *all* tacit integrations of clues—in our seeing, learning a language, solving a puzzle, and the like. But the act of integration remains mysterious because at its heart is a question. Put simply it is this: from what direction is the move of integration made? That is, is the leap across the logical gap an event *of* the subject or instead somehow *of* the other?

If the choice is a stark either-or then we can see some immediate dangers. The former, if unchecked, smacks of some Pelagian achieve-

---

44. "The expectation is that if the triune God is the source of all being, meaning and truth we must suppose that all being will in some way reflect the being of the one who made it and holds it in being." Gunton, *The One, The Three, and the Many*, 145.

ment, with our knowledge, unlike our redemption, being somehow attained by the subject alone. Yet the latter, if we are not too careful, brings with it the un-freedom of over-determination apparent, for instance, in Marxist notions of social consciousness: that is, our knowing becomes something that is done *to* us, for which we are not really responsible. But the importance of Polanyi's work is that in it such integration is somehow *both* of the subject *and* of the other. That is, integration is prefigured by the sort of universe it is that *meets* man and *calls* man, but it is also achieved by the *free* responsible exploration and effort of persons within just such a universe. In other words, the direction of the leap goes both ways. Integration is of the subject *and* of the object. It is done for us and somehow by us.

Such an apparent paradox underlines the importance of the church's endeavor to re-introduce the work of the Spirit in our conception of knowing because it is the revelation of the Spirit's work in the economy that can show how such an invasion from outside does not trample over our creaturely freedom, but instead *enables* us to be fully ourselves. As we have seen, it is the Spirit of God who perfects the creation through the Son. As Colin Gunton writes:

> When we ask how God can determine human wills without compelling them, we can understand from the life of Jesus that he does it through the Spirit, whose bidding can—in some cases—be disobeyed, as must conceivably be the case if Jesus' temptations were real ones. The Holy Spirit is . . . the one who, through Christ, enables the creation to be itself by bringing it into proper relation to God the Father. That is to say, the Spirit's historical action is to come into personal relation with human agents, liberating them to be themselves and empowering anticipations of the eschatological reconciliation of all things.[45]

Here, by implication, we find that Christology and pneumatology can have a material effect on our epistemology. As result, the theological discipline of the church can avoid the problems associated with James Dewey Watson highlighted in the introductory section of this paper. To recall: that section was entitled: *The danger of playing God when you don't know what he is like.* The argument of this paper is that in Jesus Christ the church does know who the triune God is, and this fact may helpfully contribute to the construction of any theory of knowledge.

45. Gunton, "Martin Kähler Revisited," 29.

4

Society, Skepticism, and the Problem of Moral Inversion

Reflections on Michael Polanyi's Social Philosophy[1]

ALAN J. TORRANCE

W ERE A GOVERNMENT MINISTER to suggest that the pursuit of science for its own sake was no longer appropriate and that academic scientists should concentrate their energies on the Five-Year Plan, one wonders whether the country would be unduly surprised or alarmed given our new-found culture of measurable quality assurance, demonstrable accountability, and specifiable, short-term outcomes. It was just such a statement made by Bukharin in Soviet Russia back in 1935 that was to be the trigger for Polanyi's lifelong concern with the place of free thought within society. Although heading toward his demise (and indeed, execution) three years later, Bukharin was still at this point one of the leading theoreticians of the Communist party. Polanyi had asked him about the place of the pursuit of pure science, to which Bukharin responded that "pure science was a morbid symptom of a class society; under socialism the conception of science pursued for its own sake would disappear, for the interests of scientists would spontaneously turn to problems of the current Five-Year Plan."[2]

---

1. I am greatly indebted to Dr. Tony Clark for the particularly helpful suggestions he made while I was researching this chapter and would refer readers to his excellent doctoral thesis, "Responsive and Imaginative Participation in Divine Revelation with Particular Reference to the Epistemology of Michael Polanyi."

2. Polanyi, *The Tacit Dimension*, 3 and 81.

There was an irony here for Polanyi, because it was precisely reference to independent scientific thought that sustained the remarkable "persuasive power" of socialism. Indeed, its whole appeal was underwritten by the perception that the predictions of Socialism vis-à-vis the inevitable emergence of the egalitarian society were grounded in scientific certainties. Bukharin's statement demonstrated that the scientific outlook that had generated precisely the "'mechanical conception of man and history' was now displacing science itself."[3] So what could lead to this "self-immolation of the mind," that is, to such a radical denial of the freedom of thought? There was clearly an underlying ethical agenda—a vision of universal justice, the brotherhood of man and the classless society. For Polanyi, this took the form of a kind of "moral perfectionism"—the romantic appeal of a panacea against all injustice and privilege, of dealing with the problems of society wholesale, in a unitary and all-pervasive sweep.

But the power that absolute moral renewal requires is nothing less than absolute power. As Polanyi and Prosch warn us in *Meaning*, such power inevitably translates into a "tyrannous force" that can only "destroy the moral life of humanity, not renew it."[4] The outworking of moral perfectionism meant that it became immoral to invest one's energy in anything—any discovery or research—that did not facilitate the achievement of universal brotherhood.[5]

What was required was a harmonious conception of the relationship between thought and existence—an initiative that would integrate a liberative vision of science and intellectual freedom, on the one hand, and morally responsible society, on the other. If we are to do this without engendering what will simply be an alternative, radical, theory imposed by force, we need to offer a nuanced analysis of the genetics of totalitarianism by considering the fundamental intellectual decisions that resulted from the Enlightenment.

A simplistic rendering of the factors that led to the political crises of modernity might point first to the Enlightenment's weakening of ecclesiastical authority and thus the religious sanction of moral beliefs

3. Ibid., 3.

4. Polanyi and Prosch, *Meaning*, 214.

5. One cannot help drawing the parallel again with contemporary British universities that increasingly suggest it is unacceptable to burden the taxpayer with research that does not pay its way—either by means of potential recruitment, patents, or other means!

that it sustained and, second, to the attendant scientific positivism that questioned the grounds of transcendent values. For Polanyi, however, this is insufficient as an explanation. The self-destructive tendencies of the modern mind derive rather from the marriage of scientific skepticism and "moral perfectionism," that is, a passion for moral progress. The effect of the Enlightenment was not the undermining of moral convictions but rather their displacement, generating a homeless moral fervor. It was the combination of this with the critical or absolute skepticism rooted in scientism that constituted the fundamental challenge to modern civilization. And it was this that generated fanaticism and thereby the tyranny and cruelty that ensued.[6]

In short, when the Enlightenment weakened the church's intellectual authority, Christian aspirations spilled over into secular thinking. The effect was an intensification of secular society's sense of moral responsibility. Man was obliged to step into the divine vacuum and take responsibility for social morality. Initially, the struggle against ecclesiastic authority was beneficial in that it cleared the way for political freedom and humanitarian reforms. Whereas the first-fruit of scientific rationalism was a period of intellectual, moral, and social progress, what was to emerge in the longer term was a potentially dangerous dynamic and one that has come to a head in the last hundred years. The inner tension between scientific skepticism and moral perfectionism, deeply embedded within modern thought forms, began to find expression in unhappy "hybrids of skepticism and perfectionism" embodying a "dangerous internal contradiction" that they were unable to resolve.[7] In an impressive piece of socio-intellectual analysis, Polanyi analyzes how this generated existentialism, on the one hand, and—more relevantly for this paper—totalitarian socialism on the other. Both derived from that same fusion. However, the latter, instead of affirming the individual,[8] sanctioned "the total suppression of

---

6. Polanyi, *The Tacit Dimension*, 58 and 83.

7. Ibid., 58.

8. Scientific detachment presented budding existentialists with "a world of bare facts" in which we find nothing that can serve "to justify authority or tradition." Ibid., 58. Independently of these facts, there are no controls or restrictions or conditions on human choice. But wherein lies the moral perfectionism in this so-called hybrid? It is to be found, he argues, precisely in existentialism's violent repudiation of the morality of the existing society as artificial, ideological and hypocritical. This repudiation reposes in a moral passion fused with skepticism. "Moral scepticism and moral perfectionism thus combine to discredit all explicit expressions of morality" leaving, in their wake, "moral

the individual."[9] In this case, perfectionism demanded a "total transformation of society" and, denying or discrediting explicit expressions of morality, concealed its moral motives by embodying them in a struggle for power—one that, it believed, would bring about automatically and by necessity the aims of utopia. What was to be witnessed here was a blind and fideistic acceptance of the scientific testimony of Marxism. In place of faith in Christian doctrine, blind faith was to be placed in a quasi-scientific dogma.

In sum, Marxism is an ideology that embodies human aspirations in a theory while, at the same time, concealing its ideals from skeptical doubt by means of "denying the reality of moral motives in public life." Its power, therefore, lies in the subtle unification of two contradictory forces into a single political doctrine thereby constituting a "world-embracing idea, in which moral doubt is frenzied by moral fury and moral fury is armed by scientific nihilism."[10]

This is what Polanyi famously terms "moral inversion." When the traditional forms that sustain moral ideals are destroyed and the moral needs of humanity are denied expression in terms of ideals, then those underlying moral passions all too easily find themselves diverted into the only channels that a strictly mechanistic conception of man and society leaves open. When, moreover, the channel for blind moral passion is a system of naked power, this generates a profoundly dangerous form of "moral inversion,"[11] the effect of which is to channel "moral passions into acts of violence, brutality, and cruelty in the name of sublime moral ideals."[12] The one who submits to this moral inversion not only substitutes material purposes for moral aims, but does so "with the whole force of his homeless moral passions operating within a purely materialistic frame-

---

passions filled with contempt for their own ideals." (Ibid.) Therein lies the dangerous contradiction. "And once they shun their own ideals, moral passions can express themselves only in anti-moralism. Professions of absolute self-assertion, gratuitous crime and perversity, self-hatred and despair, remain as the only defences against a searing self-suspicion of bad faith." Ibid.

9. Ibid., 59.

10. Ibid., 59–60.

11. Polanyi and Prosch, *Meaning*, 18.

12. Nagy, "Philosophy in a Different Voice, note 29.

work of purposes."[13] It is thus "a condition in which high moral purpose operates only as the hidden force of an openly declared inhumanity."[14]

These are strong claims and promise a devastating critique of the dynamics underlying so much human misery witnessed over the last century. However, all sorts of questions require to be raised as to what precisely Polanyi actually means by "moral inversion." Najder, for example, asks whether it is a process or a state. Is it a "psychological (as the terminology suggests), or a sociohistorical trend (to which the examples point), or an axiological scheme (which is implied by the general sweep of the concept)"?[15]

However "moral inversion" is to be understood, Polanyi uses the expression to denote the confused moral revolution that culminated in affirmations like Bukharin's that scientific truth would no longer be pursued for its own sake under socialism. It denotes the tragic emergence of a scenario wherein moral perfectionism found itself embodied in a scientifically sanctioned political power that left no place for truth.

IN SEARCH OF A SOLUTION

What Polanyi does *not* do in response is to offer an alternative "theory" of society or a contrasting set of moral ideals. To do so would be to reiterate the same mistake. The way forward, for Polanyi, was to seek to discover precisely how this could happen and then seek to reconceive the whole nature of knowledge and its relation to the ethical in such a way that both radical skepticism and moral perfectionism might be displaced and the inner logical tension resolved—the inherently self-destructive forces harmonized.

How does his epistemology seek to achieve this?

a) First, by demonstrating that there is a tacit dimension of thought, he challenges the Enlightenment belief in the absolute, intellectual, self-determination of humanity. If tacit thought is indispensable to all knowing—if, indeed, it is the ultimate means by which all explicit or focal

13. Polanyi, *The Logic of Liberty*, 131.

14. Polanyi, *Beyond Nihilism*, 20. Cited by Najder, "'Moral Inversion' or Moral Revaluation?" 366.

15. Najder adds, "Are its specific characteristics found in psychological processes, in sociohistorical tendencies, or in axiological structures, that is, in the way ethical systems are organised?" Najder, "'Moral Inversion' or Moral Revaluation?" 367.

knowing is facilitated and "endowed with meaning"—then it is radically inappropriate to suggest that each succeeding generation, let alone each member of it, should critically test all the teachings in which it is brought up. Given that we know a great deal more than we can tell, the whole business of understanding and discovery is grounded in and directed by the subliminal awareness of realities and levels of reality that we cannot articulate. Knowledge is not based on "wholly identifiable grounds."

b) This challenges the Napoleonic justice that sustained Enlightenment skepticism—the assumption that the contents of our minds must be assumed to be guilty until proven innocent. Just as learning requires the pupil's assumption of the teacher's authority, the transmission of knowledge from one generation to another operates on the prior assumption of the truthfulness of what is being communicated. "The most daring innovations in science spring from a vast range of information which the scientist accepts unchallenged as a background to his problem."[16]

Polanyi cites Augustine, "Unless you believe, you shall not understand."[17] Doubt presupposes assent—or as the thrust of Wittgenstein's argument in *On Certainty* suggests, doubt is parasitic on received wisdom and the advocacy of radical doubt internally incoherent. In short, Enlightenment skepticism cannot offer a coherent account of its own project. Disguised as intellectual integrity, the guardian of modern cynicism, radical skepticism preys on the misrepresentation of reality and distorts our understanding of it.

Suffice to say, Polanyi here anticipates the contemporary critique offered by Wolterstorff, Plantinga, Evans *et al.* of classical evidentialism and deontological approaches to knowledge. This is the view, traceable to Locke, that we have a duty not to believe anything except upon sufficient evidence. Or, as W. K. Clifford famously claimed a century ago, "[i]t is wrong, everywhere and for everyone, to believe anything on insufficient evidence."[18] This supposition, deeply engrained in modernity, is

16. Polanyi, *The Tacit Dimension*, 80.

17. Ibid., 61.

18. Clifford, *Lectures and Essays*, 183. Cf. Quinton, "Knowledge and Belief," 352; and Plantinga, *Warranted Christian Belief*, 89. As C. Stephen Evans summarizes this position, we have an epistemic duty not only to base our views on evidence but to "proportion the 'firmness' of our belief to the quality of the evidence." That is, we are obliged "to examine all the 'grounds of probability,' and then proportion our degree of belief to the degree of

demonstrably absurd.[19] The evidentialist's hypothesis is *itself* devoid of evidence, so should not, on its own account, be believed. In short, what is arguably one of the most widely accepted epistemological legacies of the Enlightenment is self-referentially incoherent, hoist on its own petard!

Our whole engagement with society, with other people and, indeed, with reality as a whole is sustained by an epistemic base composed of innumerable suppositions, assumptions, and believings or trustings. Of some of these we may indeed be cognizant or focally aware, but the vast majority of these believed assumptions are tacit and some are so built in to our subliminal processing of reality that few, other than the most sophisticated analytic philosophers, could even begin to make them explicit—even if we had the desire, let alone the time, to provide anything approaching a complete list. Sustaining a great deal of this epistemic web is "testimony"—the testimony of the communities in which we were brought up and in which we live and move and function. To question any belief to which these communities might provide or even merely assume testimony necessarily involves participation within (and thus tacit assent to) myriad believings to which subliminal testimony has been provided and in the context of which critical thought takes place. Society is based on trust. To the extent that politics and political philosophy repudiate that they lose not only relevance but coherence.

This brings us to Polanyi's critique of the free, detached subject. The scientist neither does nor can "sit back and choose at his pleasure a new existence . . . All his existential choices are made in response to a potential discovery . . . Every step is an effort to meet an immediate necessity; his freedom is continuous service."[20] Intrinsic to the very functioning of the knowing self is a form of indwelling within one's community and, indeed,

---

probability the evidence gives the proposition in question". Evans, *The Historical Christ and the Jesus of Faith*, 209. This suggests that we are forsaking our epistemic duties, we are being noetically sinful, if we believe something for which we don't have sufficient explicit evidence—or if we believe something with greater conviction than is warranted by the evidence.

19. We could not possibly function by ensuring that we have evidence for all that we believe. Every one of my actions performed at every moment of the day is couched in believings whose probability I could not possibly check. Even if I could quantify the probability of each, it is absurd to think that, by an act of self on self, I could alter the degree of conviction to reflect the probability rating I attribute to each belief in the light of the evidence.

20. Polanyi, *The Tacit Dimension*, 80–81.

within one's world. This indwelling is constituted by a primitive or primordial relation of trust. Society presupposes community. No political theory therefore can conceivably be imposed from scratch or *ab initio* by the detached, skeptical subject. All theories and all corrections emerge through the gradual pressure of circumstance on participants within the community and the heuristic adaptations that result from this.

Polanyi's dislike for the theories generated and imposed by modern critical philosophy is evidenced both in his approach to the philosophy of science and to ethics. As Nagy suggests, there is an Aristotelian element to Polanyi's account. His insistence in *The Tacit Dimension* that "existence precedes essence," and his advocacy of "the balanced mind secured against both critical and moral frenzy"[21] savors of the mean. And his concept of a "happy people" in a "civic home"[22] is suggestive of eudaimonistic accounts.

But does this emphasis on trust, the dislike of theory together with his critique of skepticism, not translate to an uncritical conservatism of tradition—the kind of conservatism that the Enlightenment challenged with such liberating social implications regarding slavery, superstition, and the burning of witches, not to mention the myriad other forms of religious excess? Is there any place for cultural critique and, if so, from what base?

Where the Reformed epistemologists and, indeed, Karl Barth, would variously appeal to elements in the Christian epistemic base to interpret the societal context of human flourishing—as also the ultimate grounds of the scientific enterprise—Polanyi repudiates any such move. "The enfeebled authority of revealed religion" cannot achieve the reconciliation between modern man's critical incisiveness and moral demands. Rather, he suggests, "the enfeebled authority of revealed religion" may, at best, "hope to be revived by its achievement"![23]

So where do we look? Clearly, not to any prescriptive socio-political theory! As Nagy puts it, "Whether it be Hobbes's principle of self-preservation, Locke's social contract, Kant's categorical imperative, or Mill's greatest happiness principle, the modern quest for moral perfection which is to be achieved through a supreme and universally applicable

21. Ibid., 80 and 86.

22. Polanyi, *Personal Knowledge*, 215.

23. Polanyi, *The Tacit Dimension*, 62.

moral principle, has proved futile."[24] Worse, indeed! It is not theory but the practice of a particular kind of community, the scientific community, to which Polanyi turns to find an analogue of healthy society—namely, the "society of explorers." Characterized by radical mutuality, this community constitutes an alternative paradigm to that of the dogmatic society living from some theoretical principle.[25] The scientific community is one characterized by mutual coordination, mutual adjustment, mutual authority, and mutual control, generating what he terms a "mediated consensus"[26] which derives from a principle of "mutual control."[27] "A society of explorers is controlled throughout by such mutually imposed authority."[28] "It is clear," he writes, "that only fellow scientists working in closely related fields are competent to exercise direct authority over each other; but their personal fields will form chains of overlapping neighbourhoods extending over the entire range of science."[29] Those who join the community "start their inquiries by joining the interplay of mutual co-ordination and at the same time taking their own part in the existing system of mutual control, and they do so in the belief that its current standards are essentially true and common throughout the science. They trust the traditions fostered by this system of mutual control without much experience of it and at the same time claim an independent position from which they may reinterpret and possibly revolutionise this tradition."[30] But what of hierarchy? Government, after all, has "top down" responsibilities. Yet again, the scientific community provides an analogue. In that context, authority is conceived in terms of the mutual control of independent scientists.[31]

All this seems to suggest that Polanyi would have done his shopping at the Co-operative, banked at the Alliance and Mutual, and, on Sunday mornings, attended the United Reformed Church![32] What he appears to be arguing for is the beehive or termite colony model where each termite

24. Nagy "Philosophy in a Different Voice," 22–23.

25. Polanyi, *The Tacit Dimension*, 83.

26. Ibid., 73.

27. Ibid., 73 and 83.

28. Ibid., 83–84.

29. Ibid., 72.

30. Ibid., 73.

31. Ibid., 73–74.

32. Each of these institutions in Great Britain has a co-operative, democratic ethos and constitution.

or bee freely and happily pursues his or her responsibilities virtuously in a limited and localized way trusting everyone else similarly to carry out their duties. For Nagy, Polanyi is anticipating here a second recent philosophical revolution, namely, that associated with Macintyre and Hauerwas—the abandonment of "the pursuit of an abstract ideal of moral perfection in an ethics of principle in favour of a concrete ethics of virtue and its implications for the development of moral character."[33] Whereas the former inspires moral perfection through absolute adherence to a supreme, universalizable (though often minimalistic) principle, the latter rules out any achievement of perfectionism through its concern with continuous moral growth.

The society of explorers is a community reposing on virtue in which the most revolutionary mind must choose a small area of responsibility. As and when there is a paradigm shift that impacts on the whole, it is the result of a "butterfly effect." And transformation within any domain will regard its scientific environment as its premise.[34]

THE PLACE OF POLANYI'S CONCEPT OF SUCCESSIVE LEVELS OF REALITY FOR HIS SOCIAL PHILOSOPHY

Here Polanyi's concept of levels acquires political significance. He argues that:

> all our higher principles must rely for their working on a lower level of reality . . . [that] necessarily sets limits to their scope, yet does not make them reducible to the terms of the lower level . . . Society, as an organisation of power and profit, forms one level, while its moral principles lie on a level above it. The higher level is rooted in the lower one: moral progress can be achieved only within the medium of a society operating by the exercise of power and aiming at the material advantages.[35]

33. Nagy, "Philosophy in a Different Voice," 23.

34. Clearly, this kind of approach contrasts radically with "perfectionist" outlooks that seek to "transform the whole of thought and the entire society" and that constitute nothing less than "a programme of destruction, ending up at best in a world of pretense." Polanyi, *The Tacit Dimension*, 85.

35. He then adds, "We must accept the fact that any moral advantages must be tainted by this social mechanism which alone can bring them about. To attempt to enforce absolute morality in society is therefore to indulge in fantasies that will only lead to untamed violence." Ibid., 86.

There is a limiting or conditioning effect, therefore, built in to the very business of pursuing specific beneficial aims. The political imposition of a particular program inevitably ignores localized practical concerns in favor of the realization of universal ideals. To the extent that it does this, it constitutes an act of violence by ignoring the relations of accountability between these levels. In sum, in order to facilitate real moral progress, reasoning involves assessing and analyzing practical issues at a lower level than that of moral standards or ideals. What amounts to practical wisdom must determine the scope of the appropriate application of the moral principles. Totalitarian perfectionism fails to appreciate this fact and can only damage the inherently multi-tiered nature of properly functional society.

This, however, raises questions concerning Polanyi's view of the universality of moral standards. A central affirmation of Polanyi's post-critical realism is that all our judgments, be they scientific, political or ethical, are "located." That is, no science, not least political science, can possess a God's-eye view, or occupy an Archimedean point. Is this to suggest that we interpret the claims we make as context-bound or relative? Emphatically not! All our claims are made with universal intent despite the fact that they are invariably made from within a particular context.

But wherein lies the warrant for what appears to be universal extrapolation from within an irreducibly particular or local context? Claiming universal intent is one thing; being warranted in doing so, is quite another! For Polanyi, context-specific universal intent is warranted, because what is interpreting itself to us in particular ways and in specific contexts is *reality*. The fact that access is context-mediated does not mean that we are not provided thereby with epistemic access to the way things actually *are* in some universal sense.

When we move by analogy from the physical laws as they interpret themselves to physicists to the consideration of the moral structures articulated in political philosophy, however, this kind of account becomes more problematic. It is less than clear that moral laws are to be understood on a model of scientific laws. Scientific hypotheses are generally testable, explain phenomena and are likely to be agreed on by most of the relevant communities involved to the extent that they are simply attending to the facts of the situation. But does the same apply with moral conclusions? Moral laws are prescriptive rather than descriptive. To suggest that description can generate prescriptions not only risks the naturalistic fallacy, it reiterates one of the more politically tragic confusions of recent centuries. To suggest that good scientists possess a degree of epistemic neutrality is one thing, but to extrapolate from that to suggest parallel epistemic neutrality among political scientists with respect to "moral standards" is quite another!

Now Polanyi's response might be to remind us of his claim that "moral forces" are "primary motives" for humanity.[36] This would seem to suggest that epistemic access to the ethical is hard-wired in some way. But on what grounds might one make such an assumption? In the context of contemporary science, (neuroscience, evolutionary psychology, not to mention sociology or social anthropology), this is hardly uncontroversial. Patricia Churchland is representative of a substantial section of the scientific community when she suggests that human beings are essentially nervous systems whose primary motives she articulates as follows: "Looked at from an evolutionary point of view, the principal function of nervous systems is to enable the organism to move appropriately. Boiled down to essentials, a nervous system enables the organism to succeed in the four F's: feeding, fleeing, fighting, and reproducing . . ."[37] One suspects that Polanyi would have his work cut out to persuade the scientific community in general that moral forces (as opposed to those forces that enhance human fitness and survival) are primary motives in humanity—especially if such claimed moral forces may be perceived to constitute counter-evolutionary forces.

NAJDER'S CRITIQUE

This brings us to consider briefly further criticisms that Zdzislav Najder offers of Polanyi's views on morality, conscience, freedom, and religion.

a) At the very core of Polanyi's concept of moral inversion lies his separation between moral *passions* (that are deemed to be inherent in all people) and moral *ideals* (that are not). Moral inversion results from the exercise of moral passions by those who have shed their moral ideals. But what is

36. Najder, "'Moral Inversion' or Moral Revaluation?" 367.

37. Churchland continues, "Improvements in sensorimotor control confer an evolutionary advantage . . . *so long as it is geared to the organism's way of life and enhances the organism's chances of survival.*" She also adds, "Truth, whatever that is, definitely takes the hindmost." Churchland, "Epistemology in the Age of Neuroscience," 549. Emphasis Churchland.

it that distinguishes a moral passion from an amoral passion if the difference cannot be articulated with reference to underlying moral ideals? Is it that Polanyi is himself determining what ideals actually constitute *moral* ideals?

b) Polanyi assumes that "all men's consciences" cohere by virtue of the fact that they are grounded in "the same universal tradition."[38] But what does this mean? As Najder observes, "conscience" is being used entirely ahistorically. But what then is it? Is it a general psychological faculty with its own proper objects? And if so, what are these objects if not moral principles or ideals?[39]

c) One of the essential features in Polanyi's account of moral inversion is his insistence that it results from "an unprecedented tendency to moral perfectionism."[40] What he fails to explain here, however, is that, as Najder points out, "this recent moral perfectionism or radicalism is neither theoretical nor psychological, but primarily *social*."[41] The real revolution is to be found in the fact that what took place was a move away from an *individualistic* ethical focus to a *social* one.

This leads Najder to raise further questions concerning his critique of moral perfectionism. If Polanyi's critique of socialism concerns its commitment to moral perfectionism, why is he not equally concerned with Christianity and Islam that might also be construed as involving a commitment to moral perfectionism? Furthermore, should he not also recognize that the "perfectionist" forces to which Polanyi objects reflect a concern to oppose the use of power to restrict the affirmation of human dignity to the upper echelons of society or the richer countries of the world?[42] This, in turn, raises the question as to whether Polanyi's own somewhat individualistic bent does not undervalue the significance of so-

---

38. Polanyi, *Science, Faith and Society*, 82, cited by Najder, "'Moral Inversion' or Moral Revaluation?" 367.

39. One cannot help wondering whence his own rich value structures—referred to, for example, in Polanyi, *Personal Knowledge*, 222–23—derive.

40. This is a point that Polanyi continually reiterates "stressing the disastrous consequences of excessive moral demands, imposed on man by the modern temper". Najder, "'Moral Inversion' or Moral Revaluation?" 368.

41. Ibid.

42. Ibid.

cial or group interests? In short, there were valid moral concerns leading to the Marxist revolution, and "traditional moral values" could equally be seen to have been the casualty of the localized self-interest of the wealthy, privileged, ruling classes? Is it appropriate to critique a struggle for the liberation of the working classes—even if it went awry—without also critiquing the abuse of power by ruling classes seeking to protect their vested interests?

This brings us to Polanyi's use of words like "liberty" and "freedom" that, Najder comments, he employs "in a general, unspecified sense, as if their meanings were absolutely unambiguous." This makes "no conceptual allowances for the possibility that freedom may not be a static condition, independent from historical, social and economic circumstances." By failing to appreciate the situational nature of freedom—that it is always "a freedom from or freedom to"—it comes to function for Polanyi as "a sort of magic incantation," in the same way that it did, Najder adds, for the eighteenth-century liberals.[43] There is, in short, a close connection between Polanyi's use of "moral" and his use of "free." "Moral is used in a strongly evaluative sense—the commitments fostered by a truly 'free' society are moral, but those fostered by 'totalitarian' societies are not."[44] Again, Polanyi needs a far more robust concept of "moral" if it is not to be used either emotively or in an arbitrarily prescriptive manner. The same applies to his concept of "freedom" if he is not simply to buy into reactionary political jargon.

What is required is an ontology—and Polanyi ponders whether religion can provide the necessary foundations. However, and this is my final reference to Najder's critique, Polanyi's references to God and religion are "confoundingly vague"—we simply do not know what concept of God and what kind of religion he had in mind.[45] Moreover, his references to the fact that "no society can live up to Christian precepts" and the enfeebled authority of "revealed religion" leave one wondering what kind of religion he could drum up that was not simply going to constitute divine endorsement of his own prior, locally grounded, claims as possessing not only universal significance but transcendent validity!

43. Ibid., 370.
44. Ibid., 371.
45. Ibid., 372.

In *Personal Knowledge*, Polanyi complains about "hardened utilitarians nobly upholding their logically unaccountable moral convictions."[46] The question that we find ourselves asking is how logically accountable are Polanyi's *own* convictions on moral standards and social ethics, not to mention the nature of freedom. Is he able to supply the kinds of prescriptive grounds that his own approach seems to require?

As we have seen, Polanyi appeals to the scientific community as an analogue for society. The mutuality, mutual respect, collaboration, the shared determination to build on tradition by small, localized advances, and the acknowledgement of mutual freedoms all seem to attend the spectacular explanatory success of the community. Does this not suggest that this kind of community is indeed in touch with reality? There is a subtle subliminal appeal to Polanyi's account!

But what kind of analogue is the scientific community? First, it presupposes the existence of government—i.e., the protections the state offers, systems of taxation, welfare, etc. It is against this backcloth that individuals are set free to engage in scientific research.

Second, it is not a natural community and certainly not defined, as states are, by haphazard geographical and historical contingencies. Conversely, the scientific community is defined by a highly exclusive selectivity, that is, it selects out the young, the elderly, the handicapped, the mentally ill, the criminal, and the uneducated. Indeed, the mutuality to which he refers is selected *into* the community. You only succeed in the scientific community to the extent that you not only "play the game" but are proven to do so outstandingly well—that you engage with the research of other scientists, that you are intellectually "up to snuff" and that you display the character traits with which fellow scientists can work. You do not have anti-social hobbies, you do not get drunk during the morning coffee break, go pimping in the afternoon, systematically lie to your peers or vandalize the photocopier when it lets you down. In short, you are invited to participate in the scientific community once you have satisfied the conditions of membership.

Third, its decision-making processes are less explicitly ethical. A scientist may be confronted with an ethical decision as to whether to tell the whole truth about the nature of the experimentation that led to her findings. Most of the time, however, her decisions will not be ethically

46. Polanyi, *Personal Knowledge*, 234.

problematic. A politician continually has to make choices in the light of serious moral conflicts and justify them. This, again, means highlighting aims and ideals and quantifying them, that is, showing why and how one should prioritize the investment of limited funds in healthcare for the terminally ill over the education of the young rather than the other way round. They have to justify theft as the lesser of two evils, that is, taking taxes from people who have no choice to live in any other country, who did not vote for you and whose hard-earned cash you are commandeering. The problem with Marxism may be that it absolutized certain ideals at the cost of others, but to reject the notion of moral excellence and the pursuit of moral ideals in government is surely to throw the baby out with the bath water—and not just the baby but the scientific community of explorers!

So, wherein lies the strength of Polanyi's analysis of the political problems of modernity? It may lie in part in his analyses of the misuse of science, of the impact of skepticism and its inherent confusions, and the dangers of the displacement of moral energies. There is clearly significant insight in his analysis of the concept of levels, of mutuality, that one can affirm the locatedness of epistemic access while maintaining realist commitments and in his critique of totalitarianism's use of its "quasi-scientific prediction of the march of history toward a perfect society."[47] His comments on the problems of constructing the perfect society from scratch by the radical use of power have a certain contemporary resonance given the recent history of Iraq's graphic demonstration of the chaos that can result from the radical destruction of institutions.

HOW DOES ONE RESPOND THEOLOGICALLY?

A theological response must start by recognizing, with Polanyi, the enfeebled authority of revelation in society. To the extent that the majority of people have not been given to recognize the kinship that the Eternal has established by entering time,[48] they do not recognize the presence of the kingdom and God's associated purposes for humanity. For contingent reasons the majority are not included within the sphere of God's Self-disclosure.

47. Polanyi and Prosch, *Meaning*, 17.

48. This phrase is borrowed from Kierkegaard, *Concluding Unscientific Postscript*, 508.

What does this mean? It means, for example that we cannot pre-suppose a universal *suneidesis* with God of God's purposes for humanity. What this does *not* mean, however, is that the thrust of our political philosophy should not be determined and molded by the authority of God's triune revelation! If that revelation is true, its authority is not enfeebled as the source of wisdom on all matters relating to the nature and shape of human community. In short, not only should the Christian theologian operate from a Christian epistemic base; it would be entirely irrational for her not to do so.

What are the implications of this? Negatively, it means the following: Theology knows no discipleship of an idea or an ideal—be it the ideal of freedom or equality, or the happiness of the greatest number, or a Kantian universalizability principle. Nor does it begin with any abstract idealization of the "local," the politically "small," nor with an endorsement of devolution.[49] Nor does theology translate to a theory of values. As Eberhard Jüngel has argued, the word "value" has no place within Christian thought whatsoever. At the heart of the only form of existence it affirms, he argues, is correspondence to the truth, "following the truth" or, as Paul puts it, *being true* in love (*aletheuontes en agape*).

What does "corresponding to the truth" mean positively? First and foremost, it means *being* community—not seeking to impose it by legislative means or by the use of power. At the same time, this "correspondence" does not mean being a community of loving, nor a community characterized by the pursuit of justice or "peace"—some of the church's sound-bites during the Iraq crisis have savored of intellectual and moral sloth! Nor is it about a self-conscious concern to be a community of character or virtue. Rather, it means being a worshipping community—where correspondence is defined as the gift of participating by the Spirit in the Son's communion with the Father. It is thus a community for which ethics (worthship) is also defined as the gift of participating (*koinonein*) in this same event of communion.

It is only as such and by being such that the Body of Christ can serve as the salt of the earth. What does this gift of participation involve at the political level? It involves first and foremost living out a perception. The reconciled *dianoia*, that is constitutive of Christian conversion, perceives

---

49. Although it does affirm that God takes seriously the particular, the local and the personal. With Polanyi, we can affirm that the locally conditioned and conditional may, by the grace of God, provide access not only to the universal but also to the transcendent.

the other, the non-Christian, the alien, the destitute as also the dictator, the child abuser and the ethnic cleanser as loved and unconditionally forgiven by God. The church's primary orientation to the world is thus characterized first and foremost as participating by grace in God's unconditional love and forgiveness toward the world. The offence of this, however, is that although it may have myriad implications for political policies, it can never be translated into a political program.

The political import of this has been lost to Western civilization due to a tragic history of the mistranslation of terms. When the three key biblical concepts *berith*, *torah*, and *tsedaqah* were translated via Greek into Latin, to emerge as *Foedus*, *Lex*, and *Iustitia*—or contract, (Stoic) law, and justice—they underwent a conceptual transformation that constituted a distortion, indeed violation, of their original meaning and reference. It is these concepts, torn from their Hebrew origins, that have served not only to underpin Western civilization and politics but as denoting the essential form of the Christian contribution to civilization. Sadly, the influence is profoundly distorted and distortive. *Berith* denotes the unconditional covenant commitment of God to Israel, *torah* spells out the unconditional obligations of corresponding to God's unconditional covenant faithfulness, and *tsedaqah* refers to the righteousness of the God who remains unconditionally true and faithful to his covenant commitment to humanity. This is the antithesis of a contractual system of law and justice and denotes what is, humanly speaking, an inconceivably "positive intentionality" toward the other, to use John Macmurray's expression.

So what of moral inversion? There are myriad forms of political philosophy and systems of government that could be described as forms of "moral inversion." From a Christian epistemic base, forms of civil religion that uphold a contractualism that endorses the death penalty, for example, as an outworking of contractual models of law and justice certainly constitutes moral inversion. A further example would be those forms of consequentialism that repudiate responsibility for the victims of torture by a dictator in the name of the ecclesial endorsement of "peace." Another might be the kind of political parochialism that gives financial priority to furthering space exploration over addressing the inconceivable suffering and poverty of the citizens of Darfur or the victims of the earthquakes in Kashmir and Indonesia or of Aids in sub-Saharan Africa. All of these are characterized by a reschematization and displacement of moral ideals and values that originally derived from pseudo-Christian affirmations.

What is the appropriate response? The theologian is free to make use of whatever form of argumentation that is valid and appropriate to expose the detrimental implications of the position that is being endorsed. What is not appropriate, however, is a response that assumes that political engagement must operate from universally accessible principles and ideals that then constitute the fundamental control on our political affiliations. The only political orientation that the Christian theologian affirms is one that is characterized by a Christian epistemic base and thus one that refuses to translate the person of the *Logos* into a series of *logoi*, that is, principles or ideals. It is simply irrational for a Christian to bracket out of her thinking about socio-political obligations what she believes to be true about God and humanity. The Christian knows more than she can tell—and considerably more than she can justify to the one who denies more than he can tell!

In conclusion, I would suggest that what she does know must surely include the following:

a) that the triune God affirms unconditionally the dignity of all human persons, be they sinner or sinned against—and that no form of community or society is properly functional to the extent that it does not conform to that affirmation and participate in it;

b) that the antidote to all forms of moral inversion is not a program or a political philosophy but a renewal of mind. It is the reconciliation of our minds to perceive in truth and thereby to affirm the God-given humanity and dignity of all persons—the only orientation towards others that the gospel recognizes to be "righteous";

c) that the transformation of our minds is something that the Spirit alone can accomplish and does so in and through the witness of the worshipping community—to the extent that the latter participates in the life of the "man for others";

d) that this transformation is most fully effected in response to a politics that "corresponds" to the grammar of God's covenant commitment, and emphatically not a politics grounded in contractual notions or legalistic notions endorsing the conditional acceptance of the other;

e) that the transformative impact of the gospel is to be construed in terms of evangelical repentance and not legal repentance. It is the acceptance of those who are dysfunctional that serves both to expose to them and thus to redeem their social dysfunctionality and not their isolation or rejection;

f) that it is to the extent that the church has the courage to be the church and live this life as stewards of creation that it both discerns and witnesses to God's purposes for the state;

g) that all political action is compromised in a world requiring to be reconciled. There is, therefore, no more place for the perfectionism that denies that there are grey areas than for the moral skepticism that denies that there can be shades of grey; and, finally,

h) that the church's service to the state is nothing other than the out-working of the reverent and repentant socio-political living, praying, being and doing intrinsic to the worshipping community's stewardship of creation understood in the light of the One through whom and for whom all things were created.[50]

---

50. For a considerably fuller treatment of these themes, see my chapter, "The Theological Grounds for Advocating Forgiveness and Reconciliation in the Sociopolitical Realm."

5

Michael Polanyi and Karl Barth

A Creative Congruence?

PETER FORSTER

INTRODUCTION

WHEN I WAS COMPLETING a degree in chemistry in the University of Oxford over thirty years ago, I was awarded a prize that I was obliged to take in books. In what seemed at the time a rather mad impulse, I chose several volumes of the *Church Dogmatics* and Michael Polanyi's *Personal Knowledge*. A close friend who was a doctoral student in theology encouraged me to read Barth; Polanyi was Senior Research Fellow at my College and had made the journey from chemistry to the humanities that I sensed my later life might bring.

Both Barth and Polanyi were to remain abiding influences and yet the air of the two authors seemed quite different. Although there have been some attempts to relate their thought, these have never seemed quite satisfactory and occasional attempts to use Polanyi as a means to a fundamental criticism of Barth have been unconvincing. They are increasingly acknowledged as intellectual giants of the twentieth century and were roughly comparable in age, both being born in the 1890s, yet there is no evidence that either was aware of the other's work. I hope to demonstrate that a rather deeper agreement existed between them than either they, or subsequent commentators, have noticed.

POLANYI'S EPISTEMOLOGY AND ONTOLOGY

It is best to begin with an outline of the main features of Polanyi's epistemology and ontology. His career as a scientist evolved towards the social sciences under the catalysis of political events in the first half of the twentieth century. He was deeply alarmed by the general dehumanizing influences of communism and fascism, and by the fate of free scientific enquiry under totalitarian regimes. He traced the common source to a prevailing view of the universe that was reductionist and mechanistic, and that held out to those who espoused such a view an ideal of knowledge as exhaustive, explicit, and precise. Against this, Polanyi sought to deny any fundamental opposition between faith and knowledge, and to establish across all domains of knowledge the theological maxim that he associated with Augustine: *fides quaerens intellectum*.

The epistemological case is set out in *Personal Knowledge*, starting at the point where it might be thought that Polanyi was most vulnerable: the physical sciences. Citing a series of examples as evidence, he argued that judgments of rationality and order have no ground that excludes the knowing subject. Scientific knowing is presented as a skill, that is learned, practiced, and guarded by the scientific community. Only to a degree could these skills be analyzed and formulated into rules. Polanyi sought to demonstrate that all knowledge fell in a spectrum from the physical sciences to the humanities, with the element of personal participation increasing as one moved through the biological sciences to the social sciences. He was unwilling to identify a greater degree of subjectivity in the human and social sciences, and he held that all knowledge was objective in the sense of establishing contact with a hidden reality, that would bear fruit in unexpected and unpredictable ways as the horizons of knowledge unfolded.

An example will best illustrate Polanyi's approach to epistemology. What rules guide the skill of riding a bicycle? Analyzed by the laws of physics, they are as follows. Once a cyclist starts falling in one direction he turns in that direction in order to create a centrifugal force that corrects the balance, but that then unbalances the cycle in the opposite direction. This is corrected by turning into this fall, and a cyclist progresses by executing a series of alternating curves. For a given angle of imbalance the curvature needs to be inversely proportional to the square of the speed and hence the faster you cycle the straighter the path you can take. This also explains why it is impossible to balance either while not moving, or if the front wheel is locked in position.

Do we then teach children these principles in order that they may learn to ride a bicycle? No, for two reasons. We cannot in our head perform the necessary calculation and even were we able to do so, we would fall off, because there are always other factors to be considered: wind speed, road surface, etc. The process of acquiring and holding knowledge is, for Polanyi, always an art. Rules of art can be useful, but they do not determine the practice of an art, that requires an essentially indeterminate range of skills.

In his earlier philosophical work, from the 1940s and 1950s, Polanyi was largely dependent on the principle of personal commitment. A cyclist thus committed herself to perform the art of riding a bicycle, learning in the process the skills required. In the early 1960s, he realized that this focal commitment depended on a tacit awareness of a whole range of conscious and unconscious requirements of cycling. The cyclist attended from these "tacit subsidiaries" to the focal art of cycling.

Polanyi regarded the knowledge we have of our bodies as a prime example of tacit knowledge. We only rarely focus on our own body as we attend to an external object, but we tacitly rely continually on our body in the process of observing realities outside our body. When we use a tool to perform a task, we assimilate the tool to our body. A competent cyclist is unaware of the workings of his bicycle as he concentrates on the road ahead; if he looks instead at the pedals and handlebars, or concentrates upon calculating the right angle of curvature, he is liable to fall off. Similarly, if an actor thinks directly about his script he is likely to get stage fright; the lines must come as if from the heart.

This assimilation to our bodies of the tacit subsidiary elements that we rely upon when doing or knowing something else, Polanyi calls *knowledge by indwelling*. Such knowledge is innately contingent and corrigible, offering only a partial and imprecise grasp of reality, but also holding out the prospect of revision and improvement. He develops a theory of language on this basis: just as a cyclist indwells a bicycle, assimilating it to his body in order to move around the physical world, so we indwell our words and the concepts they denote in order to understand the world. Words are thus not mirrors of reality, but the means by which we participate in reality. Language does not impose an arbitrary conceptual structure on reality, but grows out of our human participation in the wider world. Polanyi develops this into a more general account of mind and the external world, and his epistemologically driven *Personal Knowledge* was followed by a series of shorter writings in the last decade of his active life that focus more upon questions of ontology.

As we have seen, Polanyi challenged the ideal of detached, purely objective, knowledge and the associated disjunction between faith and knowledge. He traced this in its modern guise to the mechanistic worldview that had been speculatively mooted by Galileo, and elaborated much later at the Enlightenment, most strikingly by Laplace. Laplace held out the ideal of universal knowledge, that would accrue to an intelligence that possessed at one moment knowledge of the mass, position and velocity of the fundamental particles of the universe and the forces acting between them. He believed that such an intelligence would, in principle, know everything. Polanyi regarded this as quite illusory because even physical knowledge could not be deduced purely from atomic topographies, for physics requires, for example, the principle of entropy, that depends upon the quality of randomness. Laplacean knowledge would not even allow the calculation of the temperature of a given region and, far from opening up a vista of universal knowledge, it would be a recipe for profound ignorance.

In building an alternative ontology to Laplacean reductionism, Polanyi begins by analyzing an inanimate machine. Two broad conditions must be satisfied for the successful working of a machine: that it is well designed, and that components can be made to withstand operational stresses. The ontology of a machine requires a dual description. The higher-level principles of design define the meaning of the machine as a whole and the material out of which it is made, subject to the laws of physics and chemistry. A machine is controlled by these different sets of principles or laws: of engineering on the one hand and of physics and chemistry on the other. They are quite distinct; the design of a machine can be patented, but no law of nature can be patented. Machines are invented, laws of nature are discovered, and no physical or chemical investigation of an artifact can in itself reveal its purpose.

A machine can thus be said to comprise two levels, with the meaning of the machine being primarily determined by the higher level and the lower level participating in, and contributing to, the effective realization of this meaning. Polanyi applies this to a range of human endeavors, for example a literary composition. He identifies five levels: the production of sounds, or paper and ink; the utterance or writing of words; their combination into sentences; the combination of sentences into a stylistic text; and finally the meaning to be conveyed. The whole enterprise is controlled by an interaction between successive levels: voice production or lettering leaves open the combination of sounds or shapes into words, that is controlled by the vocabulary of the language concerned. The combination of words into sentences is controlled by the relevant grammar, and so forth.

Polanyi attempts to generalize this to the universe as a whole, by presenting living beings as consisting in a sequence of levels in a hierarchy. The lowest functions of life are machine-like cellular processes, comprising the two levels we saw in a machine. These leave open possibilities of growth and, in animals, the functions that permit movement around the environment. Such movement leaves open the integration of such behavior into innate patterns of behavior, that in turn can be harnessed by intelligent purpose, and intelligent purpose can be shaped by responsible moral choice. While meaning is essentially conferred by higher levels on those below, a malfunction at a lower level can disable or kill the living person.

Polanyi's metaphysics is thus a thoroughgoing attack on reductionism. Each level embodies or gives the joint meaning of events at the lower level and the meaning of each successive rising level thus becomes wider at each stage and reaches the fullest measure of meaning at the apex. This is not to underestimate the potential effect of—for example—body upon mind, if particular features of, or deficiencies at the level of, bodily/brain function restrict the fulfillment of potential at the level of personality or mind, but such "bottom up" influences, while potentially vital, are essentially negations of meaning.

This is an outline of what I take to be the chief features of Polanyi's epistemology and ontology. He was—somewhat famously—reluctant to extend his thoughts into the realm of theology or religion, although he recognized this possibility and perhaps even its inevitability. He preferred to challenge his contemporaries to rethink their understanding of the universe and the place of human beings within it, without any specific religious commitment. So what has all this to do with Karl Barth?

I have long believed that, as a theologian, Karl Barth towers above his twentieth-century contemporaries, not so much because of the prodigious volume of his output, but because his theology has an authenticity and spiritual power that is seldom encountered elsewhere among modern writers. His weakness was his reluctance to accept that his theology entailed a comprehensive world-view. His stance was a curious inversion of Polanyi's, but from a theistic perspective: he wanted to help the church to rethink the foundations of theology, without any specific philosophical commitment. Yet there is in Barth's mature theology a reasonably consistent world-view or metaphysics, and it is the contention of this essay both that the implied Barthian metaphysics is consistent with Polanyi's epistemology and ontology, and that the clarification that Polanyi can offer would take Barth's theology a little further than he was able to identify.

BARTH'S EPISTEMOLOGY

Let us begin with Barth's epistemology. For Barth, God is known as he gives himself to be known and in the process of revelation human beings are formed as subjects of the knowledge of God. Human knowledge of God therefore takes the form of faith, that Barth sometimes calls "the obedience of faith." Given that this faith is founded upon God who in his inner nature—from a human perspective—is a profound mystery, God remains intrinsically veiled in his unveiling. We know God with clarity and certainty, but only in the mystery of his being as we participate provisionally and partially, yet authentically, in the knowledge that God has of himself as Father, Son, and Holy Spirit. Barth adopts the patristic aphorism "By God alone may God be known."

Barth's strong rejection of natural theology, as an independent route to knowledge of God, follows from this belief that the true fulfillment of human knowledge of God depends upon the supremacy of God as both subject and object of that knowledge. Barth regards natural theology as an attempt to encroach upon God's sovereign initiative in Jesus Christ. The theology of the humanity of God in Barth's later writings is intended to replace and supplant what had traditionally been known as natural theology. All knowledge of God must be rooted uniquely, if thereby universally, in the humanity of God, in the person of Jesus Christ.

Barth lays considerable emphasis upon God's hiddenness in his revelation. From a human perspective God is incomprehensible, even to the point that we cannot understand how we come to know him. Indeed, we do not comprehend God at all, but we apprehend him, authentically if incompletely. This is the context in which Barth locates his much-discussed concept of the analogy of faith. It is in a dialectic of veiling and unveiling, centered both ontologically and epistemologically in Jesus Christ, that human concepts are dynamically restored to a partial correspondence with God's being. Barth speaks of a "co-existence and co-inherence of veiling and unveiling in God's revelation."[1] Veiling and unveiling are described as an "ordered dialectic," ordered by grace.[2]

There is no desire here to render the human subject a passive automaton. The grace of God is grace and not brute force and, as such, seeks to create a truly human response as it evokes and prompts acknowledgment. In the discussion in *Church Dogmatics* II.1 Barth is referring back to the central and important section in *Church Dogmatics* I.1, "The Word of God and Experience." All human activity, including the human striving for knowledge of God, is presented as genuine human self-determination that is subject to determination by God. As is well known, Barth rejected the idea that human beings determine their own existence apart from God and also the idea that there is a co-operation between God and human beings. However, he also rejects the Augustinian view that there is a "simultaneity, inter-relation and unity in tension" between the divine and human activity.[3] He rejects a concept of irresistible grace. Barth speaks of human experience of God as "genuine experience," and he emphasizes "as strongly as possible its character as human self-determination."[4] He uses the image of the action of God in judging our human action as constituting a circle within which we act as relatively, but not absolutely, autonomous agents. He wishes to avoid the circle being seen as an ellipse, with two foci, one human and one divine.

Barth's view of the relation between human self-determination and its determination by God bears an interesting resemblance to Polanyi's account of how two levels in a stratified universe interact and, particularly, to his account of how a human intelligence is open to being shaped and judged by a transcendent moral realm, that a Christian would identify with the person of God. On her own level, a human person has a relative autonomy, that, when she is in a creative relationship with the higher order of meaning that God embodies, will acknowledge and seek to cultivate that relationship. In a more fundamental sense, however, the

---

1. Barth, *Church Dogmatics*, vol II.1: 235.
2. Ibid., 2:236.
3. Barth, *Church Dogmatics*, vol I, 199.
4. Ibid., 1:208.

meaning of our lives is given by that higher level and our personhood as made in the image of God is given in that relationship. Polanyi speaks of our obligation freely to endeavor to indwell more fully the higher level of meaning and purpose that transcends us. From a Christian perspective, we would speak of God wishing to indwell the particulars of the world and, in a special way, human life, in order to relate to the world in general and to the church in a distinctive way as the Body of Christ.

Barth's epistemology can also be approached by reference to Polanyi's description of tacit knowledge. As we saw, Polanyi held that in all knowledge there are both focal and tacit components, the tacit components being a mixture of those that can be consciously identified, and those that either are not or cannot be consciously specified. Our reliance upon the tacit components in knowledge is in order to identify and understand the object of our focal attention. Let us relate this to Barth's treatment of natural theology. He denied that there is any revelation of God in the world that is independent of his revelation in Jesus Christ, that we know by reference to the witness of the Bible. He defined natural theology as follows: "By natural theology, I mean every formulation of a system that claims to be theological, that is, to interpret divine revelation, whose subject, however, differs fundamentally from the revelation of Jesus Christ and whose method therefore differs equally from the exposition of Holy Scripture."[5]

Adopting Polanyi's model, we would say that when focusing upon the reality of God's revelation in Jesus Christ—as this receives explicit testimony in the witness of Scripture—we rely tacitly upon a whole host of subsidiary clues that enable us to apprehend the knowledge that is at the focus of our search. These clues would be regarded as lower level coordinate realities, whose meaning is given from the higher level of God's revelation in Jesus Christ. However, the total venture of apprehending in faith God's revelation in Jesus Christ is critically dependent upon these lower-level realities, just as living beings depend upon food, drink, and the general functioning of their bodies. As it would be a mistake to explain the purpose of human life in terms of human appetites, or the physics and chemistry of human bodies, so also it would be a mistake to equate God's revelation in Jesus Christ with the tacitly held subsidiary clues that are required in the background, as it were, if we are to recognize

---

5. Brunner and Barth, *Natural Theology*, 74–75.

the person of Jesus Christ. The tacitly held clues to Jesus Christ must not be made to interpret revelation, but *vice versa*; they illuminate and shape our knowledge of the revelation of God in Jesus Christ only as that revelation accords meaning to those "lower level" realities.

How far is this from Barth? The later Barth affirmed that there are in the world various reflections of God's revelation, or "created lights" as he put it. It was an *independent* point of contact that Barth challenged, on the ground that to assert the independence of the world from God is precisely to prejudice the contact of God with the world. Critics of Barth have argued that without a prior natural knowledge of God, revelation will remain a message in an unintelligible language. Barth's response was that if this prior knowledge is truly independent of the knowledge of God revealed in Jesus Christ, is that not the real recipe for unintelligibility?

The traditional critique of Barth's view of natural theology, deriving originally from Brunner, has been restated by recourse to Polanyi's distinction between tacit and explicit knowledge by Paul Avis in *The Methods of Modern Theology*.[6] By contrast, it can be argued that, for Polanyi, tacit and explicit components in the knowledge of a given aspect of reality are in no sense independent. They are inter-dependent, yet cannot be reduced to each other, or linked by a logical bridge. Barth, it may be suggested, merely claims that the tacit, inarticulate, knowledge that all people of conscience have of God, when articulated apart from its source in the definitive revelation of God in Jesus Christ, will inevitably be misunderstood and distorted.

The Barth of the later volumes of the *Church Dogmatics* grants a progressively full recognition to the reality of "natural" knowledge of God, in the *Entsprechung* between God and creation, but he persists with his demand that this be correlated with its definitive and defining source in Jesus Christ, the cosmic Lord of space and time. Problems and misunderstandings arise because Barth is suspicious of all comprehensive world-views and he therefore draws back from any attempt to work out the rational structures of human understanding that correspond to this broadly conceived experience of grace. In addition, perhaps, to lacking the time and tools for this task, he would have feared a renewed confusion between the gospel and culture that has plagued the history of Protestant theology. Barth's failure to work out the structure of knowing and the

6. Avis, *The Methods of Modern Theology*, chapter 3.

ontological structures that his theology imply, could in large measure be answered by Polanyi's metaphysics. This would deepen other themes of Barth's theology.

BARTH'S DOCTRINE OF SCRIPTURE

Let us move to another area of Barth's theology that has been controversial, namely his doctrine of Scripture. Barth recognizes that human analysis can claim to identify a wide range of inconsistencies and errors in Scripture: philosophical, historical, ethical, and even theological.[7] He emphasizes that the Bible's "capacity for error" extends to its religious or theological content.[8] This aspect of Barth's theology has brought him into particular disrepute with conservative evangelical Christians, despite the parallel claim that there is an overall theological consistency in Scripture, in terms of what he calls the miracle of its witness, amid the inconsistencies, over-emphases, and errors that—humanly speaking—it contains. Barth's doctrine of Scripture evolved somewhat from a virtual identification between Scripture and the Word of God in volume I of the *Church Dogmatics*, to a later emphasis upon Scripture as *witness to* the Word. However, his treatment remains to a degree abstract: the numerous exegetical sub-sections only rarely suggest actual examples of the errors and inconsistencies that his theoretical treatment asserts as fundamental to the character of the biblical witness.

A Polanyian treatment of Scripture in terms of two co-ordinated levels—the Word of God and the word of man—would assist here. We would then say that the Word of God sets boundary conditions for the possible range of human witness and expression at the lower level. The meaning of the words of Scripture *in their purpose as Scripture* would be given from the higher level of God's revelation of himself. Diversity at the lower level would be appropriate and necessary to furnish a rich range of clues and subsidiary particulars, in order that the witness to God's revelation is properly embodied in the world. That some of the elements or emphases in the biblical witness might be misleading or even erroneous need not matter and, indeed, might emphasize the humanity of Scripture, provided that such elements were neither too numerous nor too antithetical to the overall witness of the Bible.

7. Barth, *Church Dogmatics*, I. 2:507.

8. Ibid., 2:509.

There is an analogy here with the human body. People can survive various illnesses or inconveniences that occur in the functioning of their bodies, but there are limits, set from the higher-level principles of human life, that determine when bodily life itself is threatened.

Such an analysis would support the chief lines of Barth's doctrine of Scripture in relation to its combination of fallible human witness and divine authority. It would also permit a franker dealing with problem passages than Barth normally attempts in the exegetical sections of the *Church Dogmatics*.

BARTH'S ANTHROPOLOGY

We are concerned in particular with the section in *Church Dogmatics* III.2, "Man as Soul and Body." In his anthropology, Barth emphasizes the integrity of a person as soul and body, along with an internal differentiation and structuring as body and soul. A person is held in being by the Holy Spirit and hence there can be no understanding of human persons apart from God. Nature is held in being by grace. Human beings exist as they have Spirit, but they have no Spirit as such. The Spirit is the giver of life, the principle and power that undergirds human existence. The Spirit constitutes a person as a human subject, but is not that subject. The Spirit, Barth suggests, has a special and direct relation to the soul, and through the soul an indirect but real relation to the body: an ordered relationship in which the soul is over the body.

Barth then offers three detailed sub-sections that deal with soul and body successively in their interconnection, their particularity, and their order. Just one aspect might be selected to illustrate the congruence with Polanyi's ontology: the treatment of human beings in relation to animals. For Barth, the concept of soul represents the independent life and action of a subject. Because animals clearly have a different type of subjectivity from humankind, Barth asserts that we cannot speak of the soul of an animal (or plant) unless there is a special type of animal (or plant) soul beyond our understanding.[9] Similarly, we cannot say whether or not animals are rational beings in the sense that we apply the term to human beings, because human rationality is the direct result of being addressed by God.[10]

9. Barth, *Church Dogmatics*, vol III, 2:373.
10. Ibid., 2:419.

Recast in Polanyian terms, Barth's two- or three-level view of human ontology as body and soul in relation to the Spirit of God would need to be replaced by a multi-level ontology that acknowledges that human beings share with the animal kingdom a number of levels of rational existence, uppermost being that of intelligent behavior, upon which in humanity is grafted the level of moral choice due to the human facility of response to the transcendent values of truth, justice, love, and so forth, that a Christian would identify with the creative presence of God through the Holy Spirit.

In Polanyi's view, it is the ability to acquire language that enables God—or the world of transcendent values—to summon human beings to responsible choice. This linguistic potential he believes to be due to the higher general intelligence that human beings attain through the large increase in brain size that accompanied human evolution from the apes. This enables us to understand the limited ability of some animals to reproduce certain features of humanity in expressions of feeling and, in the case of highly trained apes, the first rudiments of language.

If Polanyi's ontology helps us to understand the distinctive character of human existence, it should help us to reject the naïve distinction between human beings as rational and the rest of the animal kingdom as irrational, a distinction that, under Greek influence, took a strong root in patristic theology. Barth leaves these questions open, but Polanyi's analysis of created reality should lead us to oppose such a sharp distinction. Indeed, from Polanyi's perspective, it is human beings who are both the most rational and the most irrational animals, for whereas plant life is subject to malformation and disease, and animals to illusion and error, humanity is subject also to the possibility of moral error and moral evil. Each ontological level in a Polanyian universe has a distinctive double potential for good and evil, the good alone deriving its meaning and explanation from the succeeding level.

A final observation in the area of anthropology might be made. Barth wished to deny that there was a human "spirit," as opposed to human formation by the Spirit of God. The terminology here could be both elusive and ambiguous, but the human role cannot be regarded as essentially passive in the interplay between divine Spirit and human spirit, although meaning must ultimately derive from the higher divine level. We need to draw a clear distinction between divine Spirit and human spirit, but retention of the same term is helpful, provided that the anthropological distinction between the divine and human realms is not compromised, for example by the assumption of a master concept of spirit that underlies both. Two reasons might be given for retaining the concept of a distinct human spirit. Firstly, human beings are created in the image of God, Polanyi's account offering a fresh expression of this. Secondly, rejection of the concept of a distinct, created, human spirit could easily obscure the essential relatedness of God and humanity, as revealed and established in Jesus Christ. In his later theology, Barth showed a greater apprecia-tion of this danger of a subtle de-humanizing of humanity in the name of the all-encompassing majesty of God. The move in the later Barth is well illustrated from the latest sections of the *Church Dogmatics*, the posthu-mously published *The Christian Life*: "In the Holy Spirit God presents and attests himself to the not at all holy spirits of these people in such a way that within the limits of their spirits, and despite the very painful nature of these limits, they are summoned and raised up for experience, percep-tion, and understanding . . ."[11]

BARTH'S THEOLOGY OF BAPTISM

This trend in the later Barth to give a clearer autonomy to human exis-tence and action is also illustrated in his much-criticized treatment of baptism. He explicitly approaches baptism in terms of two levels of activ-ity that need to be brought into a proper co-ordination, if baptism is to be given its authentic place in the life of the church. The higher level is denoted by "Baptism in the Holy Spirit," the lower level by "Baptism with water," that is presented as the obedient, ethical response to the prior real-ity of Baptism with the Holy Spirit. Barth's rather notorious opposition in *Church Dogmatics* IV.4 was to a traditional interpretation of sacramental actions wherein, he claims, it has been asserted that an action at the lower level—the act of baptism with water—necessarily brings a response at the higher level, the saving action of God's Holy Spirit. For Barth, all meaning in the action of baptism must come from God and it cannot be assumed that water baptism is inherently meaningful, apart from the gift of such meaning from God. God is the *auctor primarius* of all events on earth, but God's presence and work amid the work of the human community in baptism does not supplant or displace their action. God's action in respect of the human act of water baptism "establishes and demands it as their

11. Barth, *The Christian Life* [otherwise *Church Dogmatics* IV.4] 90.

own action which is obedient to him, which hopes in him, which does not encroach but is responsible to him, which in all its genuine humanity bears witness freely to Him." God's action as Lord of the community "gives ethical meaning to their action, including their action in baptism."[12]

More clearly than in some of the earlier parts of the *Church Dogmatics*, Barth is anxious to secure the reality and relative autonomy of human activity and the earlier mathematical analogies have faded from view. The terminology has itself moved closer to that of Polanyi, with the concept of levels of reality. If recast in Polanyi's own terms, the basic correctness of Barth's view emerges, but it also becomes apparent that it was a strategic mistake to separate the treatment of water and spirit baptism as much as he did. Barth's presentation represents something of an overreaction to the tendency in sacramental theology over the centuries to confuse or conflate divine and human levels of activity. A thoroughgoing Polanyian analysis of this final full fragment of the *Church Dogmatics* would reinforce yet refine its basic shape and correct Barth's tendency to a rather over-idealized account of baptism, by rooting the action of God more clearly in the action of the church. A clearer basis for infant baptism would therefore emerge, although baptism on personal profession of faith would remain theologically normative.

CONCLUSION

Other areas of Barth's theology could also usefully be subjected to Polanyian scrutiny and clarification, for example, his doctrines of election and of providence and his basic approach to ethics. The examples discussed above serve to illustrate the creative and illuminating potential in recasting the theology of Karl Barth in the perspectives offered by Michael Polanyi's thought.

12. Ibid., 4:106.

6

Truth and Dialogue

Polanyi, Gadamer, and Theological Hermeneutics

David J. Kettle

THE WRITINGS OF MICHAEL Polanyi have attracted the attention of Christian theologians as offering an account of understanding that is comprehensive in scope, open towards the transcendent, and promising in its post-critical stance. His account of understanding appears *comprehensive* in embracing the personal, practical, passionate, and critical aspects of knowledge that are all-important for Christian faith. It appears *open* towards further meaning in which its terms might become defined ultimately by reference to the mystery of Christian revelation. And it appears to hold *promise* for the enterprise of "faith seeking understanding" by shedding new light where the self-understanding of faith has been limited or distorted by Cartesian assumptions about knowledge.

Other writers have attracted the attention of Christian theologians for similar reasons. However, it is in the writings of Michael Polanyi, I believe, that we find insights of unique value in helping us to break decisively with the Cartesianism that, often in hidden ways, so persistently shapes our thinking. Polanyi's work is accordingly of special value in helping us to assess other such writers so as to explicate and fulfill their potential contribution to theology.

Among such other writers is Hans-Georg Gadamer. In his major book *Truth and Method*,[1] Gadamer describes the pursuit of understanding and truth as this takes place historically within conversation and in

---

1. Gadamer, *Truth and Method*.

the interpretation of texts and works of art. In his hermeneutical theorizing, he shares some basic concerns with Michael Polanyi: both authors are critical of the Cartesian account of knowing; both affirm the personal, communal, and historical dimensions of understanding and the tacit role within it of tradition and authority; and both pursue an account of understanding that is open to the transcendent.

It is not my intention here to compare in detail the work of these two authors. Rather I wish to examine an image central to Gadamer's writings, drawing upon Polanyi's work to explore the clues that it offers for moving beyond the limitations and distortions of Cartesianism. The image in question is that of "horizons." I shall begin by discussing Gadamer's own talk of "horizons of questionableness." I shall conclude that this remains at key points captive to what I am calling "Cartesian habits of imagination." I shall elaborate in Section 2 below on what I mean by this phrase. Gadamer's hermeneutical theory is consequently vulnerable to a subjectivity and relativism that, within Cartesianism, always haunts objectivity and threatens to displace it. I shall then draw clues from Michael Polanyi for a fuller grasp of "horizons" and their place within the pursuit of understanding. I shall demonstrate how this opens the way to a more adequate account than Gadamer offers of the business of (a) distinguishing truth from error, and (b) being open or evasive towards the truth. In the former respect I shall endorse an understanding of truth and error wider than a Cartesian account of these; in the latter respect I shall underscore, with Polanyi, the role of heuristic passion in the search for understanding (insufficiently acknowledged in Cartesianism), and probe the phenomenon of the corruption of this passion.

The following discussion is set tacitly within the ultimate horizons of understanding disclosed in the life, death, and resurrection of Jesus of Nazareth. In the closing sections of this paper I shall reflect explicitly upon these horizons and the radical meaning they give to my discussion.

GADAMER, CONVERSATION, AND "HORIZONS OF QUESTIONABLENESS"

Gadamer accuses the Enlightenment of "extremism"[2] when it set the exercise of reason in fundamental opposition to tradition and authority. It saw the exercise of reason as directed towards establishing the truth by

2. Ibid., 249.

questioning beliefs in order to overcome the danger of "over-hastiness." Tradition and authority, by contrast, were seen as simply precluding the exercise of reason to this end.[3]

According to Gadamer, this opposition, deriving from Descartes' "method," gives a distorted picture of how tradition and authority actually function.[4] It is true, he acknowledges, that tradition and authority are sources of prejudice. However, such prejudice is not necessarily a matter of "over-hastiness"; there are such things as "prejudices productive of knowledge"[5] and it is here that tradition and authority play an important role in the pursuit of truth. Tradition and authority are not the sworn enemies of reason or truth, but belong properly to the historical exercise of reason in pursuit of truth. Conversely, the exercise of reason is never in reality a-historical, but historical; and, as such, it always involves assent—explicit or tacit—to one specific tradition and authority or another.

It follows that we must approach statements of any kind—both those of a scientific and an artistic nature (whether in the literary, musical, or visual arts)—as historical exercises of reason within a particular tradition. Moreover, importantly, we must acknowledge that our own approach to these is of a similar kind: our own exercise of reason, too, is historically embedded in tradition. Gadamer finds a model for this in the pursuit of conversation. The aim of partners in conversation is to reach a shared understanding of the truth. This involves more, on the one hand, than understanding what the other means: in conversation each finds questions of truth raised to which the other's statements are properly to be subjected. On the other hand, conversation requires that each partner allows their understanding to be questioned and changed by the other. Conversation may therefore be described as an open undertaking to which its partners submit together, and in which they are "transformed into a communion"[6] and do not remain what they were. Gadamer proposes that the hermeneutical process in general is analogous to conversation—even though, as he is aware, some of the mutuality of conversation is lost in the wider case of interpreting received texts or works of art.

3. See Ibid., 246.
4. See Ibid., 248–52.
5. Ibid., 247.
6. Ibid., 341.

Analyzing the consciousness operative in the hermeneutical process of conversation, Gadamer describes partners in conversation as each bringing to their conversation historical "horizons of questionableness." Any statements they make are to be understood against the background of questions to which these statements posit answers; these questions form their context or horizon. In conversation, partners bring both statements and the questions behind them, and these meet. Conversation is directed at once towards the truth and tacitly towards a "merging of horizons" in which not only is new understanding reached but a new, shared, horizon of questionableness is formed.

In such terms as these Gadamer posits the "hermeneutical priority of the question." Notice that here for Gadamer "the question" is not, in Cartesian fashion, something we freely conceive and then choose to apply to test a suspected prejudice. Rather "the question" *presents itself to us* in conversation, in concrete form, as a question that *arises* and that we must ask ourselves. A question discloses itself to us just as surely as does a sudden insight in which things "fall into place" or an idea that "dawns upon us." Indeed, the question offers the primary instance of such disclosure: "the real nature of the sudden idea is perhaps less the sudden realisation of the solution to a problem than the sudden realisation of the question that advances into openness and thus makes an answer possible. Every sudden idea has the structure of a question. But the sudden realisation of the question is already a breach in the smooth front of popular opinion. Hence we say that a question too 'comes' to us, that it 'arises' or 'presents itself' more than we raise it or present it."[7]

BREAKING WITH CARTESIANISM: THE "HORIZONS" IMAGE IN THE LIGHT OF POLANYI

How successful is Gadamer's account of understanding in breaking with Cartesian habits of imagination? Certainly the above account of "the hermeneutical priority of the question" breaks with the Cartesian view of the subject as the sovereign originator of questions brought to bear upon reality. However, we need to explore further Gadamer's concept of "horizons" in order to judge whether his theory leads us consistently beyond Cartesian habits of the imagination. We shall turn to Michael Polanyi for insight in forming this judgment.

7. Ibid., 329.

By way of preliminary considerations, we need to recall the central image that dominates the Cartesian imagination: that of the knowing subject as a distinct, determinate, entity among the objects in our world, standing over against that which is known. This much of the image will be readily acknowledged, of course, by Cartesian thinking itself. There is, however, another hidden, tacit, dimension to this image: as we conceive the knowing subject in this way, we unreflectively place ourselves in an empty space from which we observe the knowing subject on the one hand and the real world on the other.

Now the Cartesian image reflects well enough, for some purposes, the practice of questioning claims to possess routine information by testing these claims for correspondence with reality. However, it presents a distorted picture of that knowledge in which, as knowing subjects, we entrust ourselves to lively, responsive, personal participation in the endeavor of knowing—as in our knowledge of religious, personal, and moral subjects and agents. For it conceives the knowing subject only in negative terms, as prone to over-hastiness and subjectivity only as a limitation to be overcome in pursuit of detachment.

This negative conception of subjectivity not only gives a distorted picture of our most lively personal knowledge; it also conceals a contradiction that subverts, according to its own picture, the possibility of knowledge as such. For an insurmountable problem arises the moment we advert to our hidden, tacit self-placement in the Cartesian picture: acknowledging our own subjectivity, we see this as subverting our assumed detached knowledge of "knower" and "known." Our tacit claim to have "direct" access to the real, and to being ourselves unlimited by the determinacy of being ourselves a subject, is destroyed. All that is left is our own subjectivity (negatively conceived) and that of other "knowing" subjects whom we view. In this way objectivity is, in Cartesianism, always haunted by subjectivism and relativism. A Cartesian understanding of "objective knowledge" is always vulnerable to displacement by an understanding (that is itself still indebted to Cartesianism) in which "knowledge" is necessarily relative to the subject. In other words, in its absolute concern to avoid "over-hastiness," Cartesianism conceals a hidden premise to the effect that *all* knowledge is necessarily "over-hasty."

Does Gadamer's use of the image of horizons break with this picture? Michael Polanyi's work guides us here in recognizing that ways of understanding horizons remain captive to, and that break with, Cartesian habits of imagination. Polanyi shares Gadamer's basic concerns about Cartesianism and his work can for its own part be understood as opening the way for a decisive break with Cartesianism.[8] Moreover, parallels seem to present themselves between Gadamer's account of knowing and that given by Polanyi. Thus Gadamer's account of the question as presenting itself to us concretely, and as "hermeneutically prior," invites comparison with Polanyi's description of a "good problem": "problems," he writes, "are the goad and guide of all intellectual effort, which harass and beguile us into the search for an ever deeper understanding of things."[9] Again, Gadamer's account of understanding as directed always from questions to answers, and from horizons to objects lying within them, invites comparison with Polanyi's account of knowledge as "from-to" in structure, being directed always *from* clues we rely on, lying in our subsidiary awareness, *to* that which stands out in our focal awareness.

So let us now ask: which ways of understanding "horizons" remain captive to Cartesian habits of imagination, and that break with these habits and expose their limitations?

A *Cartesian* picture of horizons is suggested by our experience of horizons as *limitations* in our understanding. Influential here is our experience of the curvature of the earth's surface that limits what we can see on its surface, in any direction, from that surface itself. This limitation reveals itself to us when we rise above the earth in an aircraft, and things come into view that were "hidden below the horizon" at a lower altitude.

Cartesian habits of imagination may now prompt us to think of horizons in general as formed relative to a Cartesian knowing subject. We may think of them as an extension of a distinct, determinate, subject over against the real world. In so doing we are tacitly placing ourselves in an empty space outside these horizons—in a space providing horizon-less direct access to the wider world beyond these limited horizons. The usual contradiction within Cartesianism now arises: should we advert to this tacit self-placement, we shall be bound by our own Cartesian imagina-

---

8. This has been a matter of much discussion. Polanyi is not uncommonly interpreted in terms that remain secretly captive to Cartesian habits of imagination, as when he is taken to be a relativist-constructivist like Thomas Kuhn. On this tendency, see my "Cartesian Habits and the 'Radical Line' of Inquiry." Famously, Marjorie Grene feared that Polanyi himself did not appreciate the radical challenge of his own work to Cartesianism. However, this need not prevent us from ourselves affirming and developing this radical challenge where we recognize it.

9. Polanyi, "The Unaccountable Element in Science," 111.

tion to retract our claim to any such access. All that remains conceivable is mutual interaction between the (subjective) horizons of the other and our own.

Polanyi's work, however, helps us to understand horizons in another way that breaks with Cartesian habits of imagination. Let us consider the formation and operation of horizons within the realm of our tacit knowing as this has been described by him.

Consider first, the typical case in which we try to make sense visually of a landscape through which we move. Through our efforts, horizons form against which, or from which, we attend to what lies around us. Now it is vital to acknowledge here that such horizons present themselves to us precisely as *that which is unchanging*. More particularly, they summon recognition as that which we may rightly take as *definitive of* what is unchanging, as offering bearings upon which we may rely to orient ourselves and all that we see.

Such an awareness of horizons has two apparently contradictory aspects. On the one hand, horizons disclose themselves as lying *over against us*—as that unchanging reality by reference to which we may understand our changing field of perception including changes due to shifts in our own location and orientation. Fundamentally, horizons do this by disclosing what it means for us to look in a determinate direction. On the other hand, horizons form in our perceptual field precisely *though our own immersion in them*, and not through detached observation; lying over against us, we nevertheless know them as *our* horizons.

Now horizons take various forms other than the visible horizon line of a landscape, and it is fruitful to reflect on these. For example, "horizons" sometimes take the form of bearings provided by a discrete element within a "wider" setting. An example of this is the Pole Star when it is taken by seafarers for bearings at night. In such cases the character of "horizons" as standing over against ourselves and all that we see comes to the fore. Of course, it is equally true that the horizon line of a landscape stands over against us in this way *as that upon which we rely to make sense of what we see*; however this is somewhat concealed from us by the continuity of a landscape that merges into its horizon. However, the "otherness" of discrete bearings can also mislead us; we must take care lest, attending to them focally from a "wider" context, we lose sight of the fact that they themselves provide the deeper context by which we understand visually ourselves and all that we see.

In other situations, by contrast, we cannot bring our "horizons" into focal attention at all. Consider, for example, the case when we are given a set of photographs that have been taken by a person wandering around a circle of standing stones in heavy morning mist, and we are invited to make sense of them. The task of "putting together" these photos into a coherent mental picture will entail, fundamentally, our recognizing photos that have been taken at the same location, and photos that have been taken facing the same direction. Such recognition will involve discerning the "horizon"—not as visible, but as that upon which we can rely to make sense of what we see. Visibly we see only an indeterminate, white backdrop; the horizons upon which we come to rely to make sense of what we see have been discerned by us precisely through *our imaginative immersion in that which stands out from them* in the morning mist.

Whereas the example of discrete bearings highlights for us the *distinction* between horizons and ourselves and all we see, this second example highlights the *integral, tacit, role* of horizons within our efforts to make sense of things. We may say that the pursuit of understanding involves the discernment at once of that to which we attend in our focal awareness and that from which we attend in our subsidiary awareness. Our discernment of the latter—our discernment of horizons—is not a separate matter from the former, but is integral to the effort of understanding the truth.

As such, and as belonging to the wider realm of our tacit knowing described by Polanyi, awareness of horizons is integral to the continuing effort of understanding. This has two aspects. On the one side, the formation of horizons (like the self-disclosure of questions) already represents emergent understanding; as Polanyi writes with respect to a problem, clues arise *precisely in the act of pointing to their hidden solution*; they do not acquire the status of clues without doing so. On the other side, the formation of horizons never lapses in such a way that their further exploration is precluded within the project of understanding; in Polanyi's account, not only is effort required to discern what *count* as clues in the first place, but such discerning attention *always remains constitutive for* the act of understanding.

Any (Cartesian?) conception of horizons as necessarily unreflective or habitual is corrected here. Tacit awareness can remain discerning, exploratory. This is obvious enough in some cases, of course, such as when learning to ride a bicycle or learning to speak a new language. It may not be so obvious that awareness of horizons entails our discerning attention as much as does an awareness of the things we see *by reference to* these horizons. The key point is this: just as the pursuit of truth presses beyond any mistaken idea of what is true, so it presses towards true horizons beyond any mistaken idea of that by reference to which we may properly understand the world. Our search for understanding is as much for a *truly* unchanging context as it is for what stands out from it as truth.

Our search for sure bearings illustrates this process. A mountain upon which we rely for bearings within its own locality is revealed to us as an unreliable guide when we travel more widely. It no longer provides us with a fixed point lying always in the same direction; we now see the mountain as having its own location in a wider landscape, and as lying in a variable direction determined by our own location in the same landscape, the wider horizons of which now tell us what counts as "always lying in the same direction."

Thus, the question of "over-hastiness" of judgment arises not only with respect to that to which we attend focally as the truth, but also with respect to that from which we attend in the same act. The vital issue is how we conceive this question. Cartesianism, we recall, absolutizes the avoidance of over-hastiness as the way to knowledge; in so doing, it defines subjectivity negatively, distorting what is involved in the effort of understanding in the first place. In the same way here, Cartesianism defines "horizons" negatively in terms of false or over-hasty horizons and, in so doing, distorts the integral role of horizons within the effort of understanding in the first place. Just as Cartesianism is haunted by a hidden premise to the effect that all "knowledge" is necessarily "over-hasty," it is also haunted by a hidden premise to the effect that all reliance on "horizons" is necessarily "over-hasty."

Our own account allows us to describe the occurrence of limited horizons without this contradiction. It points out that "limited" horizons are by definition those that are shown precisely *not* to be our horizons, by reference to those that are indeed our horizons concretely revealed to us. But until the latter are concretely revealed, we have no reason to count the former "limited." Moreover, where the issue of horizons arises tacitly in conversation, the question where false or "limited" horizons may lie is a question we are called to pursue *together* in search of communion in truth. I shall return to this later.

GADAMER'S CONCEPT OF HORIZONS
IN THE LIGHT OF POLANYI

In the light of this understanding of horizons, let us return to Gadamer's use of this image. Having drawn upon Polanyi's insights, let us ask: does Gadamer remain captive here to Cartesian habits, conceiving horizons merely as an extension of the Cartesian self—as a limitation belonging to "subjectivity" that is to be overcome in pursuit of understanding? Or does he understand them as an aspect of tacit knowing in such a way as to break with these habits? This question invites investigation at two points in his theory. The first and most obvious is where he explains his use of the "horizons" image; the second is his understanding of the pursuit of communion in truth as the goal of conversation. Let us consider each in turn.

Gadamer explains his choice to use the "horizons" image as follows: "The concept of "horizon" suggests itself because it expresses the wide, superior vision that the person who is seeking to understand must have. To acquire a horizon means that one learns to look beyond what is close at hand—not in order to look away from it, but to see it better within a larger whole and in truer proportion."[10] According to Gadamer, acquiring such an historical horizon "requires a special effort."[11]

More frequently, Gadamer uses the "horizon" image to refer to limitations imposed upon understanding by the "situation" of the subject. Thus: "Every finite present has its limitations. We define the concept of 'situation' by saying that it represents a standpoint that limits the possibility of vision. Hence an essential part of the concept of situation is the concept of 'horizon.' The horizon is the range of vision that includes everything that can be seen from a particular vantage point."[12] Reflecting the limits imposed by the situation of the subject, horizons are thus a kind of extension of the subject, for all that they beckon beyond: "A horizon is not a rigid frontier, but something that moves with one and invites one to advance further."[13] And further, "The horizon is . . . something into which we move and that moves with us. Horizons change for a person who is moving."[14] Thus, although for Gadamer the subject pursues knowledge

10. Gadamer, *Truth and Method*, 272.
11. Ibid.
12. Ibid., 269.
13. Ibid., 217.
14. Ibid., 271.

of the truth, for him horizons limit any such knowledge. In particular, whereas the subject searches for horizons to *define what is unchanging*, for Gadamer these horizons *always change*. In terms of our discussion above, therefore, their adoption is "over-hasty." Gadamer does not apply the term "over-hasty" in this context, of course; rather he sees such changing, limited horizons as an inescapable part of historical understanding. This is why he happily acknowledges tradition as involving prejudice—albeit of a productive nature. But his own hidden self-placement here is above history; when he claims that all historical horizons change, he necessarily makes this claim by reference to that which does not change. But this is itself tacitly to claim certain horizons. Here, in the familiar self-referential contradiction within Cartesianism, he is confronted by the question of his own unacknowledged horizons.

Let us turn now to Gadamer's understanding of conversation as directed towards communion in truth. Does this account of the goal of conversation succeed in avoiding subjectivism? At first sight it would seem so—as Gadamer intends—since the goal of conversation here is said to be communion *in truth*. Gadamer enlarges upon this goal in two ways. On the one hand, he says, communion in truth is not simply a matter of putting oneself in the place of the other "to discover his standpoint and his horizon."[15] The latter, he says, "is not a true conversation, in the sense that we are not seeking agreement concerning an object." The pursuit of true conversation involves more than "the empathy of one individual for another."[16] On the other hand, true conversation is not "the application to another person of our own criteria."[17] We would not be open to pursuit of the truth if we adopted this stance in conversation. True conversation is rather, says Gadamer, a mutual encounter between partners each bringing to conversation their own "horizons of questionableness" that, in the attainment of communion, merge into a single new horizon. This always involves, for him, "the attainment of an higher universality that overcomes, not only our own particularity, but also that of the other."[18]

Does this account succeed in overcoming subjectivism? Gadamer's disavowals quoted above seem promising in this regard. However, his

15. Ibid., 270.
16. Ibid., 272.
17. Ibid.
18. Ibid.

last, positive, statement quoted above must raise doubts. The picture he offers of conversation seems to imply three claims: (1) that partners bring to their conversation horizons that are settled until this conversation challenges them, (2) that these respective horizons are necessarily complementary to each other, and (3) that the resolution of this challenge takes the form of each partner incorporating, from the horizons of the other, questions not lying within their own pre-formed horizons.

Now we may well agree with these claims in some situations—for example, where communion in truth is pursued regarding a work of art. To seek to understand a work of art as such is to enter into dialogue with it as a "way of seeing things": a dialogue in which horizons are complementary and the attainment of communion and of truth converge in the merging of these horizons. However, to apply this picture to *all* understanding would surely involve unwarranted assumptions that court the subjectivism and relativism that haunt Cartesianism. In particular, it would be to neglect the fact that in general the effort of understanding involves judging between *contested* ways of seeing things in any given situation; the possibility presents itself of seeing things in either the *right* way or the *wrong* way. It involves *weighing competing horizons* in order to adopt horizons that are trustworthy and not misleading or over-hasty.

POLANYI ON WEIGHING HORIZONS

Does such "weighing of horizons" feature at all in Polanyi's account of the pursuit of understanding? It features in two places at least. The first is in a discussion of how perceptual fields are organized. Now Gestalt psychology had described the configuration of such fields into that which stands out as "figure" (in what Polanyi calls our focal awareness) against its "ground" or background (in our subsidiary awareness). In some circumstances, however, two alternative ways of organizing a perceptual field present themselves to us. An instance of this is that familiar image of Rubin's that can be seen either as a white vase against black background or two silhouetted heads in profile facing each other against a white background. The question, "Which way round should I see this?" presents itself to us—although in this particular case the image has been deliberately contrived to be ambiguous. More normally, however, there *is* a right answer to be sought to the question, "Which way round should I see this?" Thus Michael Polanyi considers the situation when we stand on a bridge gazing down at a river that flows beneath us.[19] When the flowing water fills our field of vision, we are led easily (although without absolute compulsion) to the perception that we and the bridge are moving steadily along against the background of the water. When our field of vision widens to include the riverbank, however, this perception is inverted: we come to see the river against the background of the bank and bridge. Polanyi reminds us that we make our judgment between these two ways of seeing things tacitly by *indwelling* the data of perception and seeking their truest integration.

Polanyi's work implies what we have called a "weighing of horizons" firstly, then, in relation to acts of visual perception by an individual. A second place where this is implied relates, by contrast, to a broad act of understanding by a community of people. He considers what happens when a scientist produces experimental findings that appear inexplicable to the established scientific community and the accumulated tradition of scientific knowledge.[20] The weight of opinion among scientists will normally be towards dismissing these findings as an aberration for which there is some as yet unidentifiable explanation. On some occasions, however, such research findings prove repeatable, and may even go on to play a key part in overthrowing received scientific opinion in favor of new theoretical developments. In other words, inexplicable scientific findings raise the question: are these findings to be dismissed in the light of (that is, by adopting the horizons of) the established tradition of science, or is this tradition to be re-appraised in the light of (that is, by adopting the horizons of) these new findings? Which way round is it to be? Such a "weighing of horizons" is a weighty matter, that when it arises is likely to attract much ongoing deliberation by the scientific community.

"WHICH WAY ROUND?": HORIZONS OF QUESTIONABLENESS AND THE QUESTIONABLENESS OF HORIZONS

The pursuit of communion in truth extends, as Gadamer says, beyond seeking mutual understanding to "seeking agreement upon an object." However it also extends, we now see, to seeking *true horizons*—horizons

19. See references to this in, for example, Polanyi, *Personal Knowledge*, 150f., on scientific controversy; and in Polanyi, "The Growth of Science in Society," in Grene, *Knowing and Being*, 73–86.

20. Polanyi, *Personal Knowledge*, 143.

within which an object is seen rightly for what it is and within which other, limited horizons are seen rightly for what they are. Within such pursuit of communion in truth there may arise disagreement and this may include tacit disagreement about horizons. The goal of conversation, accordingly, may be said to include consensus upon the truth tacitly including true horizons. Where communion in truth is not attained, the question remains unresolved whether this indeterminate situation reflects complementary but mutually uncomprehending views of the truth, or contending views of the truth.

To acknowledge the possibility of competing horizons in this way is, we should note, to allow a range of possible outcomes of conversation alternative to that merging of horizons conceived by Gadamer in which both horizons are enlarged in the convergence of truth and communion.

For example, on a given occasion we may judge that our own horizons are deeper than those of our partner in conversation, and embrace those other horizons within themselves. Alternatively, we may be led to recognize that the horizons of the other are deeper than our own, and embrace our own within themselves. Moreover, on each of these occasions, we and our partner in conversation may find ourselves able to reach consensus upon or communion in the truth of this judgment. On another occasion, however, we may find it impossible to attain such communion in truth. We may be unable to agree whether our own horizons embrace those of the other, or whether the horizons of the other embrace our own, or whether our horizons complement each other. We may fail to achieve consensus. Yet another possible outcome is false consensus, in which one partner simply defers to the other; this, too, represents failure to attain "communion in truth."

How shall we understand this range of possible outcomes in conversation in the context of our discussion above of horizons? How, indeed, shall we understand disagreement upon the truth? Although disagreement upon the truth is a routine feature of conversation it receives insufficient attention by Gadamer. On some occasions, when the horizons of partners in conversation differ markedly, it turns into agreement only when partners in conversation make great efforts in mutual comprehension. How shall we describe such efforts relative to our discussion of horizons? They can be described in general, I suggest, as tacit pursuit of such questions as "Am I right to understand what you are saying in the context of where I believe horizons truthfully lie, or are you right to understand what I am saying in the context of where you believe horizons truthfully lie? Which of us is seeing things right? Which way shall we find truthful consensus?"

Let me illustrate what I mean here from my personal experience. When I moved from Britain to New Zealand in 1991, there were occasions when I was struck by some attitude or practice quite taken for granted in New Zealand culture, but which appeared to me in need of questioning. On such occasions my tacit question was "Am I confronted here with a true understanding of things, a right practice?" There were several alternative possibilities. One was that my questions reflected ignorance of the culture and that the answers to these were quite plain to anyone more familiar with the culture. If I were prepared to listen and learn, I would find my questions answered. A second possibility was that, coming from outside the culture, I could see questions that did indeed call for serious consideration but which were hidden from its own inhabitants by unthinking acceptance of their culture as "normal." Another possibility was that there could be no answer to my questions; they reflected a culturally alien way of seeing things and simply did not apply. Were I to live long in New Zealand, I would come simply to accept the attitudes or practices I questioned as "normal" and as standing in no need of justification in the terms dictated by my questions. Sometimes, of course, these distinct possibilities might arise together regarding different aspects of the same situation.

As I pursued conversation on such occasions, my tacit question was whether I had something to *learn* or something to *teach* in various regards. Framed alternatively, my tacit question was whether the truth was to be found by my *entering more fully into* the viewpoint before me, or by *standing back from it* and encouraging others to do the same. Framed in terms of the issue of horizons, my tacit question was: do my questions *find themselves already answered within* the other's horizons, or are they questions *that indeed arise for* the other's horizons and call for an answer in their own terms, that is, within my own horizons? Which way round does the truth lie? Or are our horizons simply incommensurate?

Now it is important to understand that I am not saying I faced a choice, in these circumstances, whether to adopt uncritically how others saw things, or whether to observe their views in detachment. Rather I was called in the first instance to an engagement with others that was at once receptive and critical; only within this engagement would I come to recognize which way to see things. To adopt beforehand a stance supposedly either of uncritical identification or critical detachment would have been to evade the demands of such engagement. I shall return to the issue of evasion below.

This account of conversation can be applied, I suggest, even to conversation about the truth or otherwise of a straightforward claim readily understood by both partners. When in such conversation my partner makes a statement that appears to me to be false, then an account of my situation can be offered in which I am presented with the tacit question "Is my conversation partner ignorant of something I know here, or do they know something I don't? Does my conversation partner make an unwarranted assumption here that I don't, or is it I who make the unwarranted assumption? Which way round does the truth lie?"

Now, of course, it is such conversation as this that lends itself most plausibly to a Cartesian account. The question of truth appears to be fundamentally one of *correspondence* between what is claimed by our partner in conversation and what is actually the case. However our own account above provides, I suggest, a truer, richer, and more fundamental account of such conversation.

It is worth comparing further our own and the Cartesian account of such conversation here. In such conversation, partners seek the source of their disagreement in "over-hastiness" by one or the other, and together seek to uncover where this lies. The question of "over-hastiness" presents itself, however, in a different way here in each account. In the Cartesian account, the question of over-hastiness is held to arise "a priori" and must be tested through supposedly detached examination of the correspondence or otherwise between a belief and the reality to which it refers. In our own account, however, the question of "over-hastiness" arises *in a concrete way out of incomprehension or disagreement, and together, partners in conversation test where it might lie through that weighing of horizons "from within" that belongs intrinsically to the pursuit of truth.*

Now regarding this "weighing of horizons," Polanyi's insight into knowledge helps us to understand clearly two important matters. Firstly, this weighing is *a tacit affair*. Our attention is not focally upon these two horizons, but upon pursuit of the truth and tacitly within this of true horizons. Fundamentally it is the *truth* that we weigh. Our weighing of horizons is not by attending focally to one horizon and then to the other, and then adopting each in turn as we do when testing alternative hypotheses.

To think this would be to fall back into Cartesian habits of imagination. The appearance of similarity with testing hypotheses arises only because of situations that reasonably match the Cartesian model of detached testing for correspondence because in these situations the pursuit of truth "falls out into" a decision between two alternative viewpoints.

Secondly, the weighing of horizons occurs within *an effort of integration*. It is directed towards attaining the truth through a process of integration. Our effort in this direction seeks comprehensively to incorporate all that we perceive in an act of integration. The appearance that this pursuit of truth is a process fundamentally of exclusion rather than of integration is misleading and arises only through a preoccupation with situations where the primary act of integration "falls out into" a decision between two mutually exclusive ways of configuring the world.

TRUTH AND FALSEHOOD, OPENNESS AND EVASION

I have suggested that where there arises disagreement between partners in conversation, pursuit of communion in truth can be understood as tacit pursuit of the question "Which way round does the truth lie: which horizon embraces the other?" I have granted that the outcome may be, as Gadamer assumes, the merging of two horizons within a new, wider horizon. I have emphasized, however, that the weighing of horizons may lead rather to a consensus that one horizon embraces the other.

Disagreement in conversation does not, however, always lead on to the attainment of communion in truth. Instead there may continue unresolved dispute regarding the truth. Alternatively, dispute may end with one partner "giving up" and yielding to the other in what amounts to *false* consensus.

Continuing, unresolved, dispute may have a variety of causes. In one relatively straightforward case, there is argument about the truth of a piece of information of the sort that can readily be passed on and known "second-hand" on reliable authority. Continuing dispute may arise here when conversation partners each look to, and place their trust in, differing authorities (or when one looks to authority while the other speaks from first-hand experience) and when these differences lead to differing claims about the truth.

However, continuing, unresolved, dispute also raises another vital question: whether one, or both, partners in conversation are for some reason or another evasive towards the truth. Where there is such evasion, two issues arise. The first is where this evasion lies. If we were to assume, with Gadamer, that partners in conversation carry with them into conversation established horizons and that a new horizon emerges from this that is wider than those carried to conversation, then a partner who held to their original position would necessarily appear to us evasive towards the truth. However, we have challenged Gadamer's assumption, allowing for other possibilities. In particular, we have allowed that one partner may inhabit true horizons, embracing those of the other; this partner knows the truth rather than the other. Correspondingly, where there is unresolved disagreement, we shall allow the possibility that one partner may be open to the truth when *maintaining* their horizons (because their horizons are true) while the other is not. In this situation, communion in truth will be attained only if the latter opens up to the question of truth. In other words, unresolved dispute raises tacitly the question of evasion: "Which of us is open to the truth, and which closed? Which way round does the truth lie?" Such unresolved dispute can arise concerning a range of matters varying from a straightforward piece of information to ideologically-driven claims and cross-cultural arguments where a whole "way of looking at the world" becomes the subject of critical reflection.

The second issue that arises in connection with evasion is its provenance and character as such. Evasion occurs notably in circumstances where openness to the truth makes personal demands; it is these demands that provoke evasion. Such demands are made especially by the requirement personally to embrace the loss or disruption of that to which one is personally and habitually attached. Now, should we see evasion of such demands as a response consequent upon *the perception beforehand of a truth*? Apparently not. It is not that a truth has been perceived and then, when it is seen to make such demands, it is rejected. Rather such demands are made, in the first place, by openness to the truth that involves weighing horizons. Such openness is driven, as Polanyi has shown, by *desire* for understanding: what he calls "heuristic passions" are integrally at work in the achievement of new understanding. Consider, for example, when a person is deeply committed to a received framework or horizons of understanding and is then presented with a truth that can only be grasped from within a new framework. What motivates a person to be open to such truth? It is heuristic passion that does so, leading them in response to persuasive argument to break with their familiar framework of understanding. Evasion functions already at this level: it represents a corruption of the primary heuristic passion that is integral to achieving new understanding in the first place.

To my knowledge, Polanyi does not investigate such evasion. However his account of understanding and of heuristic passion can help us to do so. When such demands upon us are mediated by conversation, we may evade them in one of two ways. Firstly, we may *dismiss* the demands of conversation by insisting upon viewing things from within our established horizons. In effect, rather than asking "Which horizons embrace the other? Which way round does the truth lie?," we may maintain uncritically that our own horizons embrace those of the other.

Now if horizons are properly understood as we have understood them in this paper, then they must be seen as undergoing a fundamental change in character when a person inhabiting them evades the demands of openness to the truth. As we have understood them, the horizons "brought to" conversation constitute a tacit openness to whatever are *true* horizons. If, in conversation, this openness is not present, however, then it has been *withdrawn*. Established horizons have now turned into closed, distorted, and ultimately *false* horizons. Now, we may note, they do indeed become horizons as Gadamer conceives them—horizons that are carried along with, and centre upon, the subject who inhabits them. And yet this is not quite true; for the subject who inhabits them is, in this moment, secretly active in employing them to resist the demands of openness to the truth. The subject maintains these horizons only in an act of inner contradiction and self-deception—the coherence tacitly granted to the subject by Gadamer's residual Cartesianism is absent.

A certain limited illustration of this may be found in the realm of our visual perception. Let us imagine that I am driving along a winding country road at night. The sky is cloudy, and I form a sense of the direction in which I am travelling by reference to the red safety beacon shining at the top of a tall radio mast. Now, however, the moon begins to show through a break in the clouds. If I continue to take bearings from the beacon, I will find that the moon appears strangely to travel along with me. The moon conflicts with the configuring of my perceptual field by reference to the beacon. This contradiction will be resolved only when I allow the moon to contribute to the continuing effort of my discerning true bearings or horizons. In this case, I will come to understand my perceptual field by reference now to the moon itself rather than the beacon. Instead, however, I may suppress the contradiction: I may resist the demands of openness to true bearings, and continue seeing the landscape and myself by reference to the beacon, actively dis-regarding the moon and concealing from myself the contradiction or dis-integration it introduces to my visual field.

I shall call this kind of evasive response a *dismissive* stance towards the demands of pursuing communion in truth. These demands are not personally great in the visual illustration above, of course, and my dismissal of them will not be a deeply personal matter. In principle, however, there are no limits to the demands we may find made upon us by openness to the truth in certain circumstances. Meanwhile the greater these demands, the more it is that we shall be resisting and the deeper our personal involvement and inner contradiction as we dismiss these demands.

A dismissive stance is thus a personal one and it presents itself in a variety of personal terms. For example, dismissiveness may make us arrogant, oppressive, or contemptuous towards the other. A dismissive stance may be directed in the first instance towards an individual whom we habitually scorn; or towards those belonging to a certain group who are devalued, or stigmatized, or victimized by the group to which we ourselves belong; or towards anyone *not* belonging among "our own" or among those to whom we look as a trustworthy source of guidance, authority, or protection; or towards particular *views*, or the *absence* of particular views, in matters where much is at stake for us.

Dismissiveness, then, shows itself in the first instance towards certain persons (or towards all except certain persons) or towards certain truth-claims (or towards all except certain truth-claims). However, it is directed more fundamentally towards communion in truth—towards whatever might amount to communion in truth in our particular situation. It is also itself a *personal* stance; it is our personal response to being engaged in a personally demanding way.

As a response, however, a dismissive stance has *self-contradictory* status: it evades precisely that towards which it is directed by way of response. This fact itself is also a matter of evasion, moreover: a dismissive stance is *self-deceived*. On this false basis both communion and truth are now reconstructed by the dismissive subject. The orientation of the *self as subject* is now ascribed definition prior to and apart from any orientation of ourselves toward *communion in truth with the other*: it is not open to that "transformation into a communion" in which, as Gadamer writes, "we do not remain what we were." Truth, for its part, is now assumed to be our own assured possession prior to and apart from orientation on our part towards truth that may yet demand new depths of personal response from us. Thus, in place of openness to true horizons in pursuit of communion in truth, a dismissive stance sets a distorted or *false* integration within perception, a *false* resolution of the search for understanding and a *false* self-orientation towards communion in truth.

Dismissiveness, then, is one form of evasion that we may adopt when the demands of responsiveness to communion in truth press upon us. However, there is another form of evasion when these demands press: we may *give up* the effort of integration. Here, rather than clinging (as in a dismissive stance) to what we have known, we yield to its loss—but without then giving ourselves to the demands of rising to the effort of renewed integration. Whereas a dismissive stance finds us repressing these continuing demands, here we take these demands into ourselves in a personal way so as pre-emptively to defeat the renewed effort of integration.

Here, in place of responsiveness to the demands of communion in truth we see *dis*-integration of the effort of perception rather than integration, *dis*-solution of effort rather than continued effort of resolution of the search for understanding, and personal *dis*-orientation rather than orientation towards communion in truth. I shall call this form of evasion a *submissive* stance towards the demands of pursuing communion in truth.

Once again, a submissive stance is a personal one, and presents itself in a variety of personal terms. It is seen, for example, where people show inappropriate deference, credulity, or impulsiveness, or act from low self-esteem and personal neediness. Submissiveness may be evoked in the first instance by various agents or circumstances—for example, by a particular individual, or group, or the holder of a particular office, or a particular set of conventions or beliefs.

Again submissiveness, like dismissiveness, is directed fundamentally towards communion in truth and is a personal response to demands arising from this. It is also both *self-contradictory* as a response and *self-deceived*. And once again, in a submissive stance both communion and truth are reconstructed. The *self as subject*, for its part, is felt to be absent or lacking apart from what is bestowed by the other; submissiveness involves a sense of self-loss of a kind lying beyond resolution. Truth, for its part, is ascribed to a world from which one is alienated and from which one is excluded as an authentic personal participant in knowledge.

How does a submissive stance affect the configuration of our perception? Is this illustrated by our picture, above, of driving winding roads at night? Now as we have already seen, dismissiveness may be pictured as like the act of blocking out the sight of the moon and continuing to take bearings from the beacon. A submissive stance may now be pictured as like the act of turning from bearings offered by the landscape to gaze at the moon—without, however, integrating the moon and the landscape in the act of achieving more adequate horizons. In this act, the moon does not become for us a new source of bearings because, although it is allowed to impinge upon our perception, we continue in a hidden and self-contradictory way to see it by reference to the bearings we have adopted but abandoned. This gives it the character of an image hovering before us, always presenting itself to us yet always displacing itself from us. Insofar as we direct our attention in this way, of course, we lose all bearings; we are disoriented and our efforts towards understanding disintegrate.

RESPONSIVENESS AND EVASION, ACTIVITY, AND PASSIVITY

Evasion, then, takes one of two forms: a dismissive or a submissive stance. Each of these involves inner contradiction and self-deception. One aspect of this self-contradiction arises in relation to the question in what sense each is active or passive in character.

Responsiveness provides, of course, the normative frame of reference here; evasion is always to be described relative to this. And here it is important to recognize how responsiveness challenges our routine understanding of activity and passivity, that is influenced by Cartesian habits of thought. The Cartesian picture posits a dichotomy between the subject as acting and as acted upon. Our foregoing reflections upon the pursuit of communion in truth, however, prompt us to revise this picture; we have seen that responsiveness is at once a matter of *receptivity* (the subject allows themselves to be acted upon by the demands of truth in communion) and of *lively activity* (the subject gives themselves in a personal way to the effort of pursuing communion in truth).

Michael Polanyi helps us to reflect on this "lively receptivity." It is a demand made upon us, in the first instance, by *truth*. This is in the first place a matter of *response* evoked as hidden reality intimates itself, beckoning us to understanding. Thus Polanyi can write of clues to the solution of a problem as harassing and beguiling us. Polanyi frequently describes the pursuit of truth as experienced as a matter of *obligation* in which we are guided by conscience. At the same time he writes of the lively creative effort, the selective and heuristic passions, and the personal commitment involved in acts of understanding.[21]

"Lively receptivity" is also, for Polanyi, entailed in that *communion* with the other that is bound up in pursuit of truth, although he usually writes of this in other terms. According to him, truth is to be pursued through participation in a community of people likewise engaged. Thus he writes on the themes of "conviviality,"[22] of the "society of explorers"[23] and of the "republic" of science.[24] The participation in community he describes is, on the one hand, *receptive*: it involves trusting other people and relying upon received wisdom in order to build critically upon their work. This participation in community is, on the other hand, a matter of *lively* personal responsibility. It is not a matter of conformity to authority within some private enterprise. Rather, the individual has responsibility personally to pursue truth; and truth when found is acclaimed "with universal intent." Once found, it is not a matter of indifference to the individual whether this truth is received by others; rather there is passion for it to win assent in the community. Polanyi identifies this "persuasive passion" as one of the intellectual passions.[25]

When viewed relative to such responsiveness, a dismissive stance and a submissive stance are shown to constitute respectively false activity and false passivity. In each case this involves inner contradiction and self-deception. Let us consider each in turn.

When we adopt a *dismissive* stance, we abandon the demands of *receptivity* to communion in truth. We abandon, firstly, *receptivity to truth*, resorting instead to familiar habits of perception: we understand the world by reference to knowledge we possess. We also abandon, in the same act, *receptivity to the other* and to communion with them: we understand the world by reference to our habitual selves alone. Such dismis-

21. Polanyi, "The Unaccountable Element in Science," 117.

22. Thus chapter 7 of Polanyi, *Personal Knowledge* is titled "Conviviality."

23. Thus chapter 3 of Polanyi, *The Tacit Dimension* is titled "A Society of Explorers."

24. Thus the title of Polanyi's article, "The Republic of Science," in Grene, *Knowing and Being*, 49–72.

25. Polanyi, *Personal Knowledge*, 150f.

siveness tends, of course, to foster continuing unresolved disagreement rather than progress towards communion in truth.

Now such a stance may suggest our autonomous action as an agent within conversation. However, it is not truly so. This is because the demands of receptivity and activity are, in reality, inseparable. Therefore, when we adopt a dismissive stance and evade the demands of *receptivity*, we thereby evade also the demands *actively* of achieving understanding. A dismissive stance does not truly constitute action; indeed it constitutes precisely our capture and paralysis as subjects—although we hide this from ourselves.

When, on the other hand, we adopt a *submissive* stance, we allow ourselves to be overwhelmed by the demands of *actively achieving* communion in truth. As our efforts towards understanding disintegrate, we suffer the loss of what is familiar to us and, in our emptiness, we may find ourselves captured and impelled by haunting mirages and specters. We experience such personal loss both with regard to the *truth* (we are overwhelmed by the demands of *taking responsibility actively for the truth*) and with regard to the *other* (we are overwhelmed by the demands of *participating actively together* in the pursuit of communion in truth). This tends, of course, to foster a premature, false, "consensus" that again falls short of communion in truth but rather constitutes oppression.

Now such a stance suggests the sheer passivity of personal loss. However, this is not truly so. This is because, again, the demands of receptivity and activity are inseparable and when the demands of *active*, responsible knowledge and participation are evaded, the demands are thereby evaded of *receptivity* to these. A submissive stance does not truly constitute passivity; indeed the unresolved personal loss and violation we experience is *actively constructed* by ourselves—although again we hide this from ourselves.

IN SUMMARY: TWO KINDS OF QUESTION

It follows, then, that when disagreement arises in conversation between ourselves and our partner in conversation we are confronted by two kinds of question. The first kind is directed explicitly towards the truth: where does the truth lie? Within such questions are incorporated various tacit questions: can we reach consensus upon the truth? Will this come about with shared recognition that my horizons embrace those of my partner in conversation, or that my partner's horizons embrace my own? Which way round does the truth lie? Or are my horizons and those of my partner in conversation complementary? These are the first kind of question confronting us. The second kind of question concerns responsiveness and evasion, and confronts us especially when it seems to us that we are making no progress towards resolving disagreement: which of us (if either) is open to the truth and which of us (perhaps both) is evasive? Where there is evasion, can this be converted into openness, leading to communion in truth?

This second kind of question—about responsiveness and evasion—arises, we should note, within our pursuit of the first question about truth. It arises fundamentally in this context, and cannot ultimately be addressed apart from this. We shall not normally be able to settle an argument between ourselves and our partner in conversation regarding which of us might be evasive except by attending to where the truth actually lies.

The question about responsiveness or evasion arises in this context, we should also note, as a dimension of the question *"which way round does the truth lie?"* Thus it is pursued *within* conversation: just as we explore from within which horizon embraces the other, so we explore from within which of us is open and which evasive. The question "which way round does the truth lie?" may be thought of as arising here in the following form. Where in conversation we remain in unresolved disagreement, the question arises "Which of the following is true?:

a) For my part I am open to the demands of pursuing communion in truth, but you are evasive towards these. Therefore, openness to the truth requires that I hold firm and bear with the non-resolution of our dispute. I must not yield to any accusation that may be leveled that I am dismissive, for this would be to yield to the creation of a false consensus and evade submissively the demands of openness to truth.

b) I must recognize that for my part I have been evasive towards the demands of pursuing communion in truth. Faithfulness to the truth requires that I seek true horizons through further attention to your own claims, allowing my own to be questioned in the process. Were I to persist in holding my own ground, I would be adopting a dismissive stance; by rejecting any resolution of our dispute that did not yield to my own demands, I would be pursuing your submission to me in order to create a false consensus.

COMMUNION IN TRUTH: THE GOAL OF THE PURSUIT

Gadamer is emphatic that conversation is directed "into the open." "A fundamental conversation" he writes, "is never one that we want to conduct . . . the people conversing are far less the leaders of it than the led . . . No one knows what will 'come out' in a conversation."[26] Nevertheless he clearly sees conversation as having a goal: the general goal of understanding and, in particular, the goal of agreement upon the truth. I have used the term "communion in truth" as shorthand for this goal.

Now, in general, the goal of conversation is agreement within a particular historical conversation upon a particular truth, such that this goal may be attained and conversation concluded, making way for other conversations. There always remain new insights into truth, new conversations to be pursued, new fathoming of horizons. Now Gadamer, we have noted, sees such further activity as leading to ever wider shared horizons and "the attainment of a higher universality." However, for our own part, we have argued that the achievement of shared wider horizons is but one possible outcome among others in conversation; sometimes, rather, the pursuit of communion in truth leads to the recognition together that one horizon embraces the other. We therefore cannot assume beforehand that, when the question arises of further pursuit of communion in truth, the goal of this will lie through the continuing further merging of present horizons into other new and wider horizons. An alternative possibility arises, in principle at least: that horizons may disclose themselves to us such that all new horizons we meet after this are embraced within them.

The possibility of such "ultimate" horizons presenting themselves to us can be known, however, only when they *do indeed arise in practice*, as a concrete eventuality. There can be no knowing them apart from such concrete self-disclosure, for this would entail knowing them from within other horizons, whereas by definition they themselves embrace all other horizons. Equally, such "ultimate" horizons can *only* be known as an arising, self-disclosing, presence; they can never lapse into habitual horizons for us, beyond which other horizons might in principle arise awakening

---

26. Gadamer, *Truth and Method*, 345.

us to themselves. Rather, our ultimate horizons present themselves to us with a presence that remains and that cannot be surpassed.

How can we ever claim to know the *ultimacy*, however, of horizons that arise for us in a concrete, historical way, when such ultimacy denotes rather the concrete outcome of potentially unlimited and unanticipated further historical encounter? To answer this let us recall how further encounter with the demands of communion in truth does actually arise for us. Such further encounter does not necessarily arise, we have argued, through further historical events or conversations. Rather, it arises first and foremost through that which challenges us to new personal responsiveness by making new personal demands upon us. Now, while these demands may indeed present themselves to us when we encounter new and different circumstances, they may also present themselves from within the depths of what is familiar to us. Our ultimate horizons are the occasion of ultimate self-disclosure of the truth to us and call us to ultimate communion in truth. As such, however, they are also the occasion of overwhelming temptation to evasion as they comprehensively subvert our habitual horizons.

Because our ultimate horizons arise for us as a concrete eventuality calling us to ultimate depths of communion in truth, they are essentially a matter of personal testimony to others. And the goal of such testimony to others is precisely such communion in truth with them; it is in this sense testimony "with universal intent." It is not a testimony that declares "for me, this is so," but one that asks "Is this not so?," inviting unqualified further acclamation from ourselves and others alike. It is testimony not to a personal *choice or exercise of freedom* so much as to *responsiveness freely to the truth* rather than evasion. The communion in truth towards which it is directed reaches beyond every limited communion that shows itself as limited when it resists further, deeper, communion in an act of evasion; it addresses every such evasion in an ultimate way by facing precisely the demands that are the ultimate provocation to evasion.

When ultimate horizons open up for us, do they simply replace all our habitual horizons? Rather, our ultimate horizons disclose themselves precisely *through* our habitual horizons, engaging us through them and renewing them as occasions of the concrete question of horizons arising for us. Our encounter with ultimate horizons is inseparable from our indwelling other such familiar horizons. On the other hand, our ultimate horizons are never identical with any such habitual horizons, but rather disclose themselves through them in a lively way as deeper, dawning horizons.

"TELESTHAI": JESUS CHRIST AND COMMUNION IN TRUTH

Integral to Christian faith is the belief that human life as such has purpose: it has been created for, and is directed towards, a goal. This purpose and goal is eternal life with God—life constituted by personal communion in truth within the divine life of the Trinity. "Communion in truth" is here given radical meaning as the goal of human life and its ultimate horizons. Seen in this setting, conversation and its pursuit of "communion in truth" are to be understood as directed ultimately towards communion in truth with God. It is the testimony of Christian faith that these ultimate horizons have been opened up to us concretely, through the initiative of God, in the events of the life, death, and resurrection of Jesus Christ and that all other horizons are set within this context. This testimony may be elaborated briefly as follows.

Jesus of Nazareth was born into the Jewish religious heritage of his time with its expectation of a coming Messiah—one through whom God would bring his promised blessings to those to whom he had bound himself in covenant. When that time came, they would know and love God and live in loving, faithful, relationship to him. Jesus believed himself raised up by God to fulfill the vocation of the Messiah and to disclose God's coming sovereign rule. He sought communion profoundly with God about this vocation, praying to him as "Father."

The truth of God's purposes, revealed to Jesus, made personal demands of an overwhelming kind. Deeply demanding, on the one hand, was the truth about the people whom God intended to bless through his Messiah: that they would reject the very fulfillment of God's purpose for themselves. Here was a matter of overwhelming grief—that God's good purpose would be resisted and seemingly defeated by its intended recipients. Deeply demanding, on the other hand, was the dawning truth about God himself: that God would seemingly abandon his own Messiah and his own purposes to violent defeat. Here again was a matter of overwhelming grief and perplexity—that God, his loving Father, could will this. It would appear inconceivable that God's intention to bless his people could come about through this. Only in radical trust could Jesus pursue communion in truth with God in the midst of these overwhelming unresolved questions, rather than evade them. Jesus showed such trust: entrusting himself to his Father, he accepted betrayal, arrest, trial, and death by crucifixion.

When Jesus is now revealed as the Risen Christ, this act is disclosed for what it was: an act of unqualified loving obedience in which Jesus entrusted everything—not only himself but the whole world he embraced within his religious heritage—to God. The resurrection testifies to an act of unqualified self-offering in love for One worthy of this love. It addresses the horizons to which Jesus' act of self-offering was addressed—every closed horizon represented by human evasion of the truth and its demands. The resurrection identifies such evasion uniquely in the rejection of Jesus, leading to his crucifixion; it reveals, in the killing of Jesus, the ultimate depths and consequences of our evasion—the worst that humankind, including ourselves, are capable of doing—now come to pass. We are met with that which most compellingly tempts us to evasion. There appears no hope for us. In the same moment, however, the resurrection addresses precisely our closed horizons, breaking them open. We find ourselves embraced by Jesus and radically freed to face the truth and shun evasion.

Jesus is disclosed here as commanding our unqualified praise and regard. We recognize the great dignity of his self-offering, his wish that we be forgiven the worst we have done, and his trust in God to bring about a new start for us even out of this. There is thus a dynamic of mutual enhancement between the dignity of Jesus and the evil he embraces: the more we grasp the stature of Jesus, the more we see the depths of evil to which evasion has led us in killing him; the more we see these depths, the more we see the dignity of Jesus displayed in forgiving us our evasion.

"Mutual enhancement" is, of course, a quite unsatisfactory way—in some respects—of describing the interaction between our grasp of the horror of Jesus' killing and the joy of God's faithfulness shown in Jesus' self-offering and God's resurrection of him. There is no harmony to be found in this interaction and no fertile power of enhancement to be found in evasion itself for its own part. The image of mutual enhancement does have value, however, in suggesting an analogy with the way that two complementary colors intensify as we look from one to the other, or the way that a resonance can amplify—when there is appropriate interaction—into forced oscillation. If we want a corrective image, meanwhile, we might invoke that of continuing deconstruction and reconstruction. Every new grasp of the exalted stature of Jesus reveals anew the horror of the act of crucifying him, deconstructing our hope; every new grasp of the horror of this act becomes the occasion of renewed self-disclosure by Jesus in his embrace of this horror, reconstructing our hope.

It is this dynamic that mediates the *ultimacy* of the horizons that open up in the death and resurrection of Jesus Christ. It is an ultimacy mediated within concrete historical encounter, but that breaks open every such encounter, itself included; it is a concrete participation in dawning horizons that are always deeper than those we have yet inhabited.

CONCLUSION: A CHRISTIAN HERMENEUTIC?

I claim that in this paper I have offered a contribution towards a Christian hermeneutic through conversation with the work of Gadamer and Polanyi. However, this claim raises questions. Must not a Christian hermeneutic necessarily *begin explicitly from* Christian revelation as testified in the Bible and in Christian doctrine? Have I not, by contrast, brought in Christian revelation only at the end of my paper? Have I not started *from elsewhere*, failing to recognize this as an alternative starting-point *rival to* Christian revelation? These questions carry additional force because Michael Polanyi himself—from whose work I have drawn extensively—seems to have resisted any explicit role for positive Christian doctrine in the formulation of his own theory of knowledge.

In reply two things need to be said. Both concern the fact that, as Polanyi's writings emphasize, starting-points can never be entirely explicit; they irreducibly involve a tacit dimension.

First, on the one hand, if we do adopt Christian revelation as an explicit framework for the project of hermeneutics, this does not guarantee that our understanding will be faithful to such revelation. Our understanding may remain, unawares and despite Christian rhetoric, *tacitly shaped by beliefs and commitments that foreclose this revelation.* Our efforts towards Christian understanding always require that we be alert to such hidden influences upon them. In this paper I have been especially concerned with the widespread hidden influence of Cartesian habits.

Second, and on the other hand, if we do not adopt Christian revelation as an explicit framework for hermeneutics, *this does not preclude the possibility that our understanding is deeply informed tacitly by this revelation.* Such tacit Christian influence can arise from Christian cultural or personal formation. However, there will always be a risk here that our explicit formulations lack integration with these tacit roots, or may come adrift from them, and may even acquire a practical status rival to Christian revelation. In order for tacit Christian influence to continue, it is necessary for us to pay continually renewed attention to Christian revelation. This may sometimes lead us, indeed, to revise our formulations; genuine openness to Christian revelation extends to openness to the transformation of our basic presuppositions and frameworks in the light of this revelation. I propose that my own paper has been rooted tacitly in Christian revelation and that it is this tacit context that has led me to identify Gadamer and Polanyi as fruitful partners in conversation in the first place and guided my critical analysis and enlargement of their work. I would also propose that this revelation informed my opening premise, in agreement with Gadamer, that conversation as such has a goal and that this goal is communion in truth. My tacit starting-point has been that this goal is fulfilled in an ultimate way in the revelation of the risen Christ; not only so, this revelation properly defines the meaning of conversation and its goal in the first place.

It should be noted that the exercise of judgment in any particular situation regarding these two issues belongs itself to the task of conversation. The judgment whether explicitly Christian formulations are tacitly distorted by false premises and whether non-religious formulations are tacitly informed by Christian revelation, belongs itself to the task of conversation directed towards communion in truth and so is itself subject to the analysis presented in this paper.

Accordingly, both explicit and implicit Christian approaches to hermeneutics have their place. They are complementary and each may correct the other when distortion creeps in. However, an explicitly Christian hermeneutic should be granted primacy. In the case of the hermeneutic of the cross sketched in this paper, extensive development will be required to relate the wider Christian Biblical and doctrinal witness to this.

What, in this case, shall we say to the objection that any theory of hermeneutics that is not founded explicitly in Christian revelation necessarily rests upon another base alternative and rival to this revelation? What of the protest that a hermeneutical theory that is framed, like the foregoing, in terms of the functioning in general of horizons of questionableness is necessarily *alternative to* a Christian hermeneutic? The answer to this objection lies, I believe, in my account itself of the relation between Christian revelation (conceived as our ultimate horizon) and horizons of questionableness in general. If openness to these ultimate horizons has tacitly shaped this account of horizons in general—as I propose it has—then the latter is not based upon an alternative to Christian revelation, but is an example of its fruitfulness. Once again, however, the judgment whether my account of horizons in general is integrally open to our ultimate horizons belongs itself to the task of conversation directed towards communion in truth.

The two fundamental questions above—concerning the desirability of an explicit Christian framework and concerning the relation of such a framework to others—receive attention in an article by Craig Bartholomew on Anthony Thiselton's well-known use of Gadamer's work in theological hermeneutics.[27] In closing, it will be illuminating to consider this article briefly in relation to my claim to contribute to a Christian hermeneutics. While he is very appreciative of Thiselton's achievement, Bartholomew refers to Thiselton's "too-ready appropriation of Gadamer."[28] He notes that "It is Gadamer's two horizons that have shaped Thiselton's work on hermeneutics to a major extent." He discerns, however, that "tacitly the *third* horizon of God and the world as his creation is always present in Thiselton's work." He suggests however that this ultimate horizon "requires to be more consciously integrated into his hermeneutic."[29]

Thiselton himself acknowledges the need to incorporate these ultimate horizons explicitly into his hermeneutical framework when he appeals for "a critique of the cross" as the larger frame by which we may understand the present: "the cross transforms present criteria for relevance: present criteria for relevance do not transform the cross. Salvation is pro-active, not re-active, in relation to the present."[30] However, this appeal for hermeneutics "from the other end" occurs, Bartholomew notes, "only at the end of seven hundred pages of *New Horizons*, and then to stave off the problem of the implications of socio-critical hermeneutics."[31] Bartholomew commends rather the approach of Lesslie Newbigin and Nicholas Wolterstorff, who he sees as arguing for scholarship to be built

27. Bartholomew, "Three Horizons: Hermeneutics from the Other End." Thiselton's two main books on hermeneutics are *The Two Horizons* and *New Horizons in Hermeneutics*.

28. Bartholomew, "Three Horizons," 132.

29. Ibid., 132–33.

30. Thiselton, *New Horizons in Hermenutics*, 610.

31. Bartholomew, "Three Horizons," 131.

unashamedly upon the foundations of a hermeneutics of the cross, or a hermeneutics (using Thiselton's terms) "from the other end."[32]

I concur that a hermeneutics of the cross is our primary requirement. However, faithfulness to such a hermeneutic is not guaranteed by explicit theological formulation, but is rather an ongoing task in which the tacit influence of faith may work even through non-theological formulations to challenge and correct distortions. In this context, the relation between horizons in general and the ultimate (or "third") horizon of Christian revelation requires most careful reflection if our understanding of this is not to be captive to Cartesian habits of imagination. This paper has been an attempt at such reflection.

32. Ibid., 131.

7

Science Meets Violence

An Anthropological Comparison of the Thought
of Michael Polanyi and René Girard

BRUCE HAMILL

BOTH MICHAEL POLANYI AND René Girard have had an enormous influence on theologians for quite different reasons. Polanyi has been seen as a savior of theological epistemology and important for exploring the relation between theology and science (although little consensus on the nature of the relation has been forthcoming). Girard has reopened discussion on atonement and the theology of the cross. In this chapter I explore the compatibility of their anthropologies.

INTRODUCTION

Michael Polanyi and René Girard seem, at first glance, to be very strange bedfellows. However, in spite of their very different philosophies it strikes me that there are some interesting comparisons to be made and some insights to be gleaned here for theological anthropology. Both thinkers are remarkable polymaths. Polanyi moved from a distinguished career in chemistry to social science and then philosophy—particularly epistemology—where the bulk of his reputation was built. Girard moved from literary criticism to philosophical anthropology. Both of them have had a mixed reception with a strong cult following. Polanyi wrote about philosophy in a way that was both consciously critical of the Anglo-American tradition and widely misunderstood by that tradition. Girard was extremely well received as a literary critic and anthropologist in the earlier part of his career; however, his popularity has narrowed with his more explicitly theological writing.[1] Both understand themselves as subversive of the mainstream tradition of Western thought and both have a following among theologians, albeit for different reasons. However, for those who discern the continuing tradition of Hellenistic religion hidden within Western philosophy, these thinkers challenge, from different angles, a common edifice of tacit assumptions. Each has their "big idea," that I will outline in brief and then attempt to examine and compare their diverse views with an eye for the central task of theology—articulating the universal relevance of Jesus Christ and thinking concretely about humanity and its assumption and redemption in Christ. It seems to me that a lot of what goes by the title of "theological anthropology" remains quite abstract, as if throwing off an old ontology by mere use of the word "relational" were enough to specify the character of humanity rather than simply to highlight a historical problem for thought.

AN ANTHROPOLOGY OF KNOWING

The old question about what science might have to do with Christian theology is not often asked as a question of anthropology. However, as the case of Michael Polanyi demonstrates, scientific thought and method cannot be fully appreciated without an understanding of the human-as-knower. Polanyi understands scientific research as essentially an aspect of the communal human search for meaning. He sees himself as part of a community of explorers who separately and together have a commitment to universality and meaning. The way this commitment inheres in the structure of *all* knowing is best explained with a short summary of what he calls the Theory of Tacit Knowing.[2]

a) Core Insight: The Theory of Tacit Knowing

According to Polanyi, knowing has a triadic structure. Knowledge is not based on passively-received data; it is an activity that can succeed or fail

---

1. For a commentary on Girard's reception and the narrowing of his audience once the theological implications of his thought become more explicit—especially with Girard, *Things Hidden Since the Foundation of the World*—see J. Bottum, "Girard among the Girardians."

2. My account is based largely on the way Polanyi describes it in Polanyi and Prosch, *Meaning*, 3.

and is an aspect of the vectorial engagement of the person with the world. As an activity, personal knowing shares its triadic structure with skillful acts. The knowing-*how* exhibited in skilful acts is the coordination of two kinds of awareness. In hammering a nail, I *attend from* the impact of the hammer handle in my hand and the functioning of my arm muscles and I *attend to* the hammer strokes on the nail. There is a knowledge relied on that is not focused on in itself. It is subsidiary. Polanyi demonstrates that this difference between *subsidiary awareness* and *focal awareness* is the same in perception. The skilful act of perception can, like any skill, succeed or fail. All skilful scientific connoisseurship shares this same structure as the scientist attends from his/her clues towards their meaning in a solution. The same structure is seen in the interpretation of the meaningful act of another person trying to communicate something. In short, knowing is an act in which two kinds of awareness are coordinated. And thus the triadic structure refers to the three elements: the knower, subsidiary elements, and focal elements. The three elements are not three separable objects, but three aspects that jointly constitute a committed act. To focus, for example, on the words on this page, rather than rely on them subsidiarily as you have been doing till now, would deconstruct the act of knowing (what they mean) in favor of another act altogether—one of regarding them as objects-in-themselves.

In this triadic act, *commitment* is an essential element. Commitment, for Polanyi, refers to the meaning-oriented (first-person singular) self-involvement of the knower in attending from the particulars of the world to their integrated meaning.[3] The structure of the act of knowing necessarily includes *dwelling in* the subsidiary elements and relying on them—as we do with our body in the world. Thus the committed act of knowing is passionate and the passion is integral to the act, but the passion is not an ego-centric or acquisitive passion. "Intellectual passions," in Polanyi's thought, contrast with the instinctive (pre-formed) "appetites" we share

---

3. Dale Cannon, in particular, highlights the irreducibility of the "first-person singular" character to commitment when he says in his reading of Polanyi: "On my view, the relationship of contact with reality that truth is, is always first-person present tense; it is not and can never be a third person relationship observable by a detached and uninvolved third party. (See *Personal Knowledge*, 303ff.)" Cannon, "Construing Polanyi's Tacit Knowing as Knowing by Acquaintance Rather than Knowing by Representation."

with other animals.[4] As Polanyi puts it: "The heuristic passion seeks no personal possession. It sets out not to conquer but to enrich the world."[5]

Polanyi understands intellectual passions as emerging from animal life[6] via "rising levels of personhood."[7] By this Polanyi means a continuous emergence from animal problem-solving—an emergence whose principal distinction is the radical power of the sign. The particular context is transcended via the symbol system, but always in a way that is grounded in the particular personal skilful acts of indwelling that are developments of animal skills.

Polanyi's theory of knowledge leads him to an understanding of humanity in which "universal intent" is central. By "universal intent," Polanyi claims that human knowing is passionate but distinguishable from self-centered appetites by its orientation towards a universal reality beyond the self. Knowing binds together in one act both passionate commitment and universal truth. "Universal intent" refers to the orientation of the knower in such an act. Every act of assertion presupposes it. The phrase "is true" does not indicate something extra predicated of a statement, but the tacit dimension of every act of assertion (and thus of co-referentiality).[8] Moreover, the tacit undergirding of knowledge means that *all* such assertions—indeed, all formalizable knowledge—depends on knowledge by acquaintance[9] with universal intent.

b) A Transcendental Orientation and Theological Connections

For Polanyi, the structure of personal knowing presupposes a transcendentally-oriented anthropology. The human-as knower exists emergent from the world of biology, but structured and governed by a truth-responsibility that is not reducible to that world.[10] It is important to understand

4. Polanyi, *Personal Knowledge*, 172–74.

5. Ibid., 174.

6. Ibid., 267–68.

7. Ibid., 373.

8. Acts of assertion are those in which our epistemological interactions with reality are shared and reference can become co-referentiatiality.

9. On this, see particularly Cannon, "Construing Polanyi's Tacit Knowing."

10. "Polanyi 'places the quest for understanding in an evolutionary, biological, psychological and socio-cultural perspective.' But Polanyi's anti-reductionist critique of each of these disciplines results in a worldview and an epistemology open to transcendence in a way that modern metaphysical naturalism characteristically does not." Cannon, "Polanyi's 'Invitation to Dogmatism?'"

that this is not a dualist transcendentalism that presupposes the classical notion of the self as a self-contained substance. Polanyi's transcendentalism is very much one of orientation beyond the self and openness to meaning beyond the self. In this Polanyi is probably not alone, particularly among theologians. However, Polanyi's unique contribution is to show, by the Theory of Tacit Knowing, how this orientation is implicit in the structure of all knowing, including scientific attention to the world. All such loving attention bears the hallmarks of Polanyi's transcendental anthropology. Thus Polanyi's account of the human-as-knower is clearly sympathetic to a Christian teleology.[11]

Although sympathetic to Christian faith, Polanyi was not a theologian. However, his understanding of the responsible search for meaning arguably renders plausible the existence of God (something he himself acknowledged). What is more, as some theologians have not been slow to recognize, his understanding of knowledge and science opens up the possibility of theology playing a key role in the search for meaning in which all scientists play a part.[12]

Polanyi's views resonate with a theological doctrine of creation in certain respects. They presuppose an ordered and meaningful world that bears exploration. They also presuppose a creature (the human-as-knower) whose existence is oriented towards meaning and is thus a potential communication partner for a communicating God. Arguably Polanyi's view of scientific knowledge portrays science as contributing to a kind of natural theology. This is not the kind of natural theology that claims to prove the existence of God, but one that recognizes that the success of science in discovering "reality" provides strong evidence indicative of a creator. Moreover, a necessary condition for the scientific enterprise is a commitment on the part of the scientist to universal meaning, the existence of which is independent of the scientific endeavor.

c) Polanyi in Context: Philosophical and Theological Questions

Polanyi's account of knowledge goes "against the grain" after Kant, Descartes, and Hume. For in this tradition once the personal act of as-

---

11. There is a political aspect to all of this. For Polanyi, this transcendental orientation is the cornerstone of the free society—a society in which the free community of science operates. If the transcendental orientation is lost, freedom reverts to some form of relatively arbitrary totalitarianism.

12. T. F. Torrance, Polanyi's literary executor, was at the forefront of this.

sertion is separated as a "belief" from the world it refers to (i.e., as a representation) then the struggle to bridge the gulf between beliefs and the world by justification (epistemology) becomes highly problematic. What usually goes by the name of epistemology in this context is something very different from what Polanyi offers. And the difference is largely anthropological. Polanyi no longer presupposes the Cartesian assumption of an ontological separation between thought and world.[13]

Rather than a mediated causal account of the relation between the world and the mind, where the mind passively receives something from beyond itself, Polanyi offers an account of the activity of knowing in the vectorial traffic that the mind has with the world. Knowing, as an activity, that can succeed or fail, both depends on and is a personal commitment to a world pre-existent with meaning. Meaning is not imposed upon isolated data caused by the external world. It is integral to the structure of knowing in the first place.[14] Percepts and concepts are integrated throughout, since perception itself is oriented towards meaningful order. Thus it is not just the character of purported knowledge that is changed, but the vision of the self changes. The Polanyian anthropology of know-

13. Cannon, "Polanyi's 'Invitation to Dogmatism?,'" summarizes Polanyi's break with modern philosophy well: "Modern theories of truth . . . take two implicit assumptions for granted: (a) the sole sense of truth that is 'of philosophical interest' is a normative property of explicit propositions—i.e., a property of representations of reality, whether verbal or mental—determined through objective critical assessment, and (b) the relationship or dis-relationship of a mind (a knowing subject or a person) to reality is a function of the truth of the propositions it believes. (Strictly speaking, this latter assumption is not made by non-realists, at least not in this form.) Mental life, the life of the knowing subject, thus subject to critical scrutiny, is assumed in principle to be representational of any objective reality it purports to know; its relationship to reality is indirect. It has no contact with reality (at least none but itself as a Cartesian cogito). It is at best directly acquainted with its immediate contents, with its representations of reality, not reality itself. To the contrary, Polanyi places the knower in the world in direct exploratory acquaintance with reality."

14. In the post-Kantian world in which epistemology has been rendered problematic, it is commonly assumed that the interests and desires of the asserter dominate the knowing process and reason is always in danger of becoming rationalization, if it is not already condemned to be so necessarily. The upshot of all of this is that in the post-Kantian and post-modern world an "intellectual" is presumed to be someone less in touch with reality by virtue of his or her insular attempts to fit reality into a theoretical framework of "knowledge." We tend to universalize the ego-centric desire leaving no place for what now appears to be an "idealistic" notion of the community of science. From the Polanyian perspective this is a predictable consequence of what Polanyi calls "objectivist" ontology and ideals, that hide from view the self's interaction with the world within the structure of commitment.

ing inverts the structure of desire from ego-centric to exo-centric within the context of commitment and universal intent. Thus for Polanyi, "commitment" describes the situation in which desire for truth results in an act of submission or self-giving to a universal reality impinging on the self's knowing processes.[15] Knowing depends on an outwardly oriented commitment to the meaningful other; the act of belief is a risk we all take on the assumption of contact with reality. And thus "every act of factual knowing has the structure of a commitment . . . to avoid believing one must stop thinking."[16]

Polanyi opens up a key aspect of a relational anthropology by rejecting Western representationalist theory and relocating the cogito in relation to the world as a universe of meaning and also in relation to transcendental restraints of truth and responsibility. However, in doing this he is not unaware of the difficulties involved in accepting our calling. He states, "Our believing is conditioned at its source by our belonging."[17]

He then goes on to acknowledge that in this social context of knowing, "every society allocates powers and profits, to which the adherents of the intellectual *status quo* lend a measure of support. Respect for tradition inevitably shields also some iniquitous social relations . . . [and thus] our motives are mixed up with the forces holding onto social privilege."[18] In spite of this, Polanyi is optimistic about the salvation of human thought. He firstly makes the logical point that these "iniquitous social relations" do not *necessarily* reduce all convictions to selfish interests[19] and then simply affirms that these conditions of belonging are "accidents of personal existence" and "the concrete opportunities for exercising our personal responsibility."[20]

Polanyi's use of an analogy with the Christian tradition is helpful for us to understand his intellectual confidence. With this revealing citation he concludes his discussion of commitment.

---

15. Polanyi's personal (and ethical) knowing is a species of responsible action and "responsible action excludes randomness, even as it suppresses ego-centric arbitrariness." Polanyi, *Personal Knowledge*, 310.

16. Ibid., 313–14. I believe this is, in effect, what most if not all of us, at a certain point, in fact do.

17. Ibid., 322.

18. Ibid.

19. Ibid.

20. Ibid.

Our personhood is assured by our simultaneous contact with universal aspirations that place us in a transcendent perspective.

The stage on which we thus resume our full intellectual powers is borrowed from the Christian scheme of Fall and Redemption. Fallen Man is equated to the historically given and subjective condition of our mind, from which we may be saved by the grace of the spirit. The technique of our redemption is to lose ourselves in the performance of an obligation which we accept, in spite of its appearing on reflection impossible of achievement. We undertake the task of attaining the universal in spite of our admitted infirmity, which should render the task hopeless, because we hope to be visited by power for which we cannot account in terms of our specifiable capabilities. This hope is a clue to God which I shall trace in my last chapter by reflecting on the course of evolution.[21]

This Pelagian passage ("technique of redemption") suggests to me that Polanyi sees in science what Augustine might have called a *vestigia trinitatis*. Science is the embodiment of human responsibility to divine grace—it involves a relationality given "from above"—the basis of which seems to be a natural tendency to self-giving in the search for meaning. Thus, unbeknown to itself, science (and to some extent human knowledge in general) bears witness to something of the close relation between knowing and loving.

However, while the transcendental calling of knowledge may remind us of the call of the triune God, the question that orthodox Christianity needs to ask of Polanyi concerns the extent to which our belonging (that conditions all our knowing) undermines that call. It seems to me that the weakness of Polanyi's liberalism lies in the overly simplistic jump from ego-centric appetites to intellectual passions. It is here that the thought of René Girard needs to be considered.

AN ANTHROPOLOGY OF DESIRE: RENÉ GIRARD

While the structure of the self exhibited in Polanyi's account of knowledge may be reminiscent of Augustine's understanding of the self conformed in relation to the triune God, Polanyi seems to share little of Augustine's pessimism regarding the possibilities of such salvation. In this respect Girard appears much more closely aligned to Augustine.

21. Ibid., 324.

a) Mimetic Desire

Rather than the transcendentally-oriented interpersonal anthropology of *knowing* that we have seen in Polanyi, Girard, in contrast, offers an anthropology of *desire* that highlights the problematic aspects of the human condition. Rather than a simple distinction between the appetites (that humans share with other animals without distinction) and intellectual desires (that clearly differentiate humans from other animals), Girard focuses on the realm of acquisitive desire in humans that is both similar to and different from other animals. Most importantly, distinctively human desire is *socially* mediated. Desire, says Girard, is *mimetic*. Girard uses the term "mimetic" to refer to imitation that goes beyond merely conscious imitation. Humans are profoundly prone to suggestion, we could say. His theory of mimetic desire shows how the suggestibility of humanity means our social order is grounded in violence and in our ways of controlling violence. For Girard, the last commandment gets to the heart of the matter since it is an attempt to resolve "the number one problem of every human community—internal violence."[22]

b) Core Insight: The Structure of Mimetic Desire and the Scapegoat Mechanism

In order to make the link between violence and mimesis we need to spell out the heart of Girard's thought as we did with that of Polanyi. Coincidentally (let me stress!) the core of Girard's anthropological theory also has a triadic structure. The fact that human desire is mimetic means that desire cannot be regarded, as it has been in the Enlightenment and Romantic traditions, as an autonomous individual relation to the object of desire, but rather as a relation to the object mediated by the desire of another or others. We model our desires on the desires of others thus desiring what they desire. As imitators, we desire what belongs to our neighbor ("near one"). Hence the three elements of mimetic desire are the self, its model and the (common) object of desire. Desire is not simply subjective or simply objective but "rests on a third party who gives value to the objects."[23]

Girard understands human nature in continuity with animal desire, which is largely—but not entirely—instinctive. However, human desire

---

22. Girard, *I See Satan Fall Like Lightning*, 9.

23. Ibid., 9.

contrasts with animal desire, not simply in terms of an intellectual desire oriented towards a universal ideal (as Polanyi does), but, first of all, in its distinctively neighbor-inspired or mimetic character. We borrow our desires from our neighbors, often without even being aware of it. "The only culture really ours is not that into which we are born, it is the culture whose models we imitate at the age when our powers of mimetic assimilation are the greatest."[24]

The second principle following from this is that such desires are usually *conflictive*. Girard describes the link between violence and mimetic desire in the following way: "Opposition exasperates desire, especially when it comes from the man or woman who inspires the desire. If no opposition initially comes from him or her, it will soon, for if imitation of the neighbor's desire engenders rivalry, rivalry in turn engenders imitation. The appearance of a rival seems to validate the desire, the immense value of the object desired."[25] The imitation of desire and rivalry go hand in hand and thus conflict is contagious. The Ten Commandments demonstrate the escalation of violence in a reverse order from murder down to its root in covetousness.[26]

Girard's theory of mimetic desire emerged from his study of various cultures and their mythologies. Hence it is helpful to see how Girard understands the impact of the basic structure of mimetic desire, not simply psycho-socially, but in cultural evolution and hominization. For Girard, mimetic desire is the dynamic that simultaneously threatens and unifies human society. Thus his core insight about mimetic desires is extended to a universal theory of human society.

Mimetic rivalry arises when the self and its model strive for the same object; the less difference in status between the self and its model, the more intense the rivalry. As rivalry intensifies the rivals tend to forget about the objects that are the cause of their struggle and become fascinated with each other and their relative prestige or "*mana*."[27] The model becomes the opponent. Acquisitive mimesis becomes simply "conflictual mimesis." Since mimesis spreads contagiously, social order breaks down unless a mechanism is developed to deal with the crisis. Girard claims

24. Ibid., 15.

25. Ibid., 10.

26. Ibid., 11–12.

27. Something like this seems to lie at the root of Alain De Botton's notion of "Status Anxiety" made popular by his recent TV series of the same name.

that comparative study of society and religion reveals scapegoating as this mechanism. At some point before all is lost in violence the protagonists converge against a common victim. A gesture of accusation is imitated and all are united against one. In this way social unity is restored. Their rage is purged in eliminating this victim who is certainly innocent, at least of the crisis that precipitated his/her demise. Just as the common rage was transferred onto this victim, so the consequence of his/her elimination is the transference of the common delight in the newfound unity. The victim is made sacred (*sacre ficio*) and the source of "peace."[28] Girard sees in his study of anthropology a history of regulations designed to avoid imitation and also public reenactment of the original violence that functions to unify the community around its representative sacred victim. Girard's research is a kind of archaeology, since he lives in a time when the mechanism of scapegoating sacrifice has been rendered largely ineffective while the underlying dynamics remain active.

Like the appetites, mimetic desires are egocentric. However, as Girard's research shows, the social context of their mimetic generation renders them a source of rivalry and potential crisis for humanity. It is through the resolution of these crises that the distinctive shape of human desire and human society emerges. However, unlike "Nietzsche's French epigones,"[29] he does not render the problematic aspects of desire *metaphysically absolute* (and to be celebrated). Girard highlights the genuine insights of post-modernity, but within a theological/biblical reading of the fall and salvation of mimetic desire.

Compared with Polanyi's ideal community of science, Girard's religious and sacrificial social order based on violence seems a stark contrast reminiscent of Karl Barth's critique of religion. However it is important not to overstate the contrast since, contra John Milbank's critique,[30] Girard does not offer an ontology of violence, but, if anything, merely an account of "ontological fragility." The tendency towards violence is not inevitable. Indeed, Girard claims that mimetic desire is not inherently evil, but rather an element of what unites humanity in the image of God. When Jesus calls his followers to imitate him in discipleship, this reflects the sense in which

28. Such peace "as the world knows" is, of course, merely a temporary containment of violence—hence the hesitation indicated by the citation marks.

29. This is Robert Jenson's category. See Jenson, *On Thinking the Human: Resolutions of Difficult Notions*, 67.

30. See Milbank, *Theology and Social Theory*.

mimetic desire is fundamental to human existence, whether it takes the form of religious violence or the kingdom of God. It is the nature of the model of desire that determines the structure of human existence. Girard argues that Jesus' call is a call to imitate him (not in any way but) specifically as he imitates the generous self-giving Father. Girard certainly does not rule out the possibility of a different kind of social order from that governed by violence. Although he may seem, at first glance, to think of evil as "substantial" and as part of the substance of the human, it is clear from his theological basis in the resurrection of Jesus and the Christian scriptures that the Aristotelian dichotomy between substance and accident simply does not apply. The self is not defined by its boundaries, but rather by its relationships—particularly by its relationships of imitation and desire. From Girard's starting point in the resurrection of Jesus, the redeemed human is still human, but a different kind of human. This is a humanity whose mimetic desire is radically reorganized by worship of the "lamb" and scapegoat of humanity. For Girard, the death and resurrection of Jesus constitute together both the unveiling and the undoing of the scapegoating mechanism. The scriptures tell the story of humanity from the point of view of its divine victim rather than from the traditional point of view of the victimizers. The community formed in conformity to this risen victim is precisely the new social order and God's new creation by the Spirit.

Girard certainly shares a notion of the human *telos* that goes beyond the imitation of our neighbors, but it is precisely the neighbor-mediated desire that renders problematic the achievement of the human *telos* and renders Girard's thought specifically theological and soteriological. "If desire were not mimetic we would not be open to what is human or what is divine."[31]

Salvation depends first of all on our openness to interpersonal and divine realities. This naturally gives rise to the question of how the mimetic openness of Jesus Christ relates to the openness needed for knowing, according to Polanyi. For Girard, sin is a distortion of desire that arises when the neighbor-model takes the place of God and becomes my rival. Sin is not substantial to human existence, but neither is it easily eliminated as if the self lived transcendently above the conflicts of desire. The identity of the self is dependent on the context of its mimesis. A new

---

31. Girard, *I See Satan Fall Like Lightning*, 16.

mimesis gives rise to a new self. The transformation is not a violent break but a communal entrancement by the Spirit of the Risen Christ. The self transformed is healed and not destroyed.

SOME QUESTIONS AND CONCLUSIONS: THE CONDITIONS OF SCIENCE AND THE AVOIDABILITY OF VIOLENCE

Neurologists know the human brain as a "powerful imitating machine." However, according to Grant Gillett[32] the notion of imitation needs to be supplemented with that of anticipation. It seems to me that these two key elements—imitation and anticipation—provide the background to the tensions between the thoughts of Polanyi and Girard. Both thinkers focus on one almost to the exclusion of the other element. For Polanyi, it is our powers of anticipation that distinguish the human mind, since we are continually drawn out of our self to indwell parts of the world as they bear on meaningful patterns yet to be discerned. Our symbol system extends this anticipatory or integrational capacity in extraordinary ways. For Girard, it is our powers of mimesis—and the consequent social orders containing its contagion and potential for conflict—that distinguish us from other animals and provide the basis and cause of the emergence of cultural and religious systems. In spite of the very different foci in the thought of Polanyi and Girard, each of them offers hints that are suggestive of the other. These can be described in terms of intention and attention.

For all his focus on attention, Polanyi knows that attention is laden with intention or desire of a particular kind, namely, universal intent— precisely the kind of intent that Girard has little to say about. This is true even in the immediacy of perception where the knower's activity usually goes unnoticed. However, the presence of universal intentionality becomes clear when we consider the case of the puzzle-picture (old woman/ young woman) where our powers of anticipation and attention are challenged and a gap opens between seeing (i.e., beginning to see) and understanding. Moreover, not only is attention desire-laden, universal intent relies in its own way on mimesis and tradition. Polanyi knows that entry into the tradition of knowing requires the mediation of the skilful intentionality of others. To become a scientist requires an apprenticeship or mimesis—to use Girard's language—in a particular domain of universal

32. In conversation.

intent. However, Polanyi does not explore apprenticeship as an aspect of the wider structure of human desire, but only as it bears on our participation in the community of science.

On the other hand, for all his focus on intention, Girard's key insight is that the intentionality of acquisitive desire is not a direct one-to-one relation between the person and the object but is mediated by the intentionality of others. Although this is often largely tacit, intention or desire is laden with a subsidiary—to use Polanyi's language—*attention* to the model/neighbor. Whereas wanting appears to presuppose knowing (I want it because I know it), on Girard's view we normally want things because others want them. The primary acquaintance is with the model and with the community of desire. Girard offers little discussion of attention outside the structures of acquisitive desire although he clearly believes in the possibility and importance of the scientific spirit.[33] Importantly, Girard sees very little evidence of the scientific spirit in the human sciences.

This raises a question for Polanyian science. Does this primary mimetic belonging rule out a disciplined acquaintance with the object? Does it rule out the kind of acquaintance that renders the object not simply the object of desire but the focus of loving attention, or even that in which the scientist dwells in order to discern a meaning it participates in? Polanyi would argue—on the basis of science and its success—that it certainly does not. Girard would no doubt agree however; Girard's view of the nature of our belonging highlights the fact that knowing requires

---

33. Girard writes: "The scientific spirit is pure expectancy. If you want proof that it is still absent in the human sciences, you have only to consider that no one, or hardly anyone, asks 'Does it work?' when discussing my hypothesis. They bring forward dogmatic and theoretical objections. For the most part, people are still prisoners of the 'metaphysics of presence.'" (Girard, *Things Hidden from the Foundation of the World*, 438.) "This complete skepticism, this nihilism with regard to knowledge is often put across just as dogmatically as the various dogmatisms that preceded it. Nowadays people disclaim any certain knowledge and any authority, but with a more assured and authoritarian tone than ever before. We are getting away from one form of Puritanism, only to fall into another. It is now a matter not of depriving mankind of sexuality, but of something we need even more—meaning. Man cannot live on bread and sexuality. Present-day thought is the worst form of castration, since it is the castration of the signified. People are always on the look-out to catch their neighbors red-handed in believing something or other." Ibid., 441–42.

a reformation of the self, since knowing implies a kind of love for the object.[34]

Both thinkers accept, in principle, the possibility of scientific truth and the notion that the scientific community must seek to indwell the order of nature in order to discern its unifying structures and meaning. Girard, however, might argue that to have accepted the possibility of science is not yet to have faced the greatest challenge to science. That is the point at which certain applications of the concept of "natural order" ought to be subject to the greatest skepticism—namely, when the object of personal knowledge is the realm of the personal itself. Here, where meaning is most needed, it is most prone to self-deception. At this point, the Christian faith holds that the meaningful ordering in question transcends nature (or creation) itself since personal existence inhabits the boundary between the theosphere and the biosphere. Personal existence is born of a conversation between creator and creation. Thus the notion of natural order (when the term "natural" becomes a normative moral category) is significantly different from that discerned in the science of the human conceived in terms of biological functioning. To attentively indwell divine communication and not simply human behavior involves "being read" as well as "reading." Thus the possibility of science is brought into sharp relief by the question of the possibility of theological science, focused on the anthropological realities of sin and salvation.

As we suggested earlier the two thinkers—perhaps because of the different foci of their thought—appear to have very different attitudes to the fallenness of the human mind. If we were to offer the Aristotelian distinction between accident and substance, Polanyi would appear to offer a view of the human in which sin was an accident of circumstance easily overcome by the responsible knower. Girard, on the other hand, appears to see sin as much more central to the substance of the human as mimetic creature. In matters of personal risk and great self-involvement our human anxiety means that our participation in violent social orders shapes us well beyond our ability to be aware of it. Neither thinker, however, adheres to the familiar Aristotelian notion of substance in his anthropol-

---

34. As Robert Jenson argues, to participate in truth such knowing must reflect God's own knowing as creator. He says, "We truly grasp any creature when we truly grasp what good God makes it for—which for currently unavoidable instance, accounts for the rancorous sterility into which biology has devolved in its refusal to take account of purpose." Jenson, *On Thinking the Human*, 58.

ogy and, interestingly both, in quite different ways, see transcendence as a key to salvation, whether it be the salvation of our attention or our intention. Of the two thinkers, it is Girard who offers a specifically theological anthropology. His theory offers an account of what it means for human nature to be redeemed by the death and resurrection of Jesus. This includes an account of the nature of our common fallenness (original sin). Our need and its resolution are revealed at the same place—the new order of (personal) creation in Christ.

It is the same human nature that fails to exemplify the kind of self-giving required by the call of God that is required for scientific research at all levels. The degree of self-giving and self-involvement will no doubt differ. However, if my analysis is correct, the scientific moment of loving-attention, when and where it exists, will, in a limited way, bear witness to the work of Jesus Christ and the work of the Spirit in human nature, since the form of existence required is the form of Christ. Girard's theological anthropology puts the scientific moment in a wider context of desire, both in the human community and in the divine.

If Polanyi is right, the knowing process involves both desire (for truth) and self-giving. In theological language, we could think of this in terms of the coordination of eros and agape.[35] Knowing includes loving in both aspects. What is desired in knowledge is something to which the self is subordinated and in which the self participates freely. In my view, both Polanyi and Girard express—in different ways—the redemption of the relational self. Once the profound impact of sin and social violence and the human community is appreciated, we can see how the Polanyian community of truth-seeking (convivial community of scientific responsibility) is, in part, an anticipation of the kingdom of God where we will know as we are known in the loving attention of God.

---

35. Jenson captures the coincidence of knowing and loving well when he writes: "There is . . . no substance to creatures but God's grasp of them, whether we think of that grasp as his loving or his knowing. If creatures existed in any way independent of God's grip on them, they could be grasped otherwise than as God does it, but as it is, if others than God are to know or love creatures, those others must act in some analogy to the way in which God does this. Thus any attempt to know a creature disinterestedly can at best be only a temporary tactic, such as that for the moment adopted by the sciences, and at worst and more likely a sinful objectification. And any attempt to love a creature ignorantly can at best be only amusing play and at worst, and more likely sinful egotism." See Jenson, *On Thinking the Human*, 54–55.

8

Michael Polanyi and the Writings
of Lesslie Newbigin

PAUL WESTON

THERE HAVE BEEN A number of assessments of the writings of Lesslie
Newbigin that have drawn attention to the influence of the work
of Michael Polanyi. But as yet there has been little sustained analysis of
this. My aim in this chapter is to explore this connection in relation to
Newbigin's later missiology. For whilst it is clear that Newbigin drew
his foundational insights into the nature of knowledge from the rich
tradition of Christian revelation, it is also clear that his understanding
found a renewed depth and conceptual coherence through a prolonged
engagement with the language and thought-forms of Polanyi's writings. It was this encounter that helped Newbigin not only to sharpen
his critique of Enlightenment assumptions, but also to develop creative
missiological responses to the epistemological challenges posed by a
post-Enlightenment West.

EARLY INFLUENCE

Newbigin had first come across Polanyi's writings following the publication of Polanyi's major treatise, *Personal Knowledge: Towards a Post-
Critical Philosophy*, in 1958. Newbigin's friend Joe Oldham had been
encouraging him for many years to read Polanyi's work[1] and Newbigin
was immediately impressed with the book. He resolved to re-read it

---

1. Wainwright, *Lesslie Newbigin*, 21.

every ten years, and commented in the 1990s that he had certainly "read it several times since."[2]

The influence upon Newbigin's thought is soon apparent. His 1966 book *Honest Religion for Secular Man* was an attempt to address the growing impact of "secularization" in the mid-sixties. In this context he devotes the third chapter of the book to the question, "What does it mean to speak of knowing God?"[3] and introduces the main discussion with the words: "Readers of *Personal Knowledge* by Michael Polanyi . . . will recognize in what follows my debt to this book."[4] Here, Polanyi's philosophical and scientific conclusions about the "personal" nature of all knowing ran parallel to Newbigin's own ideas about the "personal" nature of religious knowledge that he had first articulated thirty years earlier as a theological student in Cambridge.[5]

But it is in Newbigin's later work that the influence of Polanyi's thought becomes more pervasive. Characteristic of this "newer" reading of Polanyi is Newbigin's 1977 article, "Teaching Religion in a Secular Plural Society,"[6] that represents an early attempt to address some of the cultural questions that confronted Newbigin on his return from India in 1974. Here, for the first time, Newbigin adopts Polanyi's view that in the face of the imminent demise of the Enlightenment "project" in the West, there is a critical need for epistemological renewal. The significance of the resulting "alliance" between "epistemological" and "cultural" critiques in Newbigin's later missiological work is hard to overestimate. He introduces Polanyi's *cultural* analysis by stating: "I am haunted by a paragraph from Michael Polanyi that I think has much relevance to our subject."[7] The paragraph he quotes is taken from Part Three of *Personal Knowledge*, as follows: "The critical movement, that seems to be nearing the end of its course today, was perhaps the most fruitful effort ever sustained by the human mind. The past four or five centuries, that have gradually destroyed or overshadowed the whole mediaeval cosmos, have enriched

2. Quoted in Ibid., 22.

3. Newbigin, *Honest Religion for Secular Man*, 77.

4. Ibid., 80 n. 1.

5. The most influential of his teachers in his days as a student was John Oman (see ibid., 10; and Newbigin, *The Gospel in a Pluralist Society*, 40), who clearly influenced Newbigin's interest in thinking about religious epistemology.

6. Newbigin, "Teaching Religion in a Secular Plural Society."

7. Ibid., 84.

us mentally and morally to an extent unrivalled in any period of similar duration. But its incandescence has fed on the combustion of Christian heritage in the oxygen of Greek rationalism, and when this fuel was exhausted the critical framework itself burnt away."[8]

In the 1990s, Newbigin was to describe this passage as a "crucial point in the long argument of *Personal Knowledge*"[9] and finds in it a new perspective on the nature of the cultural crisis facing the West that begins to influence his missiological writing heavily from the mid-seventies. In many of his subsequent writings, this same passage is repeated, and occupies a position of central importance in the exposition, either being quoted directly (sometimes in full[10]), or specifically referred to at a significant point in the argument.[11]

POLANYI'S PERSONAL KNOWLEDGE
AND NEWBIGIN'S LATER MISSIOLOGY

We turn therefore to examine in more detail the influence of Polanyi's *Personal Knowledge* upon Newbigin's thought in the period following the mid-seventies. In one sense, this is to make explicit once more what Newbigin himself acknowledges at various points in his writings. In the "Preface" to his 1989 book *The Gospel in a Pluralist Society*, for example, he states that: "Throughout the work, and especially in the first five chapters, I have relied heavily on the work of Michael Polanyi, especially his *Personal Knowledge* (1958)."[12] Later, in 1996, he wrote that although it "is not easy reading," he nonetheless believed that Polanyi's work was "of great importance, not least to those who are trying to commend the Christian faith to a sceptical generation."[13] We will therefore seek to draw out these connections, arguing that Polanyi's thought not only influences the way in which Newbigin approaches the missiological questions facing

---

8. Ibid., 85, quoting Polanyi, *Personal Knowledge*, 265–66.

9. Newbigin, "Certain Faith: What Kind of Certainty?" 347.

10. E.g., Newbigin, *The Other Side of 1984,* 21; Newbigin, *The Open Secret*, 28; Newbigin, *Proper Confidence*, 52.

11. E.g., Newbigin, "Our Missionary Responsibility in the Crisis of Western Culture," 106; Newbigin, *Mission and the Crisis of Western Culture*, 6; Newbigin, *Truth to Tell*, 20; Newbigin, "Certain Faith," 347; Newbigin, *Proper Confidence*, 52.

12. Newbigin, *The Gospel in a Pluralist Society*, x.

13. Newbigin, "Foreword" in *Michael Polanyi*, iv.

Western culture, but also helps him in shaping ways in which to respond to them.

THE CRISIS OF WESTERN CULTURE

As noted above, it was during the 1970s that Newbigin's concentration upon material in "Part Three" of Polanyi's *Personal Knowledge* became critical to his own thinking. Polanyi's thesis in this section of the book is that the demise of the Enlightenment project is integrally linked to its central weakness. "[I]t has now turned out," he writes, "that modern scientism fetters thought as cruelly as ever the churches had done. It offers no scope for our most vital beliefs and it forces us to disguise them in farcically inadequate terms."[14] Polanyi responds by arguing that in order to restore "the balance of our cognitive powers," we should learn from the example of Augustine in the fourth century.[15] By drawing attention to his dictum *nisi credideritis, non intelligitis* ("unless you believe, you will not understand"),[16] Polanyi argues that Augustine "brought the history of Greek philosophy to a close by inaugurating for the first time a post-critical philosophy. He taught that all knowledge was a gift of grace, for which we must strive under the guidance of antecedent belief . . ."[17]

Polanyi therefore sets out to establish the vital inter-relationship between the "objective" and "subjective" poles of knowing in order to show that *all* knowledge functions within what he describes as a "fiduciary framework": "We must now recognise belief once more as the source of all knowledge. Tacit assent and intellectual passions, the sharing of an idiom and of a cultural heritage, affiliation to a like-minded community: such are the impulses that shape our vision of the nature of things on which we rely for our mastery of things. No intelligence, however critical or original, can operate outside such a fiduciary framework."[18] This quest for epistemological renewal is at the heart of Polanyi's project, indicated by his words a few pages earlier that: "When I gave this book the sub-title 'Towards a Post-Critical Philosophy' I had this turning point in mind."[19]

14. Polanyi, *Personal Knowledge*, 265.

15. Ibid., 266.

16. From Augustine's *De libero arbitrio*, 1.4 (cf. also 2.6).

17. Polanyi, *Personal Knowledge*, 266.

18. Ibid.

19. Ibid., 265.

Turning to Newbigin's work, we find that this insight of Polanyi's becomes foundational to his later missiological thinking. To be sure, Newbigin continues to draw general epistemological insights from Polanyi, but these are now more tightly focused within a Polanyian structure of *cultural* interpretation. There are two aspects to this: firstly, that Western culture has now reached a terminal crisis point in its search for a viable framework for knowledge; and secondly, that in response to this crisis, a fresh "starting point" for thought is urgently required that incorporates an appreciation for both the "subjective" and "objective" dimensions of "knowing." Both aspects are brought together in the opening pages of Newbigin's seminal 1983 book *The Other Side of 1984*. Here, referring to the contemporary state of Western culture, he writes:

> It is, no doubt, easy in every age to point to its obvious weaknesses. What is in question here, however, is something more precise. It is the dramatic suddenness with which, in the space of one lifetime, our civilization has so completely lost confidence in its own validity . . . The question now is whether our present self-criticism is merely the normal self-questioning of a healthy culture, or whether we are at the point where a culture is approaching death. It seems to me, and I know that I am not alone, that the truth of our present situation is nearer to the second of these alternatives than to the first.[20]

Later in the book this analysis of cultural demise is specifically developed in relation to Polanyi's thought, as follows:

> At the centre of the movement that created our modern culture was a shift in the balance between faith and doubt. After a very long period in which the European perception of how things are was controlled by a dogma based on divine revelation, the principle of doubt reasserted itself in the famous phrase "Dare to know." And who can deny that the result has been fruitful beyond the dreams of those who first used this slogan? Why, then, do we now find ourselves at what feels like a dead-end? Why has life become meaningless for so many in our culture? In a vivid parable Michael Polanyi has suggested the answer . . .[21]

At this point, Newbigin again quotes the Polanyi passage he had cited in the 1977 article referred to above and adds: "I intend to follow Polanyi

20. Newbigin, *The Other Side of 1984*, 3.
21. Ibid., 20.

in the next stage of his argument when he calls for a 'post-critical philosophy' as the necessary starting point for the renewal of our culture."[22] Polanyi's thought dominates the ensuing discussion.[23] As a result, one can suggest that the formative characteristics of Newbigin's analysis of Western culture can be shown to mirror the diagnosis of Polanyi in his *Personal Knowledge*.

Returning to Polanyi's own development of these themes in the ensuing pages of "Part Three" of *Personal Knowledge*, we suggest that the similarity between Newbigin's analysis and that of Polanyi intensifies. In order to establish this, we will follow Polanyi's argument further and then draw comparisons with Newbigin's own treatment.

To begin with, Polanyi's appraisal of the dilemma at the heart of Enlightenment epistemology is traced back to the work of René Descartes. The French philosopher-scientist had despaired of his own ability to arrive at reliable judgments and had attempted to rid them of their inherited assumptions. "Descartes," he writes, "had declared that universal doubt should purge his mind of all opinions held merely on trust and open it to knowledge firmly grounded in reason."[24] In this way, Descartes (along with Kant, who had argued that there was no room for opinion in the matter of making right judgments[25]) hoped to leave "unassailed a residue of knowledge that is completely determined by the objective evidence."[26]

But this enterprise was doomed to failure, argues Polanyi, because the exercise of doubting—upon which the whole Cartesian quest for objectivity rested—was *itself* bound up with antecedent faith-commitments exercised by the doubter. The truthfulness of statement "A" might be doubted, either because another statement ("B") is believed to be true in preference to "A"; or because there are deemed to be insufficient grounds for accepting the truth of "A." The first reason is described by Polanyi as "contradictory" doubt; the second as "agnostic" doubt.[27] Polanyi's point is that neither of these positions is devoid of "fiduciary" commitments on the part of the doubter. If a statement is doubted on the basis of some

22. Ibid., 21.
23. Ibid., e.g., 23, 25–26, and 28–30.
24. Polanyi, *Personal Knowledge*, 269.
25. Ibid., 269, referring to Kant's *Critique of Pure Reason*, B851.
26. Polanyi, *Personal Knowledge*, 269.
27. Ibid., 272–73.

other, such doubt will arise from the belief that the other statement is more reliable. It is from this new "fiduciary commitment," therefore, that doubt is cast upon the original statement. Similarly, argues Polanyi, "agnostic" doubt functions on the basis of a similar antecedent belief, either that statement "B" might be proven at some future date, or else that it could never be proven. So this, too, "implies the acceptance of certain beliefs concerning the possibilities of proof."[28] Kant's programmatic statement that only undoubtable statements are certain must therefore be seen as mistaken.[29] On the contrary, *all* statements of so-called "fact" contain "fiduciary" commitments to antecedent elements that are not strictly "demonstrable," but that nonetheless cannot be denied.

In Newbigin's work, we find a remarkably similar analysis. He, too, argues that it was Descartes' "false idea that there is or there should be available to us a certitude that does not depend upon faith" that was—in Newbigin's words—"the crucial false step, I am more and more sure."[30] To be sure, Newbigin writes that it is Descartes "who usually gets the blame for these things,"[31] but it is significant that when the French philosopher appears in Newbigin's discussions it is usually with reference to the kind of Polanyian reconstruction of epistemology that Newbigin feels is necessary as a result of Descartes' work.[32] Moreover, the Polanyian analysis of the flaw in Descartes' critical program is also directly reflected in many of Newbigin's later writings. At these points, Newbigin acknowledges his debt to the insight of Allan Bloom that it was Nietzsche who first saw the fallacy of the Cartesian method.[33] But it is significant that the way in which Newbigin articulates the grounds of this fallacy—that the Cartesian program is "inherently self-destructive" because of the "faith" position needed to doubt any proposition of truth—is pure Polanyi.[34]

---

28. Ibid., 273.

29. Ibid., referring to Kant's *Critique of Pure Reason*, B766.

30. Newbigin, "What is the Culture?" 5.

31. Newbigin, "Religion, Science and Truth in the School Curriculum," 192.

32. E.g., Newbigin, "What is the Culture?," 6–7; Newbigin, *Truth to Tell,* 35; Newbigin, "Certain Faith," 345–48.

33. E.g., Newbigin, "Mission in the World Today," 129, referring to Bloom, *The Closing of the American Mind.*

34. Cf. e.g., Newbigin, *Proper Confidence,* 23: "If you make the assertion 'I believe P,' I may say 'I doubt P because I believe Q , R, and T,' which are incompatible with P. In other words, my doubt rests upon a faith commitment."

From this analysis of Polanyi's diagnosis of the critical moment faced by the West and its influence upon Newbigin's thought, we turn now to some of the wider themes of *Personal Knowledge* and trace their influence upon Newbigin's later missiology. These comprise Polanyi's foundational notion of "personal knowledge" and the related concepts of "tacit knowing" and "heuristic passion."

"PERSONAL KNOWLEDGE"

In "Part One" of *Personal Knowledge*, Polanyi's basic concern is with the epistemological implications of assigning watertight categories to different "types" of knowledge. He writes that "modern man has set up as the ideal of knowledge the conception of natural science as a set of statements that is 'objective' in the sense that its substance is entirely determined by observation, even while its presentation may be shaped by convention."[35] Polanyi's specific purpose in writing *Personal Knowledge*, therefore, is "to show that complete objectivity as usually attributed to the exact sciences is a delusion and is in fact a false ideal."[36] By "rattling all the skeletons in the cupboard of the current scientific outlook,"[37] he sets out to establish that even within the scientific community, what is usually taken as "objective" knowledge is in fact deeply "personal." As he writes later in the book with regard to the scientist's "originality": "Originality entails a distinctively personal initiative and is invariably impassioned, sometimes to the point of obsessiveness. From the first intimation of a hidden problem and throughout its pursuit to the point of its solution, the process of discovery is guided by a personal vision and sustained by a personal conviction."[38]

Thus, a "subjective" and "personal" involvement, argues Polanyi, is intrinsic to the pursuit of scientific progress. Yet, in acknowledging this "*personal participation* of the knower in all acts of understanding," Polanyi denies that this necessarily makes "our understanding *subjective*."[39] On the contrary, "comprehension is neither an arbitrary act nor a passive experience but a responsible act claiming universal validity. Such knowing is indeed *objective* in the sense of establishing contact with a hidden real-

---

35. Polanyi, *Personal Knowledge*, 16.

36. Ibid., 18.

37. Ibid.

38. Ibid., 301.

39. Ibid., vii. Emphases Polanyi.

ity, contact that is defined as the condition for anticipating an indefinite range of as yet unknown (and perhaps yet inconceivable) true implications. It seems reasonable to describe this fusion of the personal and the objective as 'Personal Knowledge.'"[40]

As we have seen, Newbigin's use of Polanyi's notion of "personal knowledge" is much earlier than the period of his specific engagement with the problems facing Western culture. In his later work, however, there is evidence of a development in his appropriation of Polanyi's insights about "personal knowledge." He writes, for example, in his article "How I arrived at *The Other Side of 1984*," that in his quest for answers to the question "What would be involved in a really missionary encounter of the gospel with this European culture of which I am a part?," he had found "great help in Michael Polanyi's *Post-Critical Philosophy*"—specifically at the level at which Polanyi "exposed the fallacies underlying that dichotomy which is so pervasive in our 'modern' culture between 'scientific knowledge' which is supposed to be 'objective' and faith or belief, which is supposed to be 'subjective.'"[41]

Accordingly, Newbigin's material about "personal knowledge" in his later work (in his 1989 book, *The Gospel in a Pluralist Society*, for example) becomes more philosophically "aggressive" in its apologetic—in line with the original tone of Polanyi's book. To be sure, Newbigin still commends the language of "personal knowledge" to describe the epistemological implications of divine revelation.[42] But in addition, he now deploys Polanyi's argument about the "personal" element in the scientific enterprise to highlight the more "subjective" element in what the Enlightenment project took to be purely "objective." He writes, for example, that, "I have emphasized the character of scientific knowledge as—in Polanyi's phrase—'personal knowledge.' It is knowledge to which the scientist commits herself personally and on which she stakes her professional reputation. She accepts the risk that she might be wrong. If this is so, must we not say that it is part of the deep sickness of our culture that, ever since Descartes, we have been seduced by the idea of a kind of knowledge which could not be doubted, in which we would be absolutely secure from personal risk?" [43]

40. Ibid., vii–viii. Emphasis Polanyi.

41. Newbigin, "How I Arrived at the Other Side of 1984," 8.

42. E.g., Newbigin, *The Gospel in a Pluralist Society,* 61f.

43. Ibid., 48–49.

The thrust of this newer apologetic is encapsulated in Newbigin's "Preface" to the republication in 1996 of Drusilla Scott's book on Polanyi where he writes that, "Polanyi unmasks the illusion that science is a separate kind of knowledge, sharply distinguished from the vast areas of our everyday knowing that we do not call 'scientific.'" "His message," he continues, is that "we do not need to be intimidated by the claims of some populariser of 'science' to represent a superior kind of knowledge by which all the rest of our knowing is to be tested and judged."[44]

We now return to the analysis of Polanyi's *Personal Knowledge* in order to show how, from the foundational premise about the "personal" component of knowing, Polanyi himself develops a coherent "post-critical" picture both of the nature of truth and of the status of knowledge. We will then seek to show that each of these has informed Newbigin's thinking as he develops a missionary engagement with Western culture. In doing so, it will become apparent that Newbigin's indebtedness to Polanyi lies not only in an appropriation of the "deconstructive" and "critical" dimensions of Polanyi's thought, but also in the deployment of some of its key features in Newbigin's reconstructive missiological proposals.

"TACIT" KNOWLEDGE

The first of Polanyi's supporting arguments for the notion of "personal knowledge" is found in "Part Two" of the book and is summed up by its title "The Tacit Component."[45] In this lengthy section, Polanyi's purpose is to show that the reason why all knowing is "personal" is that one of its major components is the "indwelling" of assumptions and skills that are, for the moment, subconscious to a person's specific actions or thinking, but that are nonetheless real. "To affirm anything," he writes, "implies . . . an appraisal of our own art of knowing, and the establishment of truth becomes decisively dependent on a set of personal criteria of our own which cannot be formally defined."[46]

Polanyi develops this argument in both its individual and corporate dimensions, frequently making distinctions between the concepts of "subsidiary" and "focal" awareness.[47] As an example, he uses the act of

44. Newbigin, "Foreword," in *Michael Polanyi*, v.

45. Polanyi, *Personal Knowledge*, 67–245.

46. Ibid., 71. He summed up this aspect of knowing in his phrase "We know more than we can tell," in Grene, *Knowing and Being*, 172.

47. See the discussion in Polanyi, *Personal Knowledge*, 55–65.

reading a book.[48] When reading in order to gain an overall meaning or sense, a person exercises only a "subsidiary" awareness of the actual words on the page. "Focal" attention is on the sense being conveyed rather than on the words themselves. On the other hand, when proofreading a book, the reader's "focal" attention is on the actual words and syllables rather than on the wider sensual and contextual meaning. This leads Polanyi to state the broader philosophical point that "When we accept a certain set of pre-suppositions and use them as our interpretative framework, we may be said to dwell in them as we do in our own body."[49] Polanyi's point is that an acceptance of the "inarticulable" element of knowing is essential if we are to grasp its true nature and this applies as much to the scientist as to other types of investigator. New discoveries do not take place in an epistemological "vacuum," cut off from all influences except those of a supposedly pure and objective rationality. Rather, each new discovery is the result of an "indwelling" of "tacit," or "a-critical" assumptions that are nearly always accompanied by an intuitive "hunch" that seeks more formal confirmation by experimentation.[50]

With regard to Newbigin's appropriation of these insights, it is clear that he not only draws upon Polanyi's conception of "tacit" or "a-critical" knowledge and its related notion of "indwelling," but deploys them in highly significant and creative ways in his later missiology. For example, he frequently alludes to Polanyi's picture of the surgeon "using a probe to investigate a cavity into which it is not possible to look,"[51] and at one point draws out the implications of the example as follows: "Polanyi takes this as a way of entry into the whole enterprise of knowing, of probing reality. Like the surgeon using the probe, we explore reality by *indwelling* a whole range of instruments—words, concepts, images, ideas. We have to learn to use them, and while we are learning we attend to the new words, the new concepts. But when we have become familiar with their use, we no longer attend to them. We are *tacitly* aware of them, but *focally* aware of the reality they enable us to probe. We *indwell* them."[52]

48. Ibid., 92ff.

49. Ibid., 60.

50. See e.g., 130–31.

51. Newbigin, "Our Missionary Responsibility in the Crisis of Western Culture," 106–7; Newbigin, *Mission and the Crisis of Western Culture*, 7–8; Newbigin, *The Gospel in a Pluralist Society*, 33–34 and 46.

52. Newbigin, "Our Missionary Responsibility in the Crisis of Western Culture," 106. Emphasis Newbigin.

Even when not specifically referring to Polanyi, Newbigin draws upon his characteristic distinctions between "tacit" and "focal" awareness. For instance, he uses the example of a pianist's intention to communicate the *meaning* of a piece of music ("focal awareness"), rather than being preoccupied with the business of putting fingers on right notes (a skill of which a good pianist is only "tacitly" aware).[53] Or he employs Polanyi's insights in his description of how one learns to ride a bicycle, depending upon skills learnt in order to stay upright and make progress.[54] In neither instance is Polanyi specifically cited, but these examples demonstrate that Newbigin naturally operates within a Polanyian world even when he is not overtly quoting him.

"Indwelling" the Christian Story

The conceptual framework of "a-critical," or "tacit" indwelling is used by Newbigin in a number of significant ways. For example, he uses the language of "indwelling" to articulate the dynamic relationship between the community of believers and the Christian story. He writes in *The Gospel in a Pluralist Society*, "we get a picture of the Christian life as one in which we live *in* the biblical story as part of the community whose story it is, find in the story the clues to knowing God as his character becomes manifest in the story, and from within that indwelling try to understand and cope with the events of our time and the world about us and so carry the story forward."[55] He continues the description of "indwelling" by drawing on the imagery of John 15, and shifts the emphasis from indwelling the "story" to indwelling Christ: "Jesus defines for his disciples what is to be their relation to him. They are to 'dwell in' him. He is not to be the object of their observation, but the body of which they are a part. As they 'indwell' him in his body, they will both be led into fuller and fuller apprehension of the truth and also become the means through which God's will is done in the life of the world."[56]

Newbigin develops these insights in the areas of discipleship and mission. In terms of discipleship, Newbigin combines the Polanyian in-

---

53. See e.g., Newbigin, *Foolishness to the Greeks*, 57. Polanyi himself uses this example in Polanyi, *The Tacit Dimension*, 18.

54. Newbigin, *The Gospel in a Pluralist Society*, 43.

55. Ibid., 99.

56. Ibid.

sight about "indwelling" with an image drawn from George Lindbeck's book *The Nature of Doctrine.*[57] An aspect of Lindbeck's "cultural-linguistic" approach to doctrine is that the worldview created by the biblical text functions as "the interpretative framework within which believers seek to live their lives and understand reality."[58] Lindbeck uses the image of spectacles and refers to languages and religions as "lenses through which human beings see and respond to their changing worlds."[59]

Newbigin sees the value of Lindbeck's comparison between the religious discourse of the Bible and the use of language. In his essay "Truth and Authority in Modernity," for example, he writes that, "When Lindbeck uses the term 'cultural-linguistic' to describe his model for doctrine, he is rightly drawing attention to the fact that knowledge requires the ability to use a language and an accepted framework of understanding about 'how things are and how things behave' that enables us to make sense of experience. When we use language to communicate information or to share a vision, we do not attend to the words we are using; we attend *through* the words to the matter in hand."[60]

This use of Lindbeck's "intratextual" language enables Newbigin to develop an approach to revelation that builds upon the framework of "tacit" knowledge already present in Polanyi's thought.[61] As a result, what emerges in Newbigin's writings is a dynamic description of how the biblical narrative ideally functions within the life of the Christian community. On the one hand, it provides the answer to the question of Christian identity in relation to the nature of the Christian story of which the believer is a part. "To indwell the Bible," he writes, "is to live with an answer to those questions [of identity], to know who I am and who is the One to whom I am finally accountable."[62] On the other hand, the Christian story—enshrined in Scripture—also functions as the framework *through* which to "attend to" and therefore to acquire a deeper understanding of the wider world: "the Christian story provides us with . . . a set of lenses,

<hr />

57. Lindbeck, *The Nature of Doctrine.*

58. Ibid., 117.

59. Ibid., 83.

60. Newbigin, "Truth and Authority in Modernity," 73. Emphasis Newbigin.

61. Cf. Newbigin, "By What Authority?" 83; Newbigin, *Truth and Authority in Modernity*, 35, where he interprets Lindbeck's "cultural-linguistic" approach to the Bible within a Polanyian framework of "tacit knowing."

62. Newbigin, *The Gospel in a Pluralist Society,* 100.

not something for us to look *at*, but for us to look *through*. Using Polanyi's terminology, I shall suggest that the Christian community is invited to *indwell* the story, *tacitly* aware of it as shaping the way we understand, but *focally* attending to the world we live in so that we are able confidently, though not infallibly, to increase our understanding of it and our ability to cope with it."[63]

The "Hermeneutic of the Gospel"

The creative development of these ecclesiological themes leads Newbigin to a description of the missionary aspect of ecclesial "indwelling." This further dimension to the Polanyian notion of "indwelling" is encapsulated by Newbigin in his characteristic description of the local congregation as the "hermeneutic of the gospel." Newbigin had first used the phrase in his 1980 booklet *Your Kingdom Come*, where he had applied it to the world-wide church in its witness to the kingdom: "It is the Church as a whole which has to be the hermeneutic of the Gospel . . ."[64] Hereafter, the phrase is not used again until the late 1980s, when it re-emerges as a key concept in Newbigin's later missiology.

For example, Newbigin devotes a whole chapter to the idea in his 1989 book, *The Gospel in a Pluralist Society*.[65] The critical problem for the development of a truly missionary engagement with the West, he argues, is that the church itself has surrendered to the dominant assumptions of the Enlightenment. This surrender to the "reigning plausibility structure"[66] of the West must be countered by a fundamental re-orientation of outlook by the church so that it might begin to demonstrate—through its life and worship—an *alternative* "plausibility structure": "it is only as we are truly 'indwelling' the gospel story, only as we are so deeply involved in the life of the community which is shaped by this story that it becomes our real 'plausibility structure,' that we are able steadily and confidently to live in this attitude of eager hope . . . No amount of brilliant argument can make it sound reasonable to the inhabitants of the reigning plausibility

---

63. Ibid., 38. Emphases Newbigin.

64. Newbigin, *Your Kingdom Come*, 38.

65. Newbigin, *The Gospel in a Pluralist Society*, chapter 8, 222–33.

66. A concept he takes from the work of Peter Berger, defining it as "a social structure of ideas and practices that create the conditions determining what beliefs are plausible within the society in question." Newbigin, *Foolishness to the Greeks*, 10.

structure. That is why I am suggesting that the only possible hermeneutic of the gospel is a congregation which believes it."[67]

The understanding of the church as a "missionary" community is not in itself a new idea for Newbigin. From his earliest writings, he had articulated an essentially "missionary" ecclesiology that had found classic expression in such books as *The Household of God*, published in 1953[68] and in later studies that emphasized the ecclesiological implications of a trinitarian approach to mission.[69] Nonetheless, with Newbigin's more specific attention to the question of what would be involved in a "missionary engagement" with Western culture, his writing on the church is brought much more closely into line with what—through his reading of Polanyi—Newbigin had come to consider as the need of the hour. The idea of the church's "indwelling" of the gospel is, in essence, Newbigin's response to this challenge. By "indwelling" the Bible's story, the church meets the crisis of the hour both by providing the fiduciary starting point for cultural renewal and by demonstrating what this epistemological renewal looks like in practice. As a result, Newbigin brilliantly incorporates into a missionary context both the epistemological aspect of cultural "crisis" and that of cultural "opportunity" that Polanyi had called for within a scientific context.

"HEURISTIC PASSION"

Following on from the notion of "tacit" knowing, the second major offshoot of Polanyi's understanding of "personal knowledge" to find expression in Newbigin's later writing is that of "heuristic passion." One of the premises undergirding Polanyi's understanding of knowledge is that it is "objective" in the sense of "establishing contact with a hidden reality," and therefore makes claims to "universal validity."[70] Polanyi develops this idea as an intrinsic aspect of the "personal" nature of all knowing, for it involves what he calls an "originality"[71] on the part of the "discoverer" that may not immediately appear to be integrated with other known facts at

67. Newbigin, *The Gospel in a Pluralist Society,* 232.

68. Newbigin, *The Household of God.*

69. E.g., Newbigin, *One Body, One Gospel, One World*; Newbigin, *The Relevance of Trinitarian Doctrine for Today's Mission*; Newbigin, *The Open Secret.*

70. Polanyi, *Personal Knowledge,* vii.

71. See e.g., the use of this word in ibid., 301 and 311.

the point of discovery. As a result, the act of discovery represents a kind of personal intuition that involves risk. "Personal knowledge" he writes "is an intellectual commitment, and as such is inherently hazardous."[72] He describes Copernicus' anticipation of the later discoveries of Kepler and Newton as an example of the "oddity of our thoughts in being much deeper than we know and in disclosing their major import unexpectedly to later minds."[73] It can therefore be said that a theory that is accepted as "rational" can be seen to be "accredited with prophetic powers"—because it may come to yield further knowledge in the future. "We accept it in the hope of making contact with reality; so that, being really true, our theory may yet show forth its truth through future centuries in ways undreamed of by its authors."[74]

Once more, Polanyi develops this understanding in both individual and corporate settings.[75] In the case of the individual, it is the "heuristic impulse"[76] that drives and motivates the scientist towards further discovery. But this "heuristic passion" also involves a more public dimension. For the content of discovery demands by its very nature to be "published" because it bears upon "an aspect of reality, a reality largely hidden to us . . ."[77] As a result, Polanyi asserts that "By trying to say something that is true about a reality believed to be existing independently of our knowing it, all assertions of fact necessarily carry *universal intent.*"[78] Consequently, Polanyi insists that a scientist's "intimations of a hidden reality are personal" and therefore represent beliefs "which—owing to his originality—as yet he alone holds. Yet they are not a subjective state of mind, but convictions held with universal intent, and heavy with arduous projects."[79]

The scientist will want to publish findings not only in the belief that contact has been made with "reality," but because to do so will test whether conclusions can be verified in practice, thereby leading to further acts of discovery. Polanyi therefore states that, "in spite of the hazards involved,

72. Ibid., viii.

73. Ibid., 104.

74. Ibid., 5.

75. See esp. ibid., vii–viii, 64, 104, 130, and 311.

76. Ibid., 366.

77. Ibid., 311.

78. Ibid. Emphasis Polanyi.

79. Ibid.

I am called upon to search for the truth and state my findings."[80] Indeed, the discoverer "can do no more, and he would evade his calling by doing less." For the "possibility of error is a necessary element of any belief bearing on reality, and to withhold belief on the grounds of such a hazard is to break off all contact with reality."[81]

Publication with Universal Intent

We have seen that one of Newbigin's central challenges to the church in the West is that it has become subject to the dominant cultural assumptions of modernity. In particular, he claims that Christians have adopted the notion that faith is "subjective" and is therefore thought to be unconnected with the real world of "facts." Newbigin's later missiology is characterized by the attempt to counter this view and to restore confidence in the church's epistemic foundations. In attempting to describe truth as both "personal" and yet at the same time properly "objective," he regularly employs Polanyi's notion that a claim to truth demonstrates its "objectivity" by its ability to *lead the enquirer to further truth*.

In his 1991 book *Truth to Tell*, for example, Newbigin defends the idea that Christian faith "is a matter of personal commitment."[82] But this contention is framed in recognizably Polanyian terms. For though personal, this commitment is "to the understanding of a reality which is not in my mind but 'out there.' And the proof of this is in my willingness to publish it and to test it in all relevant situations."[83] Thus the idea of commitment to "truth" in Newbigin's later thought is articulated within a Polanyian framework of "heuristic" discovery. It is an understanding of truth that becomes critical to Newbigin's defense of the gospel as "public truth." In his "Conference Call" ahead of the "National Consultation" at Swanwick, England, in July 1992, for example, we recognize echoes of Polanyi both in his call for a "new starting point" and in his description of what this commitment will involve: "To affirm the Gospel as public truth is to invite acceptance of a new starting point for thought, the truth of which will be proved only in the course of a life of reflection and action which proves

80. Ibid., 315.

81. Ibid.

82. Newbigin, *Truth to Tell*, 33.

83. Ibid.

itself more adequate to the totality of human experience than its rivals."[84] In addition, Newbigin adopts Polanyi's language of "universal intent" in this context. He uses the precise phrase eleven times in all (eight of them in *The Gospel in a Pluralist Society*),[85] and does so in a way that closely connects it to the future "testing" of truth-commitments. The following quotation from Newbigin's 1988 article "Our Missionary Responsibility in the Crisis of Western Culture" illustrates these interrelated aspects: "this personal commitment is, as Polanyi says, 'with universal intent.' It is firmly anchored to the objective pole. It is made in the belief that this is the way to grasp reality more truly, not just that it is what I personally prefer. It is made in the faith that what is shown as truth is truth for all. And if it is indeed what I believe, it will prove itself so by opening the way to fresh discoveries and fresh coherences and fresh clarities."[86]

Moreover, it is precisely because faith claims have "universal intent" that they must be published. "We must seek to show others that they are valid," he argues; and "we express that intent by publishing them and inviting all people to consider and accept them."[87] By the same means, such publication will provide the grounds upon which these claims are tested for their ability to lead the enquirer to what Newbigin describes as "confirmation by further experience,"[88] "experimental verification,"[89] or "fresh discoveries and fresh coherences and fresh clarities."[90]

This framework is therefore quintessentially "Polanyian" in its linking of the concepts of "personal commitment," "objectivity," "testing" and "publication." In terms of Newbigin's particular application of the framework of "universal intent" to the church's missionary engagement with the West, three perspectives emerge.

---

84. Newbigin, "Conference Call: The Gospel as Public Truth," also Newbigin, "The Gospel as Public Truth," 1.

85. Newbigin, "Response to David M. Stowe," 151; Newbigin, "Our Missionary Responsibility in the Crisis of Western Culture," 108; Newbigin, *The Gospel in a Pluralist Society*, 35, 47, 48, 50, 77, 92, 126, and 192; Newbigin, *Proper Confidence*, 43.

86. Newbigin, "Our Missionary Responsibility in the Crisis of Western Culture," 108.

87. Newbigin, *The Gospel in a Pluralist Society*, 192.

88. Ibid., 35.

89. Ibid., 48.

90. E.g., Newbigin, "Our Missionary Responsibility in the Crisis of Western Culture," 108.

Proclamation

In Newbigin's thought, the "publication" of the gospel is naturally seen as equivalent to Polanyi's understanding of the publication of scientific discovery. In this context, Newbigin appropriates Polanyi's understanding of the "fiduciary" commitments involved in scientific "publishing" and applies them specifically to the gospel—held in "faith"—that believers are called upon to declare. As he puts it:

> If I am committed to seeking to understand what happened from within this Christian tradition, that is a decision for which I am responsible. But this decision and commitment is delivered from mere subjectivity by being made—as Polanyi would say—with universal intent. In other words, I cannot treat it as simply a personal decision; I am bound to publish it, to commend it to others, and to seek to show in the practice of life today that it is the rational tradition which is capable of giving greater coherence and intelligibility to all experience than any other tradition.[91]

Dialogue

The notion of "universal intent" (with its connected idea of "testing") also enables Newbigin to envisage a creative missiological conception of "dialogue." Such dialogue is intrinsically linked to the idea of universality in that it represents part of the "public interrogation and debate"[92] that must follow when the gospel is "published," in order to test whether its validity can be demonstrated.

There are two levels at which the notion of "dialogue" operates in Newbigin's later work. The first is in the interface between Christianity and other religions; the second in the church's dialogue with the culture of which it is itself a part. His approach to inter-faith dialogue can be illustrated from a 1977 article on the subject that opens with the statement that "All intellectual activity implies some presuppositions . . . Even the most radical scepticism can only be formulated in terms of presuppositions which are—for the moment—unquestioned." Following a reference to Polanyi's material on the "critique of doubt," he continues, "In dialogue between representatives of different faiths the participants are called upon to submit their most fundamental presuppositions, the very

91. Newbigin, *The Gospel in a Pluralist Society*, 77.
92. Ibid., 50.

grammar and syntax of their thought, to critical questioning."[93] "Cultural" dialogue is a later development in Newbigin's thought, but it operates in the same essential framework. In *The Other Side of 1984*, for example, Newbigin writes—in the context of a discussion of Polanyi's notion of "fiduciary frameworks"—that, "the supremely critical dialogue which [the church] must now face is not the dialogue with other religions (important as that certainly is) but the dialogue with the culture which took its shape at the Enlightenment and with which the European churches have lived in an illegitimate syncretism ever since . . . This is not 'dialogue insured against risk'; it is part of the ultimate commitment of faith—a commitment which always means risking everything."[94]

The Gospel as "Public" Truth

Newbigin's appropriation of Polanyi's notion of "heuristic passion" is perhaps most characteristic in his assertion that the gospel is "public truth." This phrase has come to summarize Newbigin's program, partly because he uses it so often,[95] but also because of the prominence he gives to it in his later writings.[96] It first occurs in *The Other Side of 1984*, in a discussion about the cultural dichotomy between the "private option" of religious faith and the general acceptance of "facts" that are established by the "principles which govern public life."[97] But it is significant that this statement occurs within a prolonged discussion of Polanyi's ideas—in particular the need in contemporary culture for an alternative to the objectivist stranglehold that suffocates the quest for true knowledge. In this context, Newbigin poses the question: "In what sense, then, is Polanyi asking for anything new?" After all, faith has always been "unproven." The "newness" of Polanyi's proposal—argues Newbigin—is that it calls for a cultural renewal based on nothing less than a radically new conception of epistemology. As he puts it: "What is now being proposed is that not just in the private world but also in the public world another model for understanding is needed; that this in turn requires the acknowledgment

93. Newbigin, "The Basis, Purpose and Manner of Inter-Faith Dialogue," 253.

94. Newbigin, *The Other Side of 1984*, 31, in the context of 28–32.

95. In all, Newbigin uses the phrase some 126 times in his published writings.

96. Note, for example, the use of the phrase as the subtitle to Newbigin, *Truth to Tell*; or as the article title for Newbigin, "The Gospel as Public Truth."

97. Newbigin, *The Other Side of 1984*, 26.

that our most fundamental beliefs cannot be demonstrated but are held by faith; that it is the responsibility of the Church to offer this new model for understanding as the basis for a radical renewal of our culture; and that without such radical renewal our culture has no future."[98]

Newbigin's notion of "public truth" therefore is one that builds logically upon Polanyi's concept of "heuristic passion" and frames it within a missiological context. As in Polanyi's writings, it is impossible to isolate the "public" aspects of passionate commitment in Newbigin's thought from the "fiduciary" foundations upon which they are built. [99]

CONCLUSION

It would be difficult to underestimate the importance of Polanyi's thought for an understanding of the later missiology of Lesslie Newbigin. It is clear that in Polanyi, Newbigin found his most stimulating conversation-partner, whose language and grammar were consistently conducive to his own particular theological and missiological concerns. It can also be argued that this influence has contributed to the contemporary relevance of Newbigin's writings. Newbigin's original interest in Polanyi's thought centered upon its engagement with the challenges of modernity. Here, his re-casting in apologetic terms of Polanyi's deconstructive "rattling" of the "skeletons in the cupboard of the current scientific outlook"[100] was to have a significant impact on a church that appeared to be losing its nerve in the mid-1980s.[101] But what is less often appreciated is that because of the relevance of Polanyi's thought to central *post*-modern themes (for example about the social location of knowledge, as well as its fiduciary foundations), a strong case can be made that by reflecting creatively upon these themes, Newbigin's later missiological writings are at least as pertinent in a post-modern setting as they were for modernity.[102] Part of Newbigin's

98. Ibid., 27.

99. For the connection between the idea of "public truth" and the wider Polanyian framework, see e.g., Newbigin, "Response to David M. Stowe": 151–53; Newbigin, "Our Missionary Responsibility in the Crisis of Western Culture," 105–6; Newbigin, *The Gospel in a Pluralist Society,* 35 and 48; Newbigin, "What is the Culture?," 7; Newbigin, *Truth to Tell,* 53; and Newbigin, *Proper Confidence,* 39, 47, and 50.

100. Polanyi, *Personal Knowledge,* 18.

101. See the comments by Beeby, "Mediaeval University or Post-Enlightenment Academy?," 13, and Felderhof, "Some Epistemological Questions," 20.

102. I have explored this further in Weston, "Lesslie Newbigin: A Postmodern Missiologist?"

abiding genius was his ability to develop and communicate such thinking in a way that continues to engage profoundly with the missiological questions of today.

Bibliography

Allen, R. T. "The Cognitive Functions of Emotion." *Appraisal* 3.1 (2000) 38–47.

———. "Governance by Emotion." *Journal of the British Society for Phenomenology* 22.2 (1991) 15–30.

———. "Passivity and the Rationality of Emotion." *The Modern Schoolman* LXVIII.4 (1991) 321–30.

———. *Polanyi.* Thinkers of Our Time. London: Claridge, 1990.

———. "Polanyi and the Rehabilitation of Emotion." In *Emotion, Reason and Tradition: Essays on the Social, Political, and Economic Thought of Michael Polanyi*, edited by S. Jacobs and R. T. Allen. 41–53. Aldershot, UK: Ashgate, 2005.

———. *Transcendence and Immanence in the Philosophy of Michael Polanyi and Christian Theism.* Lewiston, NY: Mellen, 1992.

Avis, Paul, *The Methods of Modern Theology.* London: Pickering, 1986.

Barnes, Barry, and David Bloor. "Relativism, Rationalism and the Sociology of Knowledge." In *Rationality and Relativism*, edited by Martin Hollis and Steven Lukes, 21–47. Oxford: Blackwell, 1982.

Barth, Karl, *Church Dogmatics*, vol. I. 2nd ed. Edited by G. W. Bromiley and T. F. Torrance. Edinburgh: T. & T. Clark, 1975.

———. *Church Dogmatics*, vol. II. Edited by G. W. Bromiley and T. F. Torrance. Edinburgh: T. & T. Clark, 1957.

———. *Church Dogmatics*, vol. III. Edited by G. W. Bromiley and T. F. Torrance. Edinburgh: T. & T. Clark, 1960.

———. *The Christian Life* [otherwise *Church Dogmatics* IV.4]. Grand Rapids: Eerdmans, 1981.

Bartholomew, C. G. "Three Horizons: Hermeneutics from the Other End." *European Journal of Theology* 5.2 (1996) 121–35.

Beeby, Dan. "Mediaeval University or Post-Enlightenment Academy." *Selly Oak Journal* 2 (January 1985) 13–16.

Bloom, Allan. *The Closing of the American Mind.* Harmondsworth, UK: Penguin, 1987.

Bottum, J. "Girard among the Girardians." *First Things* 61 (March 1996) 42–45.

Boyd, William. *Brazzaville Beach.* London: Penguin, 1991.

Brentano, Franz. *Psychology from an Empirical Standpoint.* Translated by A. C. Rancurello, D. B. Terrell, and L. L. McAlister. London: Routledge and Paul, 1973.

Brunner, Emil, and Karl Barth. *Natural Theology.* London: Bles, 1946.

Cannon, Dale. "Construing Polanyi's Tacit Knowing as Knowing by Acquaintance Rather than Knowing by Representation: Some Implications." *Tradition and Discovery* 29.2 (2002–3) 26–43.

———. "Polanyi's 'Invitation to Dogmatism?' A Response to Andy Sanders' 'Polanyian Puzzle,'" *Polanyiana* 8.1–2 (1999). Online: http://www.kfki.hu/chemonet/polanyi/9912/cannon.html.

Carroll, L. "What the Tortoise said to Achilles." *Mind* 4 (1895) 278–80.

Churchland, Patricia S. "Epistemology in the Age of Neuroscience." *Journal of Philosophy* 84 (October 1987) 544–53.

Clark, Tony. "Responsive and Imaginative Participation in Divine Revelation with Particular Reference to the Epistemology of Michael Polanyi." PhD thesis, University of St Andrews, 2004.

Clifford, W. K. *Lectures and Essays*. London: Macmillan, 1901.

Collingwood, R. G. *Faith and Reason: Essays in the Philosophy of Religion by R. G. Collingwood*. Edited by L. Rubinoff. Chicago: Quadrangle, 1967.

———. *The Principles of Art*. Oxford: Clarendon, 1938.

Collins, Harry, and Trevor Pinch. *The Golem: What Everyone Should Know about Science*. Cambridge: Cambridge University Press, 1993.

Dennett, Daniel. *Consciousness Explained*. London: Penguin, 1993.

Devitt, Michael. *Realism and Truth*. Oxford: Blackwell, 1984.

Descartes, René. *Meditations on First Philosophy*. Translated by John Cottingham. Cambridge: Cambridge University Press, 1996.

Evans, C. Stephen. *The Historical Christ and the Jesus of Faith: The Incarnational Narrative as History*. Oxford: Clarendon, 1996.

Evans-Pritchard, E. E. *Social Anthropology: Past and Present*. London: Faber and Faber, 1962.

Felderhof, Marius. "Some Epistemological Questions." *Selly Oak Journal* 2 (January 1985) 17–25.

Feyerabend, Paul. *Against Method: Outline of an Anarchistic Theory of Knowledge*. London: Verso, 1978.

Gadamer, Hans-Georg. *Truth and Method*. London: Sheed and Ward, 1975.

Girard, René. *I See Satan Fall Like Lightning*. Maryknoll, NY: Orbis, 2001.

———. *Things Hidden Since the Foundation of the World*. Stanford: Stanford University Press, 1978.

Gunton, Colin E. *Father, Son and Holy Spirit: Toward a Fully Trinitarian Theology*. London: T. & T. Clark, 2003.

———. "Martin Kähler Revisited: Variations on Hebrews 4:15." *Ex Auditu* 14 (1998) 21–30.

———. *The One, The Three and the Many: God, Creation and the Culture of Modernity*. Cambridge: Cambridge University Press, 1993.

Helm, Paul. *Eternal God: A Study of God without Time*. Oxford: Clarendon, 1988.

Jardine, Nicholas. *The Fortunes of Inquiry*. Oxford: Clarendon, 1986.

Jennings, Richard C. Review of *Leviathan and the Air-Pump: Hobbes, Boyle, and the Experimental Life* by Stephen Shapin and Simon Schaffer. *The British Journal for the Philosophy of Science* 39.3 (1988) 403–10.

Jenson, Robert W. *On Thinking the Human: Resolutions of Difficult Notions*. Grand Rapids: Eerdmans, 2003.

Kant, Immanuel. "An Answer to the Question: What is Enlightenment?" 1784. In *Immanuel Kant: Practical Philosophy*, edited and translated by Mary J. Gregor, 11–22. Cambridge: Cambridge University Press, 1996.

————. *Religion within the Limits of Reason Alone*. 1793. Translated by T. M. Greene and H. H. Hudson. New York: Harper, 1960.

Kettle, David. "Cartesian Habits and the 'Radical Line' of Inquiry." *Tradition and Discovery* 27.1 (2000–2001) 22–32.

Kierkegaard, Søren. *Concluding Unscientific Postscript*. Translated by David F. Swenson and Walter Lowrie. London: Oxford University Press, 1945.

Knorr-Cetina, Karin D. *The Manufacture of Knowledge: An Essay on the Constructivist and Contextual Nature of Science*. Oxford: Pergamon, 1981.

Kuhn, Thomas. *The Structure of Scientific Revolutions*. 2nd ed. Chicago: University of Chicago Press, 1970.

Latour, Bruno, and Steve Woolgar. *Laboratory Life: The Construction of Scientific Facts*. Beverly Hills, CA: Sage, 1986.

Lauden, Larry. *Science and Relativism: Some Key Controversies in the Philosophy of Science*. Chicago: University of Chicago Press, 1990.

Lindbeck, George. *The Nature of Doctrine: Religion and Theology in a Postliberal Age*. London: SPCK, 1984.

Macmurray, John. *Reason and Emotion*. London: Faber and Faber, 1935.

Milbank, John. *Theology and Social Theory*. Oxford: Blackwell, 1990.

Nagy, Endre. "The Hungarian Background to Michael Polanyi's Thought." In *Emotion, Reason and Tradition*, edited by. S. Jacobs and R. T. Allen, 7–20. Aldershot, UK: Ashgate, 2005.

Nagy, Paul. "Philosophy in a Different Voice: Michael Polanyi on Liberty and Liberalism." *Tradition and Discovery: The Polanyi Society Periodical* 22:3 (1995–96) 17–27.

Najder, Zdzislav. "'Moral Inversion' or Moral Revaluation?" In *Intellect and Hope: Essays in the Thought of Michael Polanyi*, edited by Thomas A. Langford and William H. Poteat, 364–85. Durham, NC: Duke University Press, 1968.

Newbigin, Lesslie. "The Basis, Purpose and Manner of Inter-Faith Dialogue." *Scottish Journal of Theology* 30 (1977) 253–70.

————. "Certain Faith: What Kind of Certainty?" *Tyndale Bulletin* 44.2 (1993) 339–50.

————. "Conference Call: The Gospel as Public Truth." *The Gospel and Our Culture Newsletter* 12 (Spring 1992) Insert 2.

————. *Foolishness to the Greeks: The Gospel and Western Culture*. London: SPCK, 1986.

————. "Foreword." In *Everyman Revisited: The Common Sense of Michael Polanyi*, edited by D. Scott, iv–v. London: SPCK, 1996.

————. "The Gospel as Public Truth." *The Gospel and Our Culture Newsletter* 9 (Spring 1991) 1–2.

————. "The Gospel as Public Truth." *Touchstone* 5.3 (Summer 1992) 1–2.

————. *The Gospel in a Pluralist Society*. London: SPCK, 1989.

————. *Honest Religion for Secular Man*. London: SCM, 1966

————. *The Household of God: Lectures on the Nature of the Church*. London: SCM, 1953.

————. "How I Arrived at the Other Side of 1984." *Selly Oak Journal* 2 (1985) 6–8.

————. *Mission and the Crisis of Western Culture*. Edinburgh: Handsel, 1989.

————. *One Body, One Gospel, One World: The Christian Mission Today*. London: International Missionary Council, 1958.

————. *The Open Secret: Sketches for a Missionary Theology*. Grand Rapids: Eerdmans, 1978.

————. *The Other Side of 1984: Questions for the Churches*. Geneva: World Council of Churches, 1983.

———. "Our Missionary Responsibility in the Crisis of Western Culture." In *A Word in Season: Perspectives on Christian World Missions*, edited by E. Jackson, 98–112. Grand Rapids: Eerdmans, 1994.

———. *Proper Confidence: Faith, Doubt, and Certainty in Christian Discipleship*. London: SPCK, 1995.

———. *The Relevance of Trinitarian Doctrine for Today's Mission*. London: Edinburgh House, 1963.

———. "Religion, Science and Truth in the School Curriculum." *Theology* 91 (May 1988) 186–93

———. "Response to David M. Stowe." *International Bulletin of Missionary Research* 12 (October 1988) 151–53.

———. "Teaching Religion in a Secular Plural Society." *Learning for Living: The Journal of the Christian Education Movement* 17 (1977) 82–88.

———. "Truth and Authority in Modernity." In *Faith and Modernity*, edited by P. Sampson *et al.*, 60–88. Oxford: Regnum, 1994.

———. *Truth to Tell: The Gospel as Public Truth*. Grand Rapids: Eerdmans, 1991.

———. "What is the Culture?" Lecture given at the 1st Regional "Gospel and Our Culture" Conference: *Mission to Our Culture in the Light of Scripture and the Christian Tradition*, High Leigh Conference Centre, October, 1990.

———. *Your Kingdom Come: Reflections on the Theme of the Melbourne Conference on World Mission and Evangelism 1980*. Leeds, UK: John Paul the Preacher, 1980.

Piaget, Jean. *The Child's Conception of the World*. Translated by J. and A. Tomlinson. London: Paul, Trench, Trubner, 1929.

Phillips, D. Z. *The Concept of Prayer*. London: Routledge and Paul, 1965.

Plantinga, Alvin. *Warranted Christian Belief*. Oxford: Oxford University Press, 2000.

Plato. *Protagoras and Meno*. Translated by W. K. C. Guthrie. London: Penguin, 1982.

Polanyi, Michael. *Knowing and Being: Essays by Michael Polanyi*. Edited by Marjorie Grene. London: Routledge and Kegan Paul, 1969.

———. *The Logic of Liberty*. London: Routledge and Kegan Paul, 1951.

———, with Harry Prosch. *Meaning*. Chicago: University of Chicago Press, 1975.

———. *Personal Knowledge: Towards a Post-Critical Philosophy*. London: Routledge and Paul, 1958.

———. "Science and Religion: Separate Dimensions or Common Ground?" *Philosophy Today* 7 (1963) 4–14.

———. *Science, Economics and Philosophy: Selected Papers of Michael Polanyi*. Edited with an introduction by R. T. Allen. New Brunswick, NJ: Transaction, 1997.

———. *Science, Faith and Society*. Chicago: University of Chicago Press, 1969.

———. "Science, Observation and Belief." *Humanitas* 1 (1947) 10–15.

———. *The Tacit Dimension*. Gloucester, MA: Smith, 1983.

———. "The Unaccountable Element in Science." *Philosophy* 37.139 (1962) 1–14.

Popper, Karl. *Conjectures and Refutations: The Growth of Scientific Knowledge*. London: Routledge and Paul, 1963.

Puddefoot, John C. "Resonance Realism" *Tradition and Discovery* XX.3 (1993–94) 29–39.

Quinton, Anthony. "Knowledge and Belief." In *Encyclopaedia of Philosophy*, vol. 4, edited by Paul Edwards, 345–52. New York: Macmillan, 1967.

Rist, J. *Eros and Psyche*. Toronto: University of Toronto Press, 1964.

Scheler, Max. *Formalism in Ethics and the Non-Formal Ethics of Value: A New Attempt toward the Foundation of an Ethical Personalism.* Translated by S. Frings and Roger L. Funk. Evanston, IL: Northwestern University Press, 1973.

———. "Liebe und Erkenntnis." In *Gesammelte Werke* Bd.6, 77–98. Berne: Franke, 1963.

———. *The Nature of Sympathy.* Translated by Peter Heath. New York: Archon, 1970.

———. *On the Eternal in Man.* Translated by Bernard Noble. London: SCM, 1960.

———. *On Feeling, Knowing and Valuing: Selected Writings.* Edited by Harold J. Bershady. Chicago University Press, 1992.

———. *Ressentiment in the Construction of Ethics.* Translated by William W. Holdheim. New York: Schocken, 1972.

Shils, Edward. *The Logic of Personal Knowledge: Essays Presented to Michael Polanyi on His Seventieth Birthday, 11th March 1961.* London: Routledge and Paul, 1961.

Skinner, B. F. *Beyond Freedom and Dignity.* New York: Knopf, 1971.

Strasser, Stephan. *The Phenomenology of Feeling.* Translated by R. Wood. Pittsburg: Duquesne University Press, 1977.

Thiselton, Anthony. *New Horizons in Hermeneutics: The Theory and Practice of Transforming Biblical Reading.* New York: Harper Collins, 1992.

———. *The Two Horizons: New Testament Hermeneutics and Philosophical Description with Special Reference to Heigegger, Bultmann, Gadamer, and Wittgenstein.* Carlisle, UK: Paternoster, 1980.

Torrance, Alan. "The Theological Grounds for Advocating Forgiveness and Reconciliation in the Sociopolitical Realm." In *The Politics of Past Evil: Religion, Reconciliation and the Dilemmas of Transitional Justice,* edited by Daniel Philpott, 45–85. Notre Dame, IN: University of Notre Dame Press, 2006.

Wainwright, Geoffrey. *Lesslie Newbigin: A Theological Life.* Oxford: Oxford University Press, 2000.

Weston, Paul. "Lesslie Newbigin: A Postmodern Missiologist?" *Mission Studies* 21 (2004) 229–48.

Williamson, Timothy. *Knowledge and Its Limits.* Oxford: Oxford University Press, 2002.

Winch, Peter. *The Idea of a Social Science.* London: Routledge and Paul, 1958.

Wittgenstein, Ludwig. *Tractatus Logico-Philosophicus.* London: Routledge and Paul, 1922.

Woolgar, Steve. *Science: The Very Idea.* London: Routledge, 1993.

Index

46427671R00113

Made in the USA
Middletown, DE
31 July 2017